BREAKING THE TIES THAT BIND

By Maureen Honey

Creating Rosie the Riveter: Class, Gender, and Propaganda During World War II (Amherst, 1984)

(editor) *Shadowed Dreams: Women's Poetry of the Harlem Renaissance* (New Brunswick, N.J., 1989)

(editor) *Breaking the Ties That Bind: Popular Stories of the New Woman, 1915–1930* (Norman, 1992)

BREAKING THE TIES THAT BIND

Popular Stories of the New Woman, 1915–1930

Edited by
Maureen Honey

University of Oklahoma Press : Norman and London

To my loving parents

and

to Russel B. Nye

Library of Congress Cataloging-in-Publication Data

Honey, Maureen, 1945–
   Breaking the ties that bind : popular stories of the new woman,
1915–1930 / edited by Maureen Honey.
      p.   cm.
   Includes bibliographical references.
   ISBN 0-8061-2467-9
   1. Feminism—United States—Fiction.   2. Short stories, American
—Women authors.   3. American fiction—20th century.   4. Women—
United States—Fiction.   I. Title.
PS648.F4H66   1992
813′.01089287′09042—dc20   92-54155
                                                                                              CIP

1   2   3   4   5   6   7   8   9   10

CONTENTS

ILLUSTRATIONS

vii

ACKNOWLEDGMENTS

When I was a graduate student at Michigan State University in the early 1970s, I had the good fortune to work with Russel Nye on my dissertation in American Studies. He was a co-founder of the Popular Culture Association and directed a graduate seminar, of which I was a member, on popular historical documents often overlooked by scholars. My own research topic for this seminar was movie magazines, as I had devoured them while growing up and felt they had something worthwhile to say about women's roles in American culture. The primary sources, however, were impossible to obtain because libraries had not bothered to collect such "trash." Thus, when Dr. Nye deposited a large carton of old movie magazines in my office, complete with a hilarious story about Canadian customs officials wondering out loud why a distinguished professor of English would be transporting such stuff from a Canadian warehouse, I was immensely grateful and relieved.

That initial experience with the delights and frustrations of doing popular culture research has increased my appreciation for all those academics who go outside of the canon for inspiration and information about how culture works, and Dr. Nye is foremost among them. I also have looked for support to a number of feminist scholars working with women's popular fiction. Janice Radway, a classmate of mine in American Studies, has since gone on to create a distinguished career in the study of Harlequin romances and gothic novels. Her lucid, respectful treatment of women's formula fiction has been a model for my own work on the fiction in women's magazines. Bonnie Zimmerman has also been an important scholar who understands the value of literature outside the canon, and her writing on science fiction and lesbian literature has opened many doors for me as well as others. African American women working on the Harlem Renaissance have been instrumental in raising my consciousness about race as a critical issue in the period that defines my study. Prominent among these are Gloria Hull, Barbara Christian, Deborah McDowell, Hazel Carby, Ann Allen Shockley, and my colleague, Joyce Joyce. Too often white feminists inadequately link the suffrage struggle to racism, and these scholars have helped me make some tentative connections between dominant culture narratives and women of color. I wish to acknowledge, too, those few people willing to look at women's magazines in a serious and scholarly way: Theodore Peterson, Frank Luther Mott, Leila Rupp, William O'Neill, Lillian Faderman, Betty Friedan, and Barbara Welter. All have contributed to the recognition of mass magazines as important carriers of American ideology about women. Finally, I must recognize the ground-breaking work of Nancy F. Cott, Rosalind Rosenberg, and Elaine Showalter, who have revised our views of the women's rights movement and the 1920s to include a more balanced assessment of their long-lasting effects. Without overstating those effects, these historians have suggested ways in which the feminist movement made deep inroads into American society and conceptions of gender.

Other sources of support helped me complete this ten-year study. The University of Nebraska provided research grants and fellowships that allowed me to work in Berkeley, New York City, and East Lansing as a supplement to the uneven collection of women's magazines available in Lincoln. I wish to thank as well my research assistants, too numerous to mention, who patiently photocopied stories out of huge, bulky volumes; and the secretarial staff of the English Department at the University of Nebraska–Lincoln, most notably Roma Rector and LeAnn Messing, who transcribed dozens of stories onto computer for me with good humor and thoughtful praise for the fiction. I would like to thank Barbara Siegemund-Broka at the University of Oklahoma Press for her help and encouragement.

Finally, I am delighted to realize that the strong women in my family hovered over me in my many hours of reading and perusing these beautiful old periodicals. As I thumbed through articles on flower gardens, recipes, dress patterns, and advertisements, I thought of my paternal grandmother, Florence Pearl Honey, who kept a lovely home during the 1920s in Detroit, Michigan, and who shaped my own household aesthetics. I also was visited by the ghosts of my maternal grandmother, Zilda Miner, and great-grandmother, "Mimi," who could have stepped out of the fantasies recorded here. Zilda was an artist at the piano and indelibly imprinted on my mind the popular tunes of her youth. Mimi was a matriarch, a New Woman, who left husband and children to adventure in Mexico in the 1910s. She then ran her own taxi service and boarding house in Detroit. Under other circumstances, she could have been one of the heroines in this collection; she will always be one of my own heroines—independent, daring, and a lover of life.

MAUREEN HONEY

Lincoln, Nebraska

BREAKING THE TIES
THAT BIND

INTRODUCTION

THIS collection of New Woman stories is the first reprinting of early American magazine fiction by women. Although periodical fiction was a central component of American popular culture between the wars, since its heyday it has received little attention from scholars and has been left largely unread, keeping silent vigil in libraries, testament to an era when the market for such literature was huge. Conservative estimates place the number of periodicals in the United States by 1923 somewhere in the neighborhood of 3,000, with a combined per-issue circulation of 128,621,000.[1] To put these figures in perspective, the population at this time numbered around 114 million; only 60,000 homes possessed radios in 1922, yet as early as 1905 there was a ratio of four magazines to every household—a figure that increased dramatically over the ensuing twenty years.[2] The mass market magazine industry took root before the advent of talking pictures in 1927, the dominance of radio in the 1930s, and the explosion of high-quality, low-cost paperback books just prior to World War II; but these media, by all accounts, did not curtail readership, which continued to grow until the 1950s.[3]

Women's magazines were the circulation leaders of the early twentieth century and, by the middle 1920s, were the type most likely to amass circulations of one million or more.[4]

3

Three of the five top leaders in advertising revenue in 1920, partially illustrating this dominance, were magazines aimed at women: the *Ladies' Home Journal, Woman's Home Companion,* and *Pictorial Review.*[5] Some analysts have suggested that the movement of middle-class women into the world outside the home was aided as well as accompanied by the rising success of women's magazines.[6] Most studies of these magazines, however, arrive at fairly negative conclusions about their content and implications, concluding that the economic forces that moved women out of the domestic sphere operated in a neo-conservative ideological context emphasizing marriage and home. Moreover, they find an unsupportive treatment of feminism in women's magazines despite the success of the suffrage movement in 1920.[7] Sound evidence supporting this view is to be found within women's magazines. Many articles appearing in the postsuffrage years attack feminism and many concern fashion and home decoration; editorials counsel restraint on women's activities in the marketplace; and thousands of ads are devoted to selling the audience on tending the hearth with miraculous new products.[8]

This anthology is designed not to refute the aforementioned view of the period so much as to supplement it with another side, which is beginning to gain recognition.[9] If there is evidence that the generation to succeed the suffragists was a nonpolitical one, alienated from what it understood by the term "feminist," so is there indication that it did not embrace a return to the Victorian doctrine of separate spheres.[10] Though some surveys at the time suggest that young women may have focused on private concerns, desiring marriage to a degree unthinkable to many women's rights advocates, they seem to have been, at the same time, dedicated to the concept of self-expression and individual freedom.[11] Current scholarship, in other words, is painting a more complex portrait of the 1920s than has been drawn in the past, suggesting that the decade built upon the Woman Movement even as that movement crumbled under the weight of rapid social change, internecine struggles, and lack of political focus.[12]

One manifestation of that complexity is the fiction that appeared in the very women's magazines that seemingly sounded the death knell for feminist ideas and unconventional life-styles. Prior to the full marketing of the paperback book at the end of the 1930s, periodical fiction formed the backbone of popular stories for the adult, middle-class reading public between the world wars. Of course this same public was buying novels and checking them out of the newly established lending libraries, but the cheapest, most accessible, and highest-quality fiction was to be found in mass market magazines.[13] The line between best-selling novels and periodical fiction was blurred by the editorial practice of negotiating with popular writers for rights to serialize their books before they were published. Edith Wharton, for example, sold *The Age of Innocence, The Mother's Recompense,* and *The Children* to *Pictorial Review* during the twenties, and Willa Cather originally published *My Mortal Enemy* in *McCall's* in 1926. These and other writers were paid large sums of money by women's magazines for stories that could attract readers in the highly competitive market.

It was the decision to include a large amount of fiction in the early teens that propelled the circulation of industry giants such as the *Ladies' Home Journal, Good Housekeeping,* and *Woman's Home Companion* into the millions and that constituted the core of their marketing strategy throughout the World War I years and twenties.[14] The case of *Cosmopolitan* is instructive. Beginning as a muckraking journalistic magazine and then gearing itself toward women, *Cosmopolitan* increased its circulation by 70 percent through serializing, in 1912, Robert W. Chambers's *The Common Law,* illustrated by well-known artist Charles Dana Gibson. Thereafter, the magazine included two serials and five or six short stories per issue, achieving a circulation of one million or more from 1915 through 1925. A new editor, Ray Long, was hired in 1918 because of his reputation for recognizing fiction that would appeal to a large audience, and, by 1931, *Cosmopolitan* enjoyed a circulation of 1,700,000, with each issue including four serials and a dozen short stories.[15]

Periodicals that originally were designed as fashion or household service magazines in the late 1800s shifted their emphasis after 1900 to fiction, gradually including more of it and hiring top book illustrators as well as best-selling authors. *Good Housekeeping,* for example, saw itself as a household management magazine aimed at the homemaker, but by 1904 it was beginning to include fiction by popular writers such as Margaret Deland and Mary Heaton Vorse. With the advent of Fiction Editor William Frederick Bigelow in 1913, *Good Housekeeping's* identity was largely shaped by its regularly featured novelists—Mary Roberts Rinehart, Kathleen Norris, Ring Lardner, and Booth Tarkington—and circulation grew from 200,000 in 1908 to over a million in the 1920s.[16] Similarly, *Woman's Home Companion* blossomed under the thirty-year editorship of newspaperwoman Gertrude Battles Lane, who began in 1911 to include two serials and four or five stories per issue. Willa Cather, Ellen Glasgow, and Mary Wilkins Freeman were all published in *Woman's Home Companion,* which was reputed to offer as much as $85,000 in the 1920s for serial rights to a novel by Sophie Kerr, Dorothy Canfield Fisher, or Edna Ferber. By 1927, the *Companion* enjoyed a circulation of two million and reached over 170 pages in length.[17]

For practical as well as ideological reasons, this wealth of material for the cultural historian barely has been tapped.[18] The sheer volume of stories in this twenty- to thirty-year period is staggering; this alone has inhibited researchers. To illustrate, the sample from which this collection is drawn numbers well over seven hundred short stories and serials.[19] Moreover, the average time it took to read one story was thirty to forty-five minutes, so anyone interested in analyzing the narrative patterns of women's magazine fiction will find merely ploughing through the raw data immensely time-consuming. In addition, most of the writers who were famous at this time have fallen into obscurity because, as with most popular literature, what they wrote fell short of critical aesthetic standards. The magazines bought formula stories, most of them romances, with archetypal characters, conventional plots, and fantasy endings; many stories were hastily and poorly written. The hallmarks of mass market fiction writers are speed, volume, and predictability, none of which aids in composing great literature.[20] Furthermore, historians have been reluctant to see this material as a reliable guide to public attitudes precisely because of its fantasy quality, its lack of correspondence to the reader's reality.[21]

In the last decade, however, women's fantasy fiction has been taken seriously as social documentation. The issue of what such stories do in fact mean has led to a variety of theoretical approaches and interpretations, ranging from Janice Radway's cautions about text-bound criticism to Tania Modleski's psychological interpretation of Harlequin romances.[22] Although scholars do not agree on what women's popular fiction represents, all advance the notion that it contains social and historical significance, if not the highest artistic merit, and that it forms a legitimate component of what we understand to be women's literature.

While a good case can be made for magazine fiction as a subject of study, there are factors complicating our interpretation of it. One of these is the determination of audience. Publishers of magazines did not conduct systematic research surveys on readers until the 1930s; as late as 1945, the Magazine Advertising Bureau complained of "the scanty data" on readership.[23] Editors had rather hazy conceptions of their audience, characterizing it as "alert," "intelligent," "average American" and claiming that their readers had "solid" or "middle-class" values.[24] Fiction was selected based on the editors' own judgment of audience appeal, and their success was determined by circulation figures rather than reader polls. The methods used then were unacceptably speculative by today's academic standards. Furthermore, due to the many changes in ownership over the years and the folding of publications, researchers cannot obtain many of the records that may have been kept on audience characteristics. About all we can say with any degree of certainty is that women made up a large proportion, if not the majority, of the readership for the magazines included in this study and that the target reader was a white, middle-class woman of rather conventional values, whatever that meant to the editors.[25]

Such sketchy information limits the conclusions we can reach about audience attitudes, even if accurate inferences could somehow be drawn on the basis of texts alone.[26] To posit a correlation between reader perspectives on a variety of issues and popular literature is, at best, a problematic endeavor; and when texts are removed from us in time, the potential for misinterpretation is even greater.[27] I do not, therefore, claim that New Woman fiction represents either the lifestyle or the personal values of the reader. Not only are the real lives of these readers obscured for us by lack of data, but the immensely complex relationship of fantasy to the consumer's value system renders all but the most tentative conclusions useless.

Nevertheless, the fiction collected here does constitute an important episode in women's cultural history, for it represents a variation of the romance that flowered after the shattering of Victorianism, one that departed significantly from standard romantic conventions. As outlined by Leslie Rabine, historically, the romance has eroticized and idealized female powerlessness while simultaneously providing one of the few acceptable outlets for women to revolt against patriarchal authority.[28] Contemporary romances similarly eroticize male dominance while covertly expressing hostility to it.[29] What distinguishes the New Woman romance from the genre's standard narrative is that the heroine's hostility to the patriarchal order is overt and grounded in her desire for self-actualization rather than eros. She embarks on a quest to find meaningful work in a world ruled by men, consistently privileging her passion for self-expression or indepedence over her romantic attachments, important as those are to her. Heroines in the conventional romance also value their independence, but they tend to betray it, either by acting against their will or by rationalizing the advent of male power into their autonomous but incomplete lives.[30] While ostensibly pursuing her own course, the romantic heroine spends most of the narrative disentangling her conflicted emotions about a man she experiences as more powerful than herself. The New Woman figure, though not immune to emotional upset or even self-betrayal, is placed more firmly in a world of her own making and either finds a mate compatible with it or recommits herself to a woman's right to have a life apart from marriage. The New Woman romance, in other words, augments the heroine's dedication to nonromantic pursuits instead of overwhelming it.

To explain fully the emergence of this story type is beyond
the scope of this study, but certainly among the relevant factors were an urbanizing, industrializing economy that pulled
increasing numbers of single women into the paid work force;
an intensified struggle for women's rights; new wartime gender roles; and the collapse of Victorian ideology, with its emphasis on family duty, sexual repression, and male control of
public activity. The parallel development of romantic fiction
in women's magazines perhaps accounts for its attention to
the heroine's place in a rapidly changing society where gender
roles were seemingly in flux. There is also evidence that, unlike
the generally conservative editorials written by the mostly
male managers of these magazines and the many features devoted to homemaking, magazine fiction tended to be open to
expansion of women's life-styles beyond marriage and domesticity. This characteristic has been acknowledged by a former
editor of *Woman's Home Companion* who went to work for the
magazine in 1908 and wrote a book about the experience:

> The First World War caused a revolution in the thinking of
> America and especially to women. . . . None of this, however,
> was shown or discussed in the 1919 women's magazines. . . .
> But often what they wouldn't say in articles or editorials, they
> would get across in fiction. . . . The heroines were women of
> much rough and varied experience in both love and life, hard
> as nails, and willing to break any rule to obtain whatever pure
> and noble ideal they were pursuing. . . . It was as close as the
> magazines could come to approving openly the new freedom
> for women.[31]

Comments from other editors made at the time echo this sentiment and indicate that the average reader was envisioned as
a woman interested in the world, in public affairs, and in
broadening her horizons. Barton W. Currie, who became
editor-in-chief of the *Ladies' Home Journal* in 1921, for instance,
stated that his readers were different than the earlier audience
for the *Journal:* "Women's magazines are no longer edited for
clinging vines . . . for helpless, submerged, and inarticulate
gentlewomen."[32]

This sense of the reader as a woman of some sophistication
who wanted more than recipes, dress patterns, or home deco-

rating schemes (although these were all regular features of the magazines) is reflected in the large number of stories that began appearing in 1914 that featured heroines with unconventional dreams and ambitious plans to make a life for themselves outside of marriage. The New Woman character predates World War I, of course, but the prewar stories about her tended to conclude in failure or serious compromise of her desire to live in the world on her own terms.[53] The aspiring writer, actress, painter, or singer left the parental home for adventure in the great metropolis with high hopes but usually returned, chastened and disillusioned, to a life-style uncomfortably similar to that of her traditional mother. Alternatively, she stuck with her career goals but was unable to form a satisfying personal life and endured much emotional deprivation.[34] Apart from the occasional endorsement of the "angel of the hearth"—a story type that made a brief comeback in the early twenties— the thrust of New Woman fiction from 1915 through 1930 was toward a positive resolution of the heroine's difficulties in forging an autonomous life of meaningful work. She was often able to have it all—financial success, satisfying activity, and a supportive intimate relationship. Even when she was unable to make a good love match, her vocational rewards tended to balance her romantic losses.

The stories selected for this collection illustrate key features of the New Woman success tale as it developed over this fifteen-year period. The fiction of these years focused on both the woman of action and the artist heroine, two figures from the turn of the century who represented fundamental challenges to the Victorian doctrine of separate spheres. One of the primary characteristics of the ideal bourgeois woman in nineteenth-century sentimental fiction was physical frailty and stasis.[35] Fragility, fainting, illness, and death were signs of the heroine's spiritual superiority and fine feelings; she was too pure for this corrupt world with its mercenary rules of commerce, cynical political machines, and brutal male power.[36] Her realm was the home, the influence of which she hoped to extend to civilization at large.[37] In contrast, the New Woman relished action and strenuous physical activity. She was athletic, healthy, eager to take on challenges in the nondomestic world. By the 1910s, the woman of action had made great headway in replacing the delicate ideal of sentimental fiction and was becoming central to a new fantasy of competence in the roughest circumstances. The bold reporter in the anthology's first piece, "The Sob-Lady" (1915), represents the triumph of this new kind of romantic heroine. Susanne Brown is a mate, a comrade, not an ethereal woman on a pedestal, a figure embodied in her rival, Angela Lake, whose name symbolizes the other-worldliness and placidity of a former era. Angela wears gowns of soft lace and "misty" pastels, whereas the down-to-earth Susanne Brown prefers suits with "mannish" hats. The contrast between these characters is mirrored in their occupation: Susanne is in a constant rush to report on life in the city whereas Angela sequesters herself in Susanne's boardinghouse in order to write "Literature." Angela's dreamy conception of writing is far removed from the hardheaded, no-frills approach taken by Susanne, who compares her newspaper stories to a fire engine, "racing into action, horses straining, driver cursing, siren screaming, smoke belching, sparks trailing—no time to look back and see what sort of fancy track they're leaving."[38]

Angela's representation of the sentimental ideal, though updated by her dedication to art, is further emphasized by her blonde hair and blue eyes, while Susanne Brown, like her surname, is dark haired, an allusion to the tendency of earlier fiction to cast active brunettes in negative roles of rebellion.[39] We are told that Susanne's girlhood companion was a dog named Rebel, in fact, and that he was by her side in childhood romps. Susanne's lack of traditional femininity is the true subject of the story, which makes repeated reference to her sweating body, disheveled appearance, and serviceable clothing. Her attraction to an old friend, Bill Ransome, is disrupted by his infatuation with the unattainable, delicate Angela, whose aloof beauty distracts him from Susanne's familiar camaraderie. Devastated by the simultaneous loss of her job and probable engagement announcement by Angela, Susanne is forced to rely on her grit for survival, ultimately winning both the man and the new position through reconfirmation of belief in herself despite what the world seems to say.

The pitting of old against new ideals forms the core of a later story included here, Vivien Bretherton's "Bird Girl" (1929). The woman of action in this piece is a pilot, Vandy Cameron, who knows as much about airplanes as her father, the owner of Cameron Aeroplane Corporation. The opening scene, in which Vandy performs dangerous aerial maneuvers while being watched admiringly by Brian Scott, the most famous pilot in the world, underscores Vandy's competence and courage. Our first glimpse of Vandy, as she emerges from her plane, reveals her "straight, boyish" figure and short dark hair as she forthrightly introduces herself to Brian, who has assumed she must be a man. All of these qualities evidence her lifelong attraction to physical risk-taking and place her in dramatic contrast to her high school friend Narcissa Elliot. Narcissa, as her name suggests, is self-absorbed, "one of those lovely, virginal-looking girls whose sly, silky little ways had never been the ways of Vandy." [40] She is as interested in the games of romance as Vandy is repelled by them and is ostentatiously squeamish about flying. It is Narcissa's helplessness and feminine glamour that appeal to Brian's regressive side, making it hard for him to recognize Vandy's own rather compelling sexual charms.

The story ultimately favors an androgynous model of women, as is typical of New Woman fiction, by making Vandy's competence essential to Brian's survival when they are forced to parachute out of her burning plane. She takes charge of the situation even though her own life is in danger and her despair over losing Brian's love has weakened her spirit. Although he saves her from drowning, she pulls him from the water and resets his dislocated arm, thus illustrating their equal strength and mutual dependence. Narcissa's artificiality is revealed to Brian, who comes to see that a pal is what he needs, not a delicate flower unsuited to the world of speed and adventure.

The woman of action could not stand on a pedestal, immobile, for she was too curious about life beyond home and marriage. Heroines of this period are frequently described as "restless" and anxious to flee the circumscribed orbit of parental authority in order to make their way in an urban environment bustling with change and possibility. They are in geographical as well as other kinds of movement, frequently abandoning small town communities for metropolitan areas. In doing so, they are rejecting settled, family-oriented life on the margins in favor of open-ended, individual effort within the heart of modern society. Blanche Gelfant has identified this journey as the heroine's existential voyage toward self-definition: "Freedom seems to [the heroine] inherent in a fluid if disorganized urban society, one that by its disorder and indifference has released her from the roles assigned to women by history and myth."[61] Anonymity gives the heroine a chance to remake herself into a New Woman in harmony with the dawning new age. Illustrating such an orientation, the women in this collection travel to New York City, Chicago, and Sacramento in pursuit of meaningful vocations and autonomy.

The flight from a small town, where the heroine's mother endured a selfless, unstimulating existence, signals the shattering of an old consensus about the nature of women and progress. Many early feminists maintained that women rightly occupied a unique space, separate from the world created by men. Their complaint was that men's sphere had grown too powerful, and they insisted on strengthening women's domesticating influence.[42] Both Rosalind Rosenberg and Nancy F. Cott argue that the distinguishing feature of modern feminism was the assertion of an essential sameness between women and men and the ensuing demand that women have equal access to the public marketplace.[43] This core tenet of new feminist thinking is fictionally represented by the small town—a dying vestige of woman's past isolation from civilization's inner workings. The New Woman heroine leaves behind whatever power she had available to her in the familial community because, while safe, it is on the periphery of life; its separation from the real workings of society make her vulnerable to following a marginalized agenda, to a deathlike passivity that comes from being irrelevant.

The impulse to relocate in a setting perceived as closer to the center of American society can be found, too, in fictional references to technology. Symbol of modernity and change, technology was also identified with men. To become comfortable with it, then, was one way a heroine could challenge gender restrictions as well as move nearer to an emerging industrial landscape. Dorothy Eades does both in "Shelter" (1916). Part of an on-going series about eight modern young women in the vaguely placed town of Chiltern, this story follows Dorothy's attempt to make a living at a time when women of her class were expected to marry and be supported by a husband. Metaphorically freeing Dorothy from these values, the town and her father's house have been destroyed by a catastrophic fire, and the patriarchal head of the Eades family loses his job as a result. With her "boyish shirts" and tailored suits, Dorothy takes charge of the family's welfare by using money from the sale of her car to finance their move to a neighboring city where she talks her way into a job selling automobiles. Dorothy's skill as a saleswoman derives from her motoring abilities and knowledge of how a car works (she boasts she can take an automobile apart and put it back together). Her familiarity with the new auto technology reflects a passionate desire to get out from under the suffocating "shelter" of middle-class domesticity for which she has been groomed and which she bitterly resents as an obstacle to real living. The male characters, most notably her father and suitor, attempt to dissuade Dorothy from her determination to enter the marketplace by warning that women need protection from the world of commerce for which she hungers. Their words may scare Dorothy, but she vows at the end of the story to raise self-sufficient daughters and fight for women's right to a larger sphere than marriage.

The technological expertise of Dorothy Eades and Vandy Cameron marks them as New Women ready to inhabit a modern era, but many protofeminist characters from this period, such as the Greenwich Village painter in Grace Sartwell Mason's "The Lotus Eater" (1918), devote their lives to art rather than technology. We first see Mary, the heroine, through the eyes of a woman friend while she is strolling down Fifth Avenue carrying a huge portfolio under her arm. This opening scene establishes her as a woman apart from the crowd, with her sensible, casual attire and her obliviousness to the commercial wares of ornamentation in shop windows with which most women concerned themselves, focused as she is on color and line, the aesthetics of her adopted city rather than its commodities. A successful portrait painter is also at the center of "The Amazing Generation" (1918), a fashion designer is the focus of "The Sleeper Wakes" (1920), an actress appears in "Half a Million" (1928), and a department store display manager carves out a career in "Henry's Divorce" (1929). These artistic characters constitute another departure from the ideology of hearth and home, for they are committed to self-expression and creative work, resisting pressures to sublimate their career goals into marriage.

The artist, whether she be painter, singer, dancer, actress, or writer, is a primary figure of New Woman fiction. Indeed, the artist herione's desire to engage in such activity alienates her from the traditional woman's world of family and community service and identifies her as a modern person. The concept of the female artist served a variety of important functions in the transition to new conceptions of women. For one thing, she worked alone and claimed private space when women's family role entailed rather constant interaction with others. In addition, she engaged in work that lasted as opposed to the unceasing chores of housework. More important, though, art bridged the gap between woman's traditional sphere and the new ideal of assimilation into public roles. It captured one aspect of nineteenth-century conceptions—the responsibility of women for cultural elevation—and merged it with the idea of individual endeavor outside the home. It could legitimize women's right to express themselves in an independent, nongender-defined way yet link that autonomy with culture and beauty.

Rachel Blau Du Plessis illuminates the transitional utility of the artist heroine in *Writing Beyond the Ending: Narrative Strategies of Twentieth Century Women Writers*. She argues that the *künstlerromane* created by women in the late nineteenth century encoded the conflict between the empowered woman and barriers to her achievement; using a romantic image of the unconventional genius, writers could legitimate the artist heroine's rejection of a traditional middle-class role.[44] She adds that the dedication to art in these characters linked the idea of visible public work with the female world. To elaborate on this concept, the artist embodied many traits associated with women's supposedly special qualities—heightened emotionalism, keen intuition, love of beauty, attraction to harmony, superior sentiment or fine feeling, and wider lattitude of self-expression. At the same time, she was a symbol of change, for the artist demonstrated her talents in a public way, calling attention to her achievements and seeking acknowledgment for them. The artist heroine, then, formed a bridge between private and public realms and was well positioned for the leap from female culture to male.[45]

As Du Plessis points out, most nineteenth-century *künstlerromanes* by women pose an unresolved conflict between the artist's happiness as a woman and realization of her vocational ambitions.[46] Love, in a word, is incompatible with work. This pattern held in women's magazine fiction until the middle of the second decade, when artist heroines found sympathetic men who admired and supported their art. This is the case in "The Lotus Eater" (1918), in which Mary learns to distinguish between false and true male support, rejecting a narcissistic dilettante for a mature man who "had a feeling for Mary's talent that was next door to reverence" and who adjusts his schedule to hers in order not to impose on her "precious time" and chances for success. The fact that he is a "plain American business man" in an automobile concern emphasizes the compatibility of Mary's artistic ambition with the emerging industrial order in which she is seeking to earn a living and of which her suitor is a representative.

The belief in successful merger—whether of public and private, male and female, or art and business—lies at the heart of much New Woman fiction. Male engineers, architects, and managers are featured consistently, for instance, as symbols of the new industrial order. They often view positively the heroine's commitment to work outside the home and consider her a comrade rather than a helpmeet. Though occasionally the suitor's old-fashioned views prove intractable, as is the case in "Shelter" (1916) and "Amy Brooks" (1927), the usual course of events leads from lack of support for the heroine's right to pursue an independent vocation to major disruptions in the romance (affairs, illness, career failure, estrangement) to final harmony and mutual dedication to work. Men who can overcome a false sense of pride at being the breadwinner or shortsighted selfishness find their wives and sweethearts eager to make them happy, as long as the women feel free to develop their talents. These are the relationships most likely to succeed, as are those in which the woman does not upset an egalitarian balance by outshining her mate.

Male chauvinists do not fare well in this fiction. Oppressive fathers are abandoned by unruly daughters and ill wives; men who insist woman's primary task is to serve their needs become paralyzed or die of a sudden heart attack; husbands with Victorian views of wives as homemakers jeopardize their marriages. In "Henry's Divorce" (1929), for example, a late-decade piece from the *Ladies' Home Journal*, the protagonist has been happily wed to a department store display manager for five years, until he gets a notion that he is being unmanly not to have a wife at home "where she belongs." Though Cookie, who has kept her maiden name, runs an efficient household, Henry goes home to mother for nursing when he contracts the flu, piqued over his feminist wife's determination to keep her job. To his consternation, he is smothered by his mother's constant attention and is intensely annoyed by her lack of interest in the news. Moreover, he is ultimately repelled by an old flame, Adele, who represents the traditional femininity he thinks he wants. Adele's demure refusal of a cigarette at lunch and her fawning attention appeal to Henry's nostalgia for the premodern era of his father, but Cookie's youthful vigor, good humor, and superior understanding of his preferences easily win him over. She is a woman who can relate to men as friends, smoke with them, move in their world, and enable them to move comfortably in hers because she has eschewed the pedestal for a level playing field.

The theme of New Women embarking on modern relationships with men supportive of their continuing commitment to a career is in harmony with studies of the 1920s that indicate hierarchical conceptions of marriage were being challenged by then with a model of companionate union.[47] However, this heterosexual egalitarianism, subscribed to in theory if not observed in fact, resulted in losses as well as gains for women.

Homophobic attacks on passionate female friendships accompanied the rising expectations of camaraderie with men, and lesbian couples were undermined in fiction after 1920.[48] The un-selfconscious college student in "The Cat and the King" (1919) who has a crush on a senior woman and flirts with her female physician was a not-uncommon figure in pre-1920 magazine fiction, but romantic implications in later woman-identified stories were either eliminated or depicted as unhealthy.[49] The business partners in "Eve Goes On" (1928), for instance, who have lived and worked together for years, are narratively marginalized and symbolically replaced by the partnership of clearly heterosexual Eve and her best friend Amy, who likewise become cafeteria owners when the original establishment is sold by the older women. Eve's romance with Amy's brother conclusively derails whatever primary attachment may have developed between Eve and Amy, who are constant companions as well as business partners.

Some scholars have argued that the weakening of feminism after suffrage was won can be traced to the dismantling of Victorian separation between woman's private and man's public spheres. The ideology of merger and equality, designed to liberate women from restricted roles, paradoxically placed them at a disadvantage.[50] The "female world of love and ritual," in Carrol Smith-Rosenberg's words, provided a strong political base as well as a protected emotional space for same-sex relationships, and its replacement by a vision of individual female achievement in the world run by men deprived women of an essential collective identity.[51] Weakening ties to other women can be detected in some of the stories reprinted here, such as "Men Are Like That" (1928), wherein a bookkeeper feels cut off from her female co-workers and the wives of men at the bank. Though Emma Morrison clearly resents the inflated male egos that blind men to her value, she blames her failure to be promoted, in part, on other women, whom she perceives as frivolous parasites. Similarly, the corporate executive of "Belinda's Importance" (1930) is alienated from her old school chums, who have become suburban matrons filling their time with idle gossip and hurtful criticism of unconventional high achievers like herself. Many, if not most, New

Woman heroines battle alone to make their way in a society riddled with prejudice against their sex, while other women are often portrayed as enemies of gender equality. There is a theme that mitigates the isolation of the New Woman heroine from female support, however, and that is her attempt to build a community of women who are themselves struggling toward fulfillment outside the family. She frequently finds a roommate, for instance, who familiarizes her with the city, or she enjoys a close friendship with a woman she respects. In addition, while the mother is usually absent, symbolizing the death of a past, home-centered community, a memory of her remains, as a negative role model, yes, but also as a source of love and moral support. Frequently, in fact, a mother or an aunt have left the heroine an inheritance that finances her escape. In other words, while she is casting her lot with male enterprise, she often relies on the help of other women. Several stories in the collection feature women who come to the aid of the heroine when she is threatened by men or in danger of losing her independence. The romantic entanglements that weaken the main character's vocational commitment are challenged by women friends, for instance, in "The Lotus Eater" (1918), "The Amazing Generation" (1918), and "Amy Brooks" (1927). In these pieces, women's friendship is vital to the heroine's successful resolution of her conflict between love of career and love of a man who interferes with that career.

Three other stories illustrate another kind of female solidarity prevalent in New Woman fiction throughout the period that stems from the woman rebel's vision of herself as part of an emerging work force. Sometimes this identification with women who are wage earners is characterized as an alternative to marital dependency, as it is in "Eve Goes On" (1928). Eve Archer has come to New York to make a new life after losing her sweetheart to a home-oriented, spoiled sister and is at once sheltered by a working-class police matron and her daughter, Irma, who provide a haven throughout Eve's struggle to make her way. Initially prejudiced against blue-collar workers, Eve quickly drops her class bias when she gets to know her fellow and sister cafeteria employees, admiring their knowledge of literature, opera, and life. Most are European immigrants whose difficulties with poverty and urban adjustment mirror her own sense of being adrift on an alien sea. As a woman supporting herself without help from husband or family, Eve views herself as a pioneer connected to all women outside the domestic realm, "the great army of women workers which she [had] joined." As Eve reflects on women wage earners, we see her growing identification with them: "There were her comrades, the poor old broken scrub woman, the stenographer, the clerk, the cook, the waitress, the seamstresses and millinery workers, the factory girls. . . . They were all fighting for their lives." [52] The story's central event—Eve's resistance to the new manager's sexual harassment, which precipitates a walk-out of the whole staff—underlines the theme of loyalty among working women.

In similar fashion, an earlier story, "*What* Would *You* Have Done in *Her* Place?" (1917), features a salesclerk who comes to see the importance of woman-to-woman loyalty during her convalescence from typhoid fever in a house of prostitution. Millie May Jewett works in such arduous conditions as a department store retail clerk that her health has been seriously weakened. After collapsing on the street from fatigue and a collision with a wealthy woman, she is nursed to recovery by a prostitute, Goldie Altamont, whose life story opens May's eyes to her own "hollow" respectability. Goldie has suffered much from the betrayal of other women and has lost job after job when her co-workers discovered that she became pregnant by an affair with her former boss, a married man. Goldie's fate demonstrates to Millie the economic reality that forces women into prostitution and the class privilege that divides women from each other, to devastating effect. Millie's ultimate failure to resist that very privilege forms the story's moral point, when she snubs Goldie at a restaurant in order to protect her engagement to a solid, respectable New Englander. Here, marriage is portrayed as an economic institution that pits women against each other and undermines the solidarity that is essential for survival in an exploitative marketplace.

A slightly different but related idea lies behind the state senatorial campaign of Doria Dean Yale in "Call of the House"

(1926). Dean becomes the first woman senator in California and, though her managers are men, it is working women who provide the crucial emotional support she needs to carve out a political career. Prohibition leader Hester McGlurk and newspaper columnist Belinda Buell are both instrumental in drumming up public support for Dean's candidacy, while Dean's nervous, homemaker mother merely wrings her hands and wishes her daughter would get married instead. Not only are McGlurk and Buell single, professional women with a toughness born of many years of public service, they reinforce for Dean the historic nature of her quest and the connection between her desire for personal challenge and her responsibility to women. This idea is strengthened further by a poor, rural woman who has helped found a Women's Improvement Club and who awes Dean by her monumental efforts to get out the female vote in her district. The fact that Dean prevails over a rival who believes women should not be in politics emphasizes the story's contention that women are linked by a common oppression and need collectively to create public space for themselves.

The idea of sisterly collectivity was undermined by the individual success story, as represented by Belinda Dale's entrepreneurial rise in "Belinda's Importance" (1930). Furthermore, the label "feminist" usually was not applied to the New Woman heroine's assertive attack on conventional beliefs. These elements worked against the ideology of suffragists, who connected individual professional goals with the advancement of women as a whole. At the same time, within the revisionist concept of feminism animating New Woman stories, there was room for sisterhood even though it was weakened by images of female betrayal. In "Eve Goes On" (1928), for example, the heroine's biological sister has stabbed her in the back by dating and eventually marrying her beau while her urban roommate, Yriane, belittles Eve's working-class occupation. These wounds are balanced, however, by the many more women who help Eve, nurture her, and ultimately establish a successful cafeteria with her. Similarly, though her pal Amy is described as "an advanced and rabid feminist" with an "abnormal complex" about men, Eve admits she is "not so crazy about men" either and bitterly resents a system that fails to teach young women how to earn a living. The characters' personal dream of going into business together is explicitly tied to economic independence for women in their vision of the planned cafeteria as an inspiration to their sex.

A parallel dynamic is at work in "Amy Brooks" (1927), though the story ends more bleakly and ambiguously. The plot seemingly follows a woman-against-woman line: the poor runaway whom Amy has rescued from suicide marries Amy's fiancé for her own selfish aims. Ironically, Amy saves her rival's life again when she performs an emergency appendectomy, thus losing one last chance at the marriage for which she has longed. Overshadowing her heroine's heartbreak and disillusionment, however, is the strong narrative presence of her reporter friend, who is telling us Amy's story with admiration and care. Clearly she will be there for Amy in a way that the conflicted lover could never have been. In addition, the world-famous woman surgeon who supervises Amy's apprenticeship acquaints her with the solace of meaningful work and assures her that it will make up for the disappointment in love: "He was a pigeon who takes a pigeon for a mate, and lets the eagle fly to the sun. . . . I will make you ready so that when June comes you will have another kind of glory." [53] Braced by the advice, Amy throws herself into her practice "with the exaltation of the chosen." Though her youthful innocence is destroyed and her idealism suffers a hard blow, the sympathy and love of other trailblazers like herself strengthen Amy's faith in her drive to be a doctor and make the world a better place for women.

The one, great, glaring omission in New Woman stories of gender solidarity and advancement is the woman of color. Racism pervaded mainstream women's magazines both in content and in the exclusion of nonwhite writers. Narrative subjugation of minorities into subordinate roles occurred regularly, and stories that did feature ethnic characters relied on racist stereotypes of the white-identified Indian maiden, the exotic "Oriental," or the tragic mulatto who longs to join white society. This racial insensitivity is reflected, among other ways, in the invisibility of a black maid in "*What* Would

You Have Done in *Her* Place?" (1917), the subservient portrait of an Asian servant in "Call of the House" (1926), the lack of concern with apartheid in "Half a Million" (1928), and the absence of African-Americans from urban, working-class districts portrayed in "Amy Brooks" (1927) and "Eve Goes On" (1928). The whiteness of New Woman stories reflected the racist practices of white editors, their exclusionary view of the market for magazine fiction, and the failure of the suffrage movement to make race a priority in the struggle for women's rights.[54] The social debate over gender had been framed for years by racist arguments, acceptance of segregation, and reference to white, middle-class models of feminism, so it is not suprising—though no less reprehensible—that the fantasy of gender equality in mass-produced periodicals rested on white supremacist assumptions.

Women of color were interested in sexism as well as racism in the multifaceted movement to end slavery and Jim Crow segregation, but they worked primarily within their own organizations and wrote for their own journals.[55] The Harlem Renaissance was under way by 1918 and black women played a major role in it, contributing much poetry and fiction to *The Crisis*, founded by the National Association for the Advancement of Colored People (NAACP) in 1910, and *Opportunity*, begun by the Urban League in 1923.[56] Although not quite analogous to mainstream magazines such as the *Ladies' Home Journal* that had circulations in the millions, these middle-class, African-American journals were among the only places where black women could publish anything like comparable stories about modern life.[57] I have included here one such story by Jessie Fauset to correct partially the racism of the day. Not only was Fauset literary editor of *The Crisis* from 1919 until 1926, but her fiction was the formulaic type of romance favored by the mass market and thus is comparable to the other pieces in this collection.[58] The fantasylike, popular nature of her writing and its central place in the middle-class, African-American community of this time period support its inclusion here.[59]

"The Sleeper Wakes" (1920) provides a revealing contrast to the other New Woman stories of Jessie Fauset's time, for it features a nonwhite heroine who shares some typical characteristics of the dominant culture figure. Amy Kildare has left a traditionally run home to make a career for herself in New York City, where she is befriended by a bohemian white artist, Zora, and supports herself as a fashion designer. Although Fauset uses the motif of an adventurous artistic young woman searching for life experience in the big city, she quickly entwines the focus of this standard plot, gender conflict, with issues of racism. Amy's mysterious ethnic origins are shrouded in secrecy. She knows she was adopted by a black family in New Jersey, but her fair skin and ignorance of her biological parents enable her to pass for white once she runs away from home. Passing gives Amy the illusion that the American dream of success is possible for her, a notion that is shattered by her marriage to a white man and symbolically represented by the story title's reference to awakening from a false dream.[60]

Fauset's narrative is concerned with race as much as the standard New Woman plot ignores it. Colors are featured prominently and pointedly, for instance, while white things are disparaged. Amy prefers colored jewels to diamonds or pearls, which she describes as "hard," "cold," and "dead," and her drawing room is "a wonderful study in browns." Later on in the story, when Amy goes into dress designing, we are told that the figures she uses are of many colors and shapes to account for nonwhite women, a sensitivity that Amy has picked up from the variety of skin colors she found in the black community as a child. Amy's rejection of the dominant culture's beauty ideal is central to her growing revulsion toward her husband's bigotry, symbolized by his skin's "awful whiteness" and the fact that he comes from one of the South's oldest families.

Furthermore, Amy is better able to link her disempowerment as a woman to the commercial center's exploitation than are her white counterparts. The husband, Stuart Wynne, a wealthy, retired broker, represents that center to a large extent. Not only does his racism demoralize those in his employ, but he encourages Amy to be childish, vain, and shallow, utterly dependent on him. Earlier, in fact, we are told that Wynne's first two marriages failed due to his dominant nature. Amy realizes that her desire to be beautiful and gain success through marriage has made her weak and demeaned her, that she has been blinded to the ugly reality behind the screen images she absorbed as a child. The economic dependence of wives and people of color on patriarchal racists like Wynne becomes the story's focal point as Amy rebuilds her self-esteem through earning a living and returning Wynne's alimony. Moreover, Amy ultimately perceives Wynne's perverse desire for her as a microcosm of white imperialism and the colonization of dark people throughout the world.

This critique of the economic center is far more muted in mainstream women's periodicals. Commercialism is corrupting in the standard New Woman story and male power threatens the heroine, but these problems are not portrayed as endemic or insurmountable. While the public arena or marketplace is riddled with exploitative practices, the heroine is able to rise above them and pursue her independent course without moral compromise. Dean Yale in "Call of the House" (1926), for example, is surrounded by unsavory politicians, but she votes her conscience in the climactic final scene. Similarly, Belinda Dale's business savvy as manager of a large company in "Belinda's Importance" (1930) fails to destroy her commitment to social betterment, represented by her policy of hiring ex-convicts. The New Woman heroine overcomes prejudice against her gender within a system that is basically open to any person with talent, fortitude, and ambition even if backward beliefs and individuals put women at a disadvantage. Her dedication to work and social progress are ennobling, making it possible for her to improve the modern scene as well as enter it. The more profoundly skeptical treatment of success in Jessie Fauset's story highlights the race privilege behind challenges to sexism in women's periodicals and indicates the accommodationist framework in which they were posed. The New Woman fantasy was more than a Cinderella tale with a feminist heroine, then; it was also a moral fable that posited female individual triumph within a male-dominated system that, nonetheless, made room for the woman of talent and ambition.

Despite their contradictions and biases toward white, middle-class, heterosexual characters, these New Woman stories of the World War I and postsuffrage years deal seriously and progressively with many contemporary feminist issues: lack of professional advancement, sexual harassment, prostitution as alienated labor, enfeebling marital dependency, and the importance of female solidarity. Above all, they endorse a woman's right to meaningful paid work outside the home, her right to choose what her destiny is to be regardless of gender, family obligation, tradition, or prejudice. It is easy to see these stories as individualistic and naive, but we need to keep in mind that the demand for women's right to professional and creative work was a relatively new idea and that the fantasy of an individual woman making her way in the outside world challenged deeply rooted patriarchal assumptions about woman's nature and proper role.[61] Public work became synonymous at this time with not only individual freedom, but an expanding universe for all women and their independence from the restricted experience of family duty.[62] A triumph for one, then, was portrayed as a victory for all. That this belief was, perhaps, maintained too unrealistically and selectively should not blind us to its historical usefulness in the struggle for women's right to a full, unimpeded life.

Similarly, although the homophobic exclusion of lesbian relationships must temper any positive assessment of the 1920s, the implicit demand that a woman ought not to have to choose between work and an intimate relationship—one in which she is nurtured as well as nurturing—was another significant assertion. New Woman stories refused to sacrifice automatically the heroine's love of her work to the need for love and companionship. If she were forced to compromise either, it was a sad sign that the times were not yet enlightened enough to recognize the human requirement for both. Most New Woman characters from this era did not have to choose between love and work though they needed patience, faith in themselves, and a passionate drive to do something "useful." It is, perhaps, the harmonizing of the personal and vocational spheres that best distinguishes this fifteen-year period from what went before and what came after, for the fantasy of female achievement dates back to the Civil War and continues beyond the 1920s.[63] With the Great Depression, however, attacks on married career women multiplied and depictions of lesbians were almost nonexistent in popular culture.[64] The New Woman archetype did not disappear until the late forties, but her image was never again quite as composed.[65]

How typical were the kinds of stories reproduced in this volume? To gather a reliable sample, I studied seven mass magazines with circulations of one million or more, five of which are represented here: *Good Housekeeping,* the *Ladies' Home Journal, Woman's Home Companion, Cosmopolitan, McCall's, Pictorial Review,* and the *Delineator.*[66] I read an average of one story per monthly issue of *Good Housekeeping* and *Ladies' Home Journal* from each of the fifteen years between 1915 and 1930 and one story per monthly issue from every other year for the rest.[67] Some of these magazines were more likely to publish New Woman fiction than others. *Pictorial Review* and the *Delineator* were relatively conservative, for instance, while *Good Housekeeping, Ladies' Home Journal,* and *Woman's Home Companion* published such stories regularly. With the exception of the early 1920s, when New Woman characters fell on hard times (most likely due to a postwar backlash), a reader could expect to find one story every month about a work-oriented, positively treated character in these latter three journals. For the rest, one could be found every three or four issues throughout the period. Other pieces were not necessarily about characters with traditional values, though a fair number were, but they concerned narrowly focused courtships, murder mysteries, westerns, historical romances, or childhood. The New Woman success story, therefore, was one of many generic tales that appeared. My perusal of these magazines suggests that admirable New Woman characters were not unusual, but editors included all sorts of storylines, home-centered ones among them, in order to cover a variety of fantasy needs for the readers.

Without exaggerating the numerical strength of these narratives, it is fair to say that they constituted a major story formula at the time. They were published in all the top women's magazines, in some quite frequently, and they often were the showcased piece—a serial, say, with elaborate illustration and cover advertising. Some of the most popular writers from the period wrote New Woman stories and are included in this anthology: Sophie Kerr, Josephine Daskam Bacon, Zona Gale, Booth Tarkington, Mary Synon, Edith Barnard Delano, and Juliet Wilbor Tompkins.[68] It is not necessary to demonstrate, in other words, that all fiction in all women's magazines supported the New Woman plotline to acknowledge its key place in popular culture or to conclude that it held wide appeal for a middle-class audience.

A completely representative anthology, of course, would include all the major story formulas found in women's magazines. What I have done instead is to select stories that are representative of one prevalent formula that has continuing resonance in today's world. Within that framework, I have chosen the best-written pieces with the most relevance for contemporary readers. I have also tried to be as inclusive as possible, giving visibility to working-class, lesbian, and older characters as well as those with nontraditional occupations. Most stories in the formula featured young, middle-class, heterosexual women in adventurous roles, however, and the anthology reflects this orientation. I made an effort to represent a number of periodicals and to cover comprehensively the entire spectrum of time when the New Woman success tale was a staple of women's magazine fiction. The final selection favors *Good Housekeeping* and the *Ladies' Home Journal* because the study sample favored them. It did so because I wanted an in-depth look as well as a broadly based reading of the most popular journals and because these two magazines have been among the most influential and long-lasting of their type. In addition, these two magazines symbolize traditional domestic roles, so the prominence of unconventional heroines in them underscores dramatically the complexity of middle-class women's culture in the early twentieth century. Balancing these disparate factors generated some conflicts, which I generally resolved by putting writing quality and striking presentation of issues over other considerations. If there is a bias to the collection, then, it is in the direction of readable prose with continuing appeal to modern readers. Fortunately, the best-written material tended to be the most representative of archetypes, themes, fictional trends, and writers. I elected to order the pieces chronologically as a way to indicate how this narrative pattern developed over time and to demonstrate its resilience; by the end of the 1920s, the New Woman romance was as strong, if not stronger, than it was at the peak of the suffrage campaign.

There are lessons to be learned from this moment in women's literary history, crystallized here in the form of fifteen stories covering fifteen years. Some of these are negative: a heritage of racism within the struggle for women's rights, marginalization of lesbians, too uncritical an embrace of American institutions and success myths. It is hoped that the current women's movement, now in a second wave of feminism, can avoid these pitfalls and build truer representative models of sisterhood and liberation. On the positive side, however, we can see that contemporary issues were around seventy years ago and that this early awareness constitutes a strong historical legacy for anyone working toward equal rights for women. The existence of early popular literature with feminist overtones suggests widespread interest in new ways of thinking about women, an openness to female autonomy that can inspire our own visions of change. Fantasies are powerful potential motivators, for they are not limited by reality, with its hobbling restrictions. They can paint a possible world of dreams grasped and limitations transcended that points toward a bright future and away from a frustrating present.[69] These stories were pioneers in this area, and they animate, still, egalitarian ideals that are yet to be realized.

One final benefit to be gained from this backward glance is that it strengthens our assessment of the suffrage movement. The depressing notion that women turned their backs on those who fought to expand their options can be balanced by reference to the continuing presence of work-centered romances in women's periodicals. As Elaine Showalter cautions in her study of the twenties, it distorts our history to maintain that women gave their freedom away at this time. She concludes that this was, at worst, a decade of postponement and emphasizes the survival of female desires for adventure and public service that had been articulated by the suffragists.[70] New Woman stories are evidence of that continuing interest in expanded horizons. It was far from revolutionary, yet the fiction in women's magazines kept alive transformative dreams issuing from the long fight to secure the vote and created an image of competence in nondomestic arenas. New Woman stories undoubtedly fabricated rather than mirrored reality, but they affirmed the notion that women were primarily individuals with human needs for substantive work as well as political rights and who possessed an appetite for all the adventures possible to imagine.

NOTES

1. Theodore Peterson, *Magazines in the Twentieth Century* (Urbana: University of Illinois Press, 1964), 58–59.

2. Ibid., 50; Richard Ohmann, "Where Did Mass Culture Come From? The Case of Magazines," *Berkshire Review* 16 (1981): 85–101.

3. Peterson, *Magazines,* 1964, 52.

4. Ibid., 63.

5. Ibid., 84.

6. James P. Wood, *Magazines in the United States* (New York: Ronald Press, 1971), 122; Helen Woodward, *The Lady Persuaders* (New York: Ivan Oblansky, 1960), 2.

7. William Chafe, *The American Woman: Her Changing Social, Economic, and Political Roles, 1920–1970* (New York: Oxford University Press, 1972), 104–107; Leila Rupp, *Mobilizing Women for War: German and American Propaganda, 1939–1945* (Princeton: Princeton University Press, 1978), 57–73; Ruth Schwartz Cowan, "Two Washes in the Morning and a Bridge Party at Night: The American Housewife Between the Wars," *Women's Studies* 3 (1976): 147–72. Other studies of the 1920s that do not focus on magazines but conclude that popular culture and women's values were unsupportive of feminism include Winifred Wandersee, *Women's Work and Family Values, 1920–1940* (Cambridge: Harvard University Press, 1981); Joan M. Jensen and Lois Scharf, *Decades of Discontent, The Women's Movement, 1920–1940* (Westport, Conn.: Greenwood Press, 1983); June Sochen, *Herstory: A Record of the American Woman's Past* (Van Nuys, Calif.: Alfred Publishing, 1981), 258–60.

8. The emphasis on woman as consumer in the 1920s is discussed in Carol Lopate, "Selling to Ms. Consumer," *College English* 38 (April 1977): 824–34.

9. A revisionist history of this period is provided by Nancy F. Cott, *The Grounding of Modern Feminism* (New Haven: Yale University Press, 1987); Paula Fass, *The Damned and the Beautiful: American Youth in the 1920's* (New York: Oxford University Press, 1977).

10. Feminist attacks by the twenties generation on this ideology are re-

corded in Rosalind Rosenberg, *Beyond Separate Spheres: The Intellectual Roots of Modern Feminism* (New Haven: Yale University Press, 1982).

11. William O'Neill comments extensively on what he calls young women's privatized vision in the era after suffrage, concluding that they lost interest in careers but acknowledging that they had hazy desires for self-fulfillment. *Everyone Was Brave: A History of Feminism in America* (New York: Quadrangle Books, 1971), 306–308. O'Neill's conclusion that careerism disappeared in the 1920s is belied somewhat by a 1924 survey of teenage women he cites in which over half of 347 respondents said they wanted careers and by a 1928 article to which he refers that reflects this interest. Similarly, reports of disillusionment with the women's movement are balanced by evidence of support for female self-expression and individual productive work at this time in Elaine Showalter, *These Modern Women: Autobiographical Essays from the Twenties* (New York: Feminist Press, 1978), 16.

12. Good descriptions of the crumbling feminist movement are provided by Chafe, *American Woman,* 1972, 112–32; O'Neill, *Everyone Was Brave,* 1971, 233–95; Nancy F. Cott, "Feminist Politics in the 1920's: The National Woman's Party," *Journal of American History* 71 (June 1984): 43–68.

13. Histories of the popular book market include Russel Nye, *The Unembarrassed Muse: The Popular Arts in America* (New York: Dial Press, 1970), 10–87; Alice Payne Hackett and James Henry Burke, *Eighty Years of Best Sellers, 1895–1975* (New York: R. R. Bowker, 1977); James D. Hart, *The Popular Book: A History of America's Literary Taste* (New York: Oxford University Press, 1950); Frank Luther Mott, *Golden Multitudes: The Story of Best Sellers in the U.S.* (New York: Macmillan, 1947).

14. Peterson, *Magazines,* 1964, 126.

15. Frank Luther Mott, *A History of American Magazines, 1885–1905,* vol. 4 (Cambridge: Harvard University Press, 1957), 491–503.

16. Frank Luther Mott, *A History of American Magazines, 1905–1930,* vol. 5 (Cambridge: Harvard University Press, 1968), 133–36.

17. Mott, *History,* 1957, 766–72.

18. Only a few studies have been published on magazine fiction from the early twentieth century: Patricke Johns-Heine and Hans Gerth, "Values in Mass Periodical Fiction, 1921–1940," *Public Opinion Quarterly* 13 (Spring 1949): 105–13; Martin Martel and George McCall, "Reality-Orientation and the Pleasure Principle: A Study of American Mass-Periodical Fiction (1890–1955)" in *People, Society, and Mass Communications,* ed. Lewis Dexter and David Manning White (Glencoe, Ill.: Free Press, 1964); Ellen Hoekstra, "The Pedestal Myth Reinforced: Women's Magazine Fiction, 1900–1920," in *New Dimensions in Popular Culture,* ed. Russel B. Nye (Bowling Green: Popular Press, 1972); Donald Makosky, "The Portrayal of Women in Wide-Circulation Magazine Short Stories, 1905–1955" (Ph.D. diss., University of Pennsylvania, 1966); Esta Seaton, "The Changing Image of the American Woman in a Mass-Circulation Periodical, the *Ladies' Home Journal,* 1890–1919" (Ph.D. diss., University of Minnesota, 1967). Of these, only Hoekstra, Makosky, and Seaton focus on images of women. Their contrasting assessments of the

conservative messages within periodicals suggest both the complexity of the image and the varying degree of thoroughness managed by each study. Seaton's conclusions more closely match my own, as she sees a clear break between the 1890–1914 period and the war years, describing the latter as a time when the *Ladies' Home Journal* endorsed models of activity outside the home.

19. The core sample for this study consists of 180 stories from the *Ladies' Home Journal*, 180 from *Good Housekeeping* (one per monthly issue from 1915 through 1929), and 84 each from *McCall's, Woman's Home Companion, Cosmopolitan, Pictorial Review,* and the *Delineator* (one per monthly issue for every other year). The total number of stories I read from these seven magazines during this period was 780. I also, however, read many stories from the 1910–1914 period, which are not included in this figure, from *Good Housekeeping,* the *Delineator, Cosmopolitan,* and the *Ladies' Home Journal* to create a context for the era in which I was most interested. I looked at an average of one story each issue for every other year from these four magazines for a total of 144 stories. The grand total, then, is 924 short stories and serials from 1910–1929, accumulated over a period of nine years. I supplemented the core sample with stories that seemed to concern the New Woman, some of which appeared outside of the main sample.

20. Because of the distinguishing features characterizing popular fiction, it has been suggested that different aesthetic standards be developed for criticism of it. John Cawelti, *Adventure, Mystery, and Romance: Formula Stories as Art and Popular Culture* (Chicago: University of Chicago Press, 1976), 8–20.

21. This issue is explicated well by R. Gordon Kelly, "Literature and the Historian," *American Quarterly* 26 (May 1974): 141–59.

22. Janice Radway, *Reading the Romance: Women, Patriarchy, and Popular Literature* (Chapel Hill: University of North Carolina Press, 1984); Tania Modleski, "The Disappearing Act: A Study of Harlequin Romances," *Signs* 5 (Spring 1973): 435–48.

23. Peterson, *Magazines,* 1964, 56, 115.

24. Mott, *History,* 1957, 498, 551, 769.

25. In 1890, subscription lists for women's magazines were overwhelmingly dominated by women consumers; editorials and advertising throughout the first decades of the twentieth century continued to address a female audience. Ibid., 353.

26. Janice Radway discusses the dangers of text-bound analyses of popular romances in *Reading the Romance,* 1984, 11. Radway's reader-response criticism draws heavily on the work of Stanley Fish; see *Is There a Text in This Class? The Authority of Interpretive Communities* (Cambridge: Harvard University Press, 1980).

27. A good overview of the difficulties involved in using popular literature as a mirror of reader values is provided by Cawelti, *Adventure,* 1976, 20–36.

28. Leslie W. Rabine, *Reading the Romantic Heroine: Text, History, Ideology* (Ann Arbor: University of Michigan Press, 1985). See also Kay Mussell, "Ro-

mantic Fiction" in *Handbook of American Popular Culture,* vol. 2, ed. M. Thomas Inge (Westport, Conn.: Greenwood Press, 1980).

29. Modleski, "Disappearing Act," 1980; Ann Barr Snitow, "Mass Market Romance: Pornography for Women Is Different," *Radical History Review* 20 (Spring/Summer 1979): 141–61; Janice Radway, "The Utopian Impulse in Popular Literature: Gothic Romances and 'Feminist' Protest," *American Quarterly* 33 (Summer 1981): 140–62.

30. Recent studies argue that women's romances became more egalitarian in the 1980s, frequently emphasizing the heroine's right to a career. Nevertheless, the story continues to focus on a passionate romance as primary to the heroine's life and on her power to attract male attention. Mariam Darce Fremier, *Good-bye Heathcliffe: Changing Heroes, Heroines, Roles, and Values in Women's Category Romances* (Westport, Conn.: Greenwood Press, 1988); Carol Thurston, *The Romance Revolution: Erotic Novels for Women and the Quest for a New Sexual Identity* (Urbana: University of Illinois Press, 1987).

31. Woodward, *Lady Persuaders,* 1960, 115–16.

32. Mott, *History,* 1957, 551.

33. Carl S. Smith, *Chicago and the American Literary Imagination, 1880–1920* (Chicago: University of Chicago Press, 1984), 7–9. My own perusal of New Woman stories from women's magazines in the 1910–1914 period confirms this observation.

34. Well-known examples of novels with this perspective include Elizabeth Stuart Phelps's *The Story of Avis* (1879); *The Awakening* by Kate Chopin (1899); and Ellen Glasgow's *Phases of an Inferior Planet* (1898).

35. Overviews of the restricted ideal for women in nineteenth-century popular culture and sentimental fiction include Barbara Welter, "The Cult of True Womanhood, 1820–1860," *American Quarterly* 18 (Summer 1966): 151–74; Herbert Ross Brown, *The Sentimental Novel in America, 1789–1860* (New York: Octagon Books, 1975), 100–200; Rachel M. Brownstein, *Becoming a Heroine: Reading About Women in Novels* (New York: Viking Press, 1982), 32–77.

36. One of the most famous female characters in nineteenth-century women's fiction, for instance, is Beth March in Louisa May Alcott's *Little Women* (1868), whose prolonged illness and ultimate death symbolize her innocence and goodness. Nina Baym brilliantly discusses the appeal of such an image for women readers of sentimental fiction in *Women's Fiction: A Guide to Novels by and about Women in America, 1820–1870* (Ithaca: Cornell University Press, 1978), 15, 78–85.

37. Ibid., 22–50. See also Aileen Kraditor, *The Ideas of the Woman Suffrage Movement, 1890–1920* (New York: Columbia University Press, 1965), 110. Although the ideology of women's uniqueness underwent considerable revision at the turn of the century, it was not until the 1920s that it was replaced by an integrative model, according to Rosalind Rosenberg, *Separate Spheres,* 1982, 84–113.

38. Elizabeth Frazer, "The Sob-Lady," *Good Housekeeping* 61, no. 3 (September 1915).

39. The blonde ideal and her brunette antithesis are typified by the sisters in Mary Jane Holmes's *Tempest and Sunshine* (1854).
40. Vivien R. Bretherton, "Bird Girl," *Good Housekeeping* 88, no. 3 (March 1929).
41. Blanche H. Gelfant, "Sister to Faust: The City's 'Hungry' Woman as Heroine," in *Women Writers and the City: Essays in Feminist Literary Criticism,* ed. Susan Merrill Squier (Knoxville: University of Tennessee Press, 1984).
42. Rosenberg, *Separate Spheres,* 1982, 14–17, 152–53.
43. Ibid., 54–83; Cott, *Modern Feminism,* 1987, 278–83.
44. Rachel Blau Du Plessis, *Writing Beyond the Ending: Narrative Strategies of Twentieth Century Women Writers* (Bloomington: Indiana University Press, 1985), 84–104.
45. Maureen Honey, "Gotham's Daughters: Feminism in the 1920s," *American Studies* 31 (Spring 1990): 23–38.
46. Du Plessis, *Beyond the Ending,* 1985, 87.
47. Cott, *Modern Feminism,* 1987, 157–61; Fass, *Damned and Beautiful,* 1977, 80–83.
48. The upsurge in attacks on lesbians is discussed in Carroll Smith-Rosenberg, *Disorderly Conduct: Visions of Gender in Victorian America* (New York: Oxford University Press, 1985), 280–96. See also Lillian Faderman, *Surpassing the Love of Men: Romantic Friendship and Love Between Women from the Renaissance to the Present* (New York: William Morrow, 1981), 332–56.
49. Lillian Faderman, "Lesbian Magazine Fiction in the Early Twentieth Century," *Journal of Popular Culture* 11 (Spring 1978): 800–17.
50. Estelle Freedman, "Separatism as Strategy: Female Institution Building and American Feminism, 1870–1930," *Feminist Studies* 5 (Fall 1979): 512–29.
51. Carroll Smith-Rosenberg, "The Female World of Love and Ritual: Relations Between Women in Nineteenth Century America," *Signs,* 1 (Autumn 1975): 1–29. Female disenchantment in the 1920s with political solutions to women's problems and the tendency to not identify with women as a group is discussed in O'Neill, *Everyone Was Brave,* 1971, 308. See also Elaine Showalter, *These Modern Women: Autobiographical Essays from the Twenties* (New York: Feminist Press, 1978), 9–16.
52. Sophie Kerr, "Eve Goes On," *Ladies' Home Journal* 45, nos. 3–5 (March–June 1928).
53. Mary Synon, "Amy Brooks," *Good Housekeeping* 84, no. 3 (March 1927).
54. Racism within the suffrage movement is described in Rosalyn Terborg-Penn, "Discrimination Against Afro-American Women in the Women's Movement, 1830–1920," in *The Afro-American Woman: Struggles and Images,* ed. Sharon Harley and Rosalyn Terborg-Penn (Port Washington, N.Y.: Kennikat Press, 1978).
55. Erlene Stetson, "Black Feminism in Indiana, 1893–1933," *Phylon* 44 (December 1983): 292–98.
56. Women writers of the Harlem Renaissance are discussed in Barbara

Christian, *Black Women Novelists: The Development of a Tradition, 1892–1976* (Westport, Conn.: Greenwood Press, 1980); Gloria Hull, *Color, Sex, and Poetry: Three Women Writers of the Harlem Renaissance* (Bloomington: Indiana University Press, 1987); and Ann Allen Shockley, *Afro-American Women Writers, 1746–1933* (Boston: G. K. Hall, 1988).

57. Circulation for *The Crisis* reached a peak of 95,000 in 1919 and dipped to 30,000 by 1930 due to an early start of the depression for African-Americans. Abby Arthur Johnson and Ronald Maberry Johnson, *Propaganda and Aesthetics: The Literary Politics of Afro-American Magazines in the Twentieth Century* (Amherst: University of Massachusetts Press, 1979), 35.

58. Fauset's editorial and literary activities are the subject of Deborah McDowell, "The Neglected Dimension of Jessie Fauset," in *Conjuring: Black Women, Fiction, and the Literary Tradition,* ed. Hortense Spillers and Marjorie Pryse (Bloomington: Indiana University Press, 1985); and Abby Arthur Johnson, "Literary Midwife: Jessie Redmon Fauset and the Harlem Renaissance," *Phylon* 39 (June 1978): 143–53.

59. An excellent history of Fauset's literary achievements is provided by Carolyn Sylvander, *Jessie Redmon Fauset: Black American Writer* (Troy, N.Y.: Whitston, 1981).

60. The same theme is used in Fauset's novel *Plum Bun* (1928) and explicated by Deborah McDowell in her Introduction to the reprint of that novel (London: Pandora Press, 1985).

61. Rosenberg, *Separate Spheres,* 1982, 1–27; Smith-Rosenberg, *Disorderly Conduct,* 1985, 182–96.

62. LeeAnne Giannone Kryder, "Self-Assertion and Social Commitment: The Significance of Work to the Progressive Era's New Woman," *Journal of American Culture* 6 (Summer 1983): 25–30.

63. Carolyn Forrey, "The New Woman Revisited," *Women's Studies* 2 (1974): 37–56; Susan Ware, *Holding Their Own: Women in the 1930's* (Boston: Twayne, 1982), 171–96.

64. Jane Humphries, "Women: Scapegoats and Safety Valves in the Great Depression," *Review of Radical Political Economics* 8 (Spring 1976): 98–121; Rupp, *Mobilizing Women,* 1978, 60–73.

65. Betty Friedan describes images of achievement in women's magazine fiction through World War II in *The Feminine Mystique* (New York: Dell, 1963), 28–61. The appearance of New Woman figures throughout the forties in film is analyzed in Molly Haskell, *From Reverence to Rape: The Treatment of Women in the Movies* (New York: Holt, Rinehart, and Winston, 1974), 189–230. One of the last New Woman heroines in American popular culture is the lawyer, Amanda Bonner, marvelously played by Katharine Hepburn, in the film *Adam's Rib* (1949).

66. With the exception of *Cosmopolitan,* these magazines were known as the "Big Six" at the end of World War I due to their dominance of the women's market. Circulations varied from magazine to magazine and grew over the time period under consideration. By the mid-twenties, all had passed the million mark, and by 1930, most had passed two million. The *Ladies' Home*

Journal was the pacesetter, enjoying a circulation of one million as early as 1904 and reaching nearly three million by the end of the 1920s. Peterson, *Magazines,* 1964, 60–63.

67. Specifics on the story sample are provided in note 19.

68. I was forced to exclude, due to space limitations, many other writers who were published frequently in their day and who created New Woman characters. Some of those I most regret are Kathleen Norris, George Weston, Elizabeth Jordan, Phyllis Duganne, I. A. R. Wylie, and Clarence Budington Kelland. Writers who are better known today, such as Susan Glaspell, Willa Cather, Edith Wharton, Fannie Hurst, Gertrude Atherton, and Mary Austin, are not included because their works are available elsewhere. In addition, this group's writings depart significantly from the more conventional works of their peers, and the emphasis of this anthology is on formulaic patterns in women's magazine fiction rather than artistic innovation.

69. Cheri Register alludes to this property of mass market fiction when she urges its inclusion within the female literary tradition: "If the mythos of the woman artist is a story of confinement, while some popular fiction celebrates community, then we must ask whether 'serious' literature by women defined as artists is the best or only source for discerning the female mythos. If we really want to know what stories women tell about female experience in order to form a group identity, our definition of literature ought to include popular literature and the oral traditions of illiterate populations of women." "Literary Criticism," *Signs* 6 (Winter 1980): 268–82.

70. Showalter, *Modern Women,* 1978, 27.

THE SOB-LADY

Elizabeth Frazer

ANGELA Lake, Bill Ransome's girl, or rather, to be strictly truthful, the girl to whom Bill wanted to be engaged, but who was solemnly betrothed to Literature—to high, noble, puissant Literature, not to the ordinary, everyday proletarian kind of literature that finds its way into current magazines and is greedily devoured by a plebeian public—Angela Lake stood on the dusky upper step of her boarding-house at the close of a thick, oppressive day in New York, bidding good-by to a lady who was surreptitiously weeping.

"Now, Mother," said Angela gently, but with the faintest edge of irritation in her liquid young voice, "don't cry. What is there to cry about? You ought to be glad!"

"I know, dear," breathed Mrs. Lake, furtively dabbing away a trickling water-course of tears; "and I am glad. I'm glad you're here. It seems a nice, clean, well-ordered house, with good food and pleasant young people. I'm glad I thought to write that Miss Brown about a boarding-place for you. She's doing newspaper work on one of the big dailies, the landlady told me. Perhaps she can help you with your work and go about with you."

From *Good Housekeeping* 61, no. 3 (September 1915).

In the dark, the girl's pretty lips curled a trifle disdainfully, but her voice was quiet. "I should hardly think of giving my things to a person who writes for the newspapers to criticize; and as for going about with her—Mother dear, you don't understand. I'm not going about with anybody. Not a soul. I'm just going to write. Study and write. That's what I came down here for, away from disturbances: to write. Some days it will be a paragraph, some days only a line. But each word living, final." She stood, a slim, white figure, staring into the thickening gloom of the street. "I intend," she said gravely, "to become a great stylist."

A shabby, unwashed individual, hatless, and with wild, bloodshot eyes, staggered toward her from the pavement, reached the bottom step, and halted, swaying slightly on his feet. He held out at arm's length one hand cupped in the other, and muttered huskily.

Angela looked at him sternly. "Go away!" she said. "Go away, I say."

The intruder blinked rapidly at her, frowned, then wheeled without a sound, and made his unsteady way back into the middle of the street.

"He's intoxicated," said Angela. "How revolting!"

"I don't know," murmured Mrs. Lake, peering after him uncertainly—"I thought he said something about being burned—his hand—and he looked frightfully pale."

A clanging ambulance tore furiously by, and behind it another. "I wonder what's the matter," said Mrs. Lake eagerly.

"It's an ambulance street," replied Angela carelessly. "Here comes your cab dear. Good-by. Don't fret about me." They embraced each other in the gloom.

A slender, dark girl in a tailored suit, with a stiff, mannish little hat dragged down over her nose, brushed by them and climbed the steps wearily, pulling out her hat-pins as she came. Before her, the vestibule door suddenly flew open, and a red-haired snub-nosed telephone-boy sprang out like a lively hop-toad.

"I been watchin' for youse!" he exclaimed, a thrill of excitement in his fresh young voice. "Mr. Garden sent in a hurry call."

"What does he want, Pinky?" asked the girl languidly. She collapsed weakly into the nearest chair.

"He wants de sob-lady, Miss Susanne, and he wants her quick. 'Hello, Pink,' he says, 'is Miss Brown there?' 'She ain't come in yet,' I says. 'Any message?' And he says, 'Keep your eye peeled for her, Pink, and when she comes in tell her to beat it over to Thirtieth Street. There's a big fire on de Second Avenue L—four cars ablaze, burnt men and women and kids droppin' like a shower of scorched flies onto de street below,' he says. 'Tell her not to monkey wit' de news end—that's covered—but to come down on all fours onto de story-book part; wedder de bad, naughty motor-man done it or wedder he didn't done it, and what kind of a tie was he wearin'. Play up de kiddies and mudders, Come across wit' de sobs for de dear, sob-lovin' public. And step lively—see?'"

Miss Susanne Brown, sob-lady on *The Earth,* whose ability to make her readers laugh and cry over her vivid little human-interest stories had won her that elegant title, and also a precarious foothold on the big, sensational daily, threw up her hands.

"Oh," she groaned, "what luck—what beastly, rotten luck! I'd rather be shot than thumb-screw a story out of those poor wretches tonight. This heat has wrecked me. And I've had a nail in my shoe all day as high as the Matterhorn!"

Pinky gazed sympathetically. "I bet you're tired, Miss Susanne."

"You win!" she said grimly. "I'm so tired I'd sell my immortal soul for a bath and to crawl in between cool, fragrant sheets. How hot was it today, Pinky?"

"A hundred and umpty-ump in the shade, and no shade," grinned Pinky. "It's a grand night for a fire. Say, Miss Susanne, can I come along and help gadder in a few sobs?"

Susanne laughed. "If you want to. I dare say I can get you through the lines on my pass." She pulled herself reluctantly together, and stood up on one stockinged foot, swinging by its laces a very grubby, stub-toed, little brown boot—the one containing the offending nail.

"Gimme de shoe here," demanded Pinky, capturing the laces. "Youse go on up-stairs. I'll hammer down de nail."

"Go away!" a clear, musical voice came to them out of the darkness. "Go away, I say!" At the same moment Angela appeared on the threshold. She had put on a pale gown of some misty-green substance, spangled all over with little silvery disks that trembled and winked like the sequinned pathway of the moon across a twilight sea. Above the soft lace rose a slender white throat and a small, well-poised, golden head. She looked slim and lovely and distinguished, and cool as a summer wave.

Susanne stared at the vision. Then involuntarily her glance sought her own crumpled linen blouse with the ink-splash across the cuff; the serviceable serge skirt, the small, stockinged foot. The contrast was complete and brutal. A grim laugh escaped her.

"Hello, Miss Lake," she said, and extended her hand.

Angela's delicate brows puckered into a frown. "Who—I can't seem—I—don't—"

"No," said Susanne simply, "you probably don't. Your mother wrote me about you and asked me to recommend a boarding-house; she got my address from Bill Ransome. I'm Susanne Brown, who lived in the small green house at the end of your street, and had a big curly white dog that you were afraid of. I was a grade behind you at school, but we were in the same spelling-class, you and Bill and I. Do you remember? And Bill used to miss words on purpose so you could go ahead, but he would never miss for anybody else!" She laughed, and turning her gray eyes aside asked casually: "How is Bill these days? Do you ever see anything of him?"

Angela colored ever so slightly. "Oh, he's terribly well," she said. "And I see him—occasionally. But he's a bridge-builder now, you know, and very busy."

Susanne nodded. "I know. The year before I left he used to come over to my house in the evenings and talk of it by the hour. I think he waked and slept and dreamed and ate bridges! I got to know them all by heart—suspension, cantilever, tension, truss, skew-bridge, girder, pontoon, tu—" The whirring of the clock by the switch-board broke in upon the list. It chimed eight clear notes. Susanne sucked in her breath sharply.

"Good gracious!" she gasped. "My job—what am I thinking of!" She stooped for her hat, pinned it on hastily, shrugged herself into her coat, and swept up her purse and gloves from the table. "Give me the shoe, Pin," she ordered crisply. "I sha'n't have time to change now."

"She's fixed," announced Pinky triumphantly, emerging from the corner. "Try her on." He dropped on his knees before her.

Susanne slid in her foot, and stamped the boot on, wincing. "It'll do," she said grimly. She dropped into a chair, and began manipulating the laces with lightning fingers.

Angela looked down at the resolute profile curiously. "Why are you going out again, if you are so tired?" she asked.

"Fire," said Susanne briefly. She stood up, buttoning her gloves. "Not far from here. I've got to report it."

There was a sudden flash of illumination in Angela's clear blue eyes. "Of course," she said. "Mother told me. You write for the papers."

"You might call it that," laughed Susanne. "I call it splash-work—word splashes. Violent, screaming, red and black splashes. For example, take tonight: four burning elevated cars, packed end to end with working men and women and children. Someone else does the news; I go over and write the picture. I tick down the stuff, red-hot, just as I see it: men and women shrieking, raving, cursing, clawing, fighting to escape alive from that burning pen. I see it, and I dash it down without time to draw breath or change a line. Sometimes it's good; sometimes it's bad as perdition." She smiled a farewell at Angela and opened the hall door.

A hatless, stub-bearded man leaning up against it from the outside pitched heavily into the hall. He took one staggering step forward, and stood glaring from blood-shot eyes. His eyebrows and lashes were singed off as if a clean flame had licked over his face; his cheek-bones were blackened; a coat-sleeve, wrenched bodily from its socket, hung by a dirty inner lining; and he held one hand outstretched before him, as if he were leading himself, manacled, to jail. Susanne saw that the entire palm of his right hand had been burned and torn away, and hung, a jungle of bloody fingers, by a few shreds to his wrist.

"F-fire!" mumbled the man thickly. "On th' L." His knees

suddenly caved under him; he gave a sort of lurch; Susanne sprang forward just in time, and supported him to a chair. He looked up into her face, his own working convulsively. "Ghastly!" he stuttered. "Fought like mad beasts—fought and clawed—clawed me—me!" he uttered a little, gasping cough, and began, quite grotesquely, to cry.

"Steady!" said Susanne, with her arm tight round his shoulders. "Don't do that. It's all over now! You're safe and with friends. Pinky," she cried sharply, "get some brandy—quick! Then call the ambulance." She turned back to get her story, come to her so strangely from the street. But the man had crumbled off into unconsciousness.

The next morning, Angela, looking very pretty in pale-blue linen, sat at her round breakfast-table, spooning her grapefruit, and rereading, with a faint curl of scorn on her lips, certain paragraphs of Bill's letter. For Bill had dared to give unsolicited advice on a subject which was outside of his bridge-building province. Angela read:

DEAR: I want to say something to you—three somethings—which I'm afraid you won't like. Or me either! But that can't be helped. There must be brute truth between you and me—anything else is fatal. So I'm going to hit out straight from the shoulder, just as if you were a man—almost!

First off, then, brother: I think you're on the wrong road to do good work, cooping yourself up in that little room to learn the mechanics of writing. Dear, that makes me set my teeth, and long to shake you. It's so fatally artificial! It's all well enough to say you must be master of your materials, but what if you have none, no bricks or mortar to build with? What have you loved, suffered, sweated, or starved for in all your sweet young life? Nothing. And you know the Law: *Out of nothing, nothing comes!* . . . I said you would hate me!

That's number one. Number two is better. I have made a wonderful discovery. All by myself, alone, I made it, in the middle of the night—the night after we sat together on the steps, and I would, and you wouldn't! The discovery is this: that the fame of book-writing, and of bridge-building, and every other kind of fame, big and little, on the earth—the whole thing—is not to be compared with a certain other beautiful

"'F-fire!' mumbled the man thickly. 'On th' L.' His knees suddenly caved under him; Susanne sprang forward and supported him to a chair. 'Steady!' she said. 'It's all over now! You're safe with friends.' 'Pinky,' she cried sharply, 'get some brandy—quick!'" Illustration by John Alonzo Williams. From "The Sob-Lady," *Good Housekeeping* 61, no. 3 (September 1915), p. 316.

little business—which same I have already named to you! For that also is the Law. And so I say to you again, solemnly and gaily, leave that stuffy room and come live with me and be my love; and I will teach you, and you shall teach me, and we'll learn things together. And then perhaps, some day, if you are very good, you'll be permitted to beget some real stuff, a book so live that it'll make all the old, one-eyed critics in the shop stand up on their hind legs together and yell, "It isn't Art!" And we'll tell 'em to go to—Hoboken!

Number three is about your what-you-call-him professor-man, who is to teach you the essentials of Art. Somehow, I don't like that man! I bet he's an esthete, a sissy. It's as some fellow said, "Those who can, do; those who can't, teach." And, darling, he can't teach you the things you should know. He can't put power into your pretty power-house. Only you can do that—and you won't! Is this rough sledding, little brother? That last, I'll admit, is simply the abysmal brute in me rearing its ugly head—I'm j—l—s of that writing-Johnny! But all the rest is a true bill. It's because I lo—"

Here the letter trailed off into mere irrelevant personalities of the sort Angela had forbidden.

A shadow fell across the open page of the letter, and Susanne slipped into the other chair. "May I gobble a bite opposite you," she asked, "before I go down to the office and get eaten alive?"

"Who's going to eat you?" asked Angela pleasantly. "And what for?" She restored the letter to its envelop. Susanne caught the heavy superscription, and her eyes went from gray to black.

"I fell down," she stated grimly, nodding at the folded newspaper by her plate. "Fell down with an awful plunk! Pinky could have done better. And now I suppose I shall lose my job."

Angela, regarding her curiously, noted the faint violet shadows beneath the eyes, and wondered at what unearthly hour the girl before her had got in last night.

"Do you like that—that sort of work?" Angela asked. "Should you care very much if you lost it?"

"Care!" Susanne reached for a roll, broke it, and spread it with creamy fresh butter. "Well, I care to eat and pay my board and buy a new hat now and then; and I can't do any of those pleasant things if I lose my job. Yes, I care. I dare say it shows a very low, materialistic streak in me; but I care like the dickens. You see," she went on soberly, "Madame Rosie, here, is really beyond my present means. A hall bedroom is more my price. But if you knew what deadly, pinched, and bleak little horrors those places are to come home to in the evening! My heart used to sort of sicken every time I turned the key in the lock. And one hot night I couldn't bear it another minute! I put on my hat and walked out. Fortunately, Madame Rosie had a vacant skylight room. It's hot, up under the tin roof, but the food here is jolly."

The entrance of the maid with her breakfast-tray stopped further speech. But Susanne looked up presently to say: "Your mother wrote that you were coming here to write. I'd like to see some of your stuff." She continued to study Angela through narrowed, intent eyes, as if she were going to draw her. "I believe," she said slowly, "that you could do a certain sort of thing, and do it very well. I dare say you have style to burn."

Angela felt secretly gratified, but she replied modestly, "I haven't anything to show at present. I'm just studying. I write—little fragments, you know; and then once a week I go for criticism up to Professor Tappan. You've heard of him, perhaps? He wrote 'Dawn Over the Horizon'—an exquisite thing!" She spoke in a hushed voice. "It's just—himself."

Then she reached politely for the paper. "I'd like to read your article."

"All right!" Susanne said, flushing. "Read it if you wish. I told you it was bad. I have no style. Style means time; I have no time. I say what I think without thinking. Newspaper writing is like a fire-engine racing into action, horses straining, driver cursing, siren screaming, smoke belching, sparks trailing—no time to look back and see what sort of fancy track they're leaving. They've got to reach that fire!" Laughing, she turned away, but at the door turned gaily back again. "Pray for me in fifteen minutes," she said. "I shall be in the lion's den."

But Susanne escaped out of the lion's den. She did not lose her job that day. It is doubtful whether she would have lost it at all had not her nerves been affected by the heat, and by sundry square envelopes which continued to arrive with discreet regularity, to be laid at Angela's plate and read under Susanne's nose as coolly as if they were nothing more than a bill for a typewriter ribbon. Susanne marveled at that. Sometimes, glancing up absently from such a missive, Angela would find her companion, her brows knit, her eyes shining like diamonds, her cheeks aflame as from some inward fire. At which, in her turn, Angela marveled.

It was about this time that Susanne contracted the habit of not sleeping, or when she did, of dreaming wild, hateful dreams. She dreamed that she was flying, slowly, with great anguish, a little distance above the house-tops, while underneath, closely pursuing, was an enemy, vague, but most malignant, who was waiting to catch her when she dropped, as drop she surely must from sheer fatigue, to the ground. This dream-enemy might have been the editor, whose growls of late had become simply terrific; or it might have been the heat which, like a thick blanket, enveloped the city in a sticky, yellow haze, and rendered the tiny skylight room under the tin roof a place of diabolical torment. The violet shadows beneath her eyes became permanent. More alarming still, she stopped eating.

And then, suddenly, the letters ceased. They ceased for a whole puzzling week, at the end of which time Bill himself appeared in their stead. After that, things for Susanne took a distinct turn for the worse. Bill carried off Angela, lovely as a dream (some dreams!) to a gay roof-garden; or Bill thought Angela might like to motor up the river in the refreshing cool of the twilight; or Bill and Angela strolled bare-headed together in the warm, breathing city night under a glamourous crescent moon.

Meantime, the temperature soared to a record-breaker. Fat citizens, given to grog, fell down in purple fits on the pavements; pallid little shop-girls fainted in the subway crush; in Battery Park, on the waterfront, columns of men lay shoulder to shoulder on the parched grass at night, like an encamped army; the Ghetto spread its frowsy bedclothes on the fire-escapes, or slept on the sidewalks.

And during this cheerful spell of mid-summer madness, Susanne (for her sins, most likely) was assigned to report the suicides. She still possessed a lingering sense of humor which had not been killed off by being in love or by brooding over the uncertain tenure of her job, and she perceived a certain grim fitness in these particular cases being given to her. For most of the weary wretches, she discovered, died for one of two reasons: they were hungry or they were in love, and when they could endure it no longer, they walked off the pier, or turned on the gas, or used a razor, or a revolver. Susanne wished savagely that somebody would kill himself just once for an original reason—so that she might hand in a good story. As days passed she grew light-headed from the heat, from the strain of uninspired suicides, from sleeplessness—and Bill.

And then one night she met him in the hall. She had stumped in and cast herself, a pallid, untidy little heap, on the nearest chair.

"I wish," she grumbled aloud, "that all the weary lovers in the world would dispatch themselves in one fell bunch to-night—line up at once, and leap to death together!"

A smothered chuckle from a shadow at the end of the hall caused her to call crossly, "Pinky, I don't want to hear any laughter tonight!" The shadow uttered another laugh, came forward, and turned up the light so that it cast a cruel glare on the draggle-plumed little figure.

"How d'you do?" said Bill genially, giving her fingers a cordial squeeze. "What have you got against the weary lovers?"

"They keep killing themselves," she murmured weakly. "It's tiresome." She stared steadily at his white tie, not daring to lift her gaze higher to his eyes. For Bill's eyes were his best card. They were a particularly jolly tint of deep ultramarine, very straight and keen and gay.

Bill laughed again. "And you want them to get together—form a union, eh?—and all walk out together! 'Weary Lovers of the World Unite!' Oh, let 'em alone, poor things. They make literature."

"Not they!" scoffed Susanne. "There's not a gleam of color or technique among the lot!" Susanne, though she did not intend to betray it to Bill, had that very day lost her job, and all on account of the unspeakable dullness displayed by the suicidal mind.

"I interviewed one this morning," she said. "At the morgue."

"No!" cried Bill. "What a grisly job for a girl!" he added under his breath. He stared down at her as she stood, mechanically straightening her glove. "What did the poor devil have to say for himself?" he asked, still looking down.

"Oh, same old thing," said the girl wearily. "He was a shoe-clerk—wife ran off with another man—he couldn't stand it—last night threw himself off the bridge—that's all. That's all; but it's not enough, you know; not when it happens everyday. People want to hear something different."

"I see," said Bill soberly. "So what did you do?"

"I frilled it up a bit, and handed it in." She omitted to mention the very regrettable result. "And after that I sat on a bench in the park, between two down-and-out gentlemen, and we three watched the feet of the world go by, rich man, poor man—"

"But what did the editor say?" interrupted Bill, his consecutive mind refusing to be side-tracked.

Susanne hesitated. "He said, 'Bow! Wow! Wow!' Also, 'Gr-r-r! Gr-r-r!' several times and very much indeed." She barked with such savage realism, straining at the end of an imaginary chain, that Bill was transported back across the years to a summer lane and a skinny-legged little girl racing through the faint-starred dusk beside a big, ghostly-white dog. He laughed outright.

"By Jove," he said, "how *is* Rebel? How he used to charge the squinch-owls at night on the hill behind our house! D'you remember?"

"Rather."

"And do you remem—"

A soft rustling behind him made him spin round on his heel. Angela was descending the stairs, dressed in her green mermaid gown splashed over with bright sequins, and carrying a long white cloak over her arm. Bill stared up at her, his eyes narrowed ever so little, and straight-way squinch-owls and dogs and editors and tired reporter-girls dwindled in his mind to the size of a shadow at noonday. And then Susanne slipped away, unheeded.

The hot weather continued. Susanne's surplus fund melted like fat men's collars in the subway. By day she haunted newspaper offices, pulling such scant wires as she knew; and by night, in the grilling little bedroom under the eaves, she doffed her sticky outer garments and washed out her bits of laundry. After which she lit the green student-lamp, selected the least stumpy of her outcast heap of pencils, and sat down in the heat to work.

I hope that at this point no one is tempted to pity Susanne. She was young, tingling with life, and mightily in love with Bill. Nevertheless, she was a week behind on her board. One evening after dinner Madame Rosie broached the subject delicately; business was business, and slack at this season; she had her own bills to meet. Susanne, in return, gave her the exact state of the market: five dollars in her pocketbook; she might have a job over-night or not for several months. She agreed, if nothing turned up before, to leave at the end of the week. That night in her own little room, she sat a long time in the darkness.

The next morning she awoke in a room several degrees more habitable. The heat wave had passed. The big, water-girt city was its breezy self again. Susanne, who was persuaded that her luck was somehow bound up with the weather, treated herself to a fresh white blouse, and Angela to a smile at breakfast, the first in several weeks. In payment, and because she really liked Susanne, Angela invited her to accompany Bill Ransome and herself uptown that afternoon, wait at the university while she had her Friday conference with Professor Tappan, and later have tea on the terrace overlooking the river. And Susanne consented.

After breakfast she betook herself to a certain fabulous bargain emporium, where she invested heavily in white gloves, fresh frills for her last year's gray mull dress, and a splashy red rose for her black tulle hat. These vanities mounted up to $3.98, leaving out of the five dollars a scant margin of $1.02

for current expenses—which was shaving it pretty fine, even for Susanne. But gaming spirits will understand her mood; she was nailing her luck to the wall! And then, after all, Bill didn't see her. He was there, to be sure, faultlessly arrayed in flannels, sitting close beside her in the big, red touring-car he had rented for the day, but after his first rather blank recognition of her as a third person in the party, he noticed Susanne not at all. In a little while, as he sat quiet, immobile, answering in monosyllables or sunk within himself, she stole a quick sideglance at him. His fair, slightly heavy face was serious, the strong mouth set, the blue eyes cloudy with resolution. Evidently he had planned to do "it" that very afternoon!

Of the remainder of that stricken day, Susanne had only wild and disjointed recollections: of Bill stalking restively across the lawn, awaiting Angela's reappearance from the conference; of Angela and Professor Tappan—who turned out to be a boyish-looking instructor with chiseled, academic features—standing a moment upon the steps with their heads very close together; of a grotesque tea-party upon a windy terrace; and finally, of Bill setting down his cup and turning his eyes upon her in a look which said, with brutal plainness, "Begone!"

And Susanne went. She got on her feet, pale as Bill himself, and murmured hurriedly, "There's a cunning little circular path I've been watching—I want to see where it goes." Behind her, almost before she turned, Bill took Angela's hand in his, and began to speak.

Susanne escaped down the cunning little path. Presently she sank upon a bench and closed her eyes. A little imagination is a terrible thing; but a big one is worse, and Susanne's had been trained in her business. She opened her eyes again, and saw before her on the path a sailor kissing his holiday girl. Susanne sprang up and hurried on. To steady herself, she began mentally to pack her trunk for the morrow, garment by garment; and still packing, she completed the circle of the path, and came once more upon Bill and Angela, but from the opposite quarter. She saw Bill suddenly reach out a big arm, draw Angela to him, and kiss her on the mouth almost roughly.

And at that, hot as fire all over, Susanne suddenly came to

her senses and fled. She fled away from that scandalous little kissing path, studded with summer lovers; and leaving a message with the chauffeur of the car, she betook herself home in the subway. But in her mind there kept rising the look on Bill's face as he bent tenderly above Angela; and over and over, in unison with the vibration of the rushing train, the refrain of a foolish, cheap little song kept beating itself out:

> One kiss more! One kiss more!
> Never let a lady lack for one kiss more!

And yet no longer ago than that morning a certain little idiot had dared to bet on her luck!

After dinner she packed her trunk in earnest; and then she drifted through the front hall, and sat down on the steps. Tomorrow at breakfast, Angela would, perhaps, announce her engagement. Or no, being Angela, she would do no such ordinary thing! Susanne dragged her thoughts away from them. There was a dull, physical oppression at her heart, as if it were beating painfully under a heavy stone. Tomorrow would bring another day, and she would lodge her trunk in some dingy little room, and sally forth upon the search of that elusive job; tomorrow she would be herself again, gay, hardy, resourceful, as a young adventurer must needs be in the big, fickle town. But tonight she felt weak, tired, not a bold adventurer; just a girl.

In the parlor some joyous soul started a nasal rag-time waltz on a phonograph. Suddenly, without warning of any sort, Susanne's breath caught fast in her throat; her emotion, dammed up so sturdily through long, hot weeks of unemployment, broke loose; a big sob wrenched its way onward; another followed, and another. The sob-lady bowed her face down to her knees and wept unrestrainedly.

And it was in this position, a short time later, that some one discovered her. Flinging himself blindly from Angela and from the house, choked with the fury and pain of his defeat, he stumbled directly over the abject little figure at his feet—and swore.

And that swear-word of Bill's really finishes the story. For the next few months Bill, like every other rejected lover, firmly believed he was drinking life's cup of sorrow to its bitterest lees, but one sunny morning, not so very long after, as the gods measure time, he suddenly woke up healed, recalled his rudeness to Susanne—but that is another episode.

After his departure, Susanne sat on the steps, very still in the cool darkness, scarce daring to believe the astounding thing that had befallen! Angela didn't want Bill! The oppressive, stony weight mysteriously rolled itself away from her heart, leaving her tremulously light and happy. It was in this mood that Pinky, returning home from a "movie" show, found her, and delivered a belated telephone message: Mr. Garden wanted Miss Brown to report the following noon at his office. A full minute of silence followed this announcement. And then Pinky heard a queer choking sound—he couldn't be certain whether it was a laugh or a sob. It sounded a bit like both. He repeated the good news. And this time he heard a sure enough, shaky little laugh. Susanne stood up and laid her arm across the boy's shoulders.

"Pinky," she said, "let me give you a piece of advice. When you bet on your luck and it looks as though you would lose, don't cry like a silly girl in the middle of the game, but double the stakes and go on. Just double the stakes—and go on!"

SHELTER

Juliet Wilbor Tompkins

The character of Dorothy Eades was created by Beulah Marie Dix in the October 1915 issue of Good Housekeeping *in the first story of a series about eight high school friends, recently graduated and making places for themselves in the work world. Dorothy is the leader and organizer of the group, which includes Julia Earle, who establishes a child care center with her sister; Marion Eastman, a real estate agent in New York; and Margery Eliot, who becomes head librarian in Chiltern, their home town. Each story was written by a different author but the pieces are linked by the high value each character places on independence and challenging work. Dorothy has captained the basketball team in high school and in this, the last, story of the series applies her assertiveness to selling cars.*

IT seemed to Dorothy as though the smell of smoke would never get out of her life. Every garment and possession breathed it; even her hair, shaken down at night, shook out smoke about her. In the smoldering blocks the first fresh outpouring had been drowned out, but the acrid breath of wet smoke hung over the ruined town. The women spoke of it with shudders when their flying paths crossed, then raced on from relief committee to shelter tent with bright eyes and elated voices. "It is so horrible!" they insisted, rushing down to the supplies headquarters at seven in the morning to rejoice over the big

From *Good Housekeeping* 62, no. 6 (June 1916).

bundles that came in and to give out shoes and groceries with happy kindness. Everybody knew everybody and loved everybody, everybody was needed: the dully prosperous little town had at last given a chance to the most pitiable of unemployed, the wives and daughters of its dully prosperous leading citizens. Only the old and the sick felt what all were declaring they felt—heartbreak.

Dorothy Eades, being a sturdily honest young person, presently realized something of this. She had come racing in her car—not home, for home was now a welter of blackened stone and writhing iron, but to the cousinly roof, five miles from burned Chiltern, that had given temporary shelter. The sky was splashed with autumn stars, and the crisp cold had poured over her for the eight glorious minutes of the run. (Dorothy considered the speed laws abrogated for the present.) She found her mother piled up with relief garments, making them whole and neat with absorbed industry, but her father sat by the fire, his dropped head on his hand. Dorothy's awakened glance passed from one to the other.

"You know, Father, it's awfully hard on you—being ruined and all that, but mother and I are having the time of our lives," she said. Mrs. Eades uttered the usual shocked protest, but Dorothy's eyes were on her father. She planted herself on the hearth rug, her hands clasped at her back. She always wore tailored suits, rather squared off and short, with obvious pockets, and boyish shirts of soft white silk.

"I never really knew what fun was before," she went on. "I've run that silly car till I thought I was tired to death of it—but running it to get things done—citizen things—why, Daddy, I'm the trustiest little messenger on the force! I've had the mayor on board today, and two policemen with a looter squirming between them, and a stunned child—he got a brick in the head, but he's all right—and about fourteen loads of stuff. Oh, we have to keep saying it's pitiful, because it is, frightfully, but I never had such sport in my life."

Some vision of the girl's unused strength, the force that had had to expend itself on games and restless trips, might have touched a different man, but Mr. Eades had an old-fashioned caution where women were concerned. He believed that they ran grave dangers outside the safe routine of dull prosperity. "I wish you could have some older person with you," he said worriedly.

Dorothy sighed aloud. "Age doesn't always mean sense," she explained to him. "If you would only believe that I can take care of myself!"

The shadow on her father's face deepened. "If I were only sure I could always take care of you," he muttered. Under his haggard eyes, ruin suddenly became a more real thing. She fell into musing silence that presently ended in an abrupt, "Why on earth haven't you brought me up to know something!"

A different man might have felt the reproach, but Mr. Eades acknowledged only one way to bring up girls. "A man expects to provide for his wife and child," he said sorrowfully, and Dorothy, seeing how he sagged in his chair, forgave him.

But the problem began to go through the busy days with her. She faced it in all its aspects: ruin—that incredible thing that happened in the newspapers to people one didn't know. *Ruin.* In all her life she had never gone without, and she tried to picture what was coming, but she could not keep down a growing thrill. Like a tightening of new muscles, the thought strung her erect every time it came: "I must do something! I must go out into the world and make my fortune!"

Dorothy's charitable activities came to an abrupt end a few days later with the sale of her car. The money took them to the neighboring city, where friendly influence had secured a small position in a bank for Mr. Eades, and set them up in as dismal a little bunch of rooms as ever advertised light-housekeeping facilities. Or so Dorothy thought them. Mrs. Eades, who had been killing time for twenty prosperous years, went back to the occupations of her youth with surprised energy, sweeping rooms in mauve satin and peeling potatoes in brown broadcloth, for there was no money to replace the excellent clothes they had saved. She sang sometimes when she thought no one could hear. But Dorothy looked on the new surroundings and occupations with frowning distaste.

"What can I do?" she asked herself over and over. There she

was, young, vigorous, handsome, unafraid—and idle. A son in her place would have found occupation at once. "But he would know something; he'd have trained himself for something," she protested. "Father would have hounded him till he did—just as he's sat on me till I didn't. Parents didn't know much when I was young." The last sentence was spoken aloud, across the bed she and her mother were making.

"They knew how to lay a counterpane straight, anyway," was the somewhat sharp answer. Dorothy, with an internal laugh, relaid the counterpane.

"I adore it when you hit back," she said. "But, you know, you really ought to have given me a trade. Except for running a car—" She stopped short. An idea grew in her face from a pin-point of wonder to a broad laugh.

"What is it?" her mother asked uneasily.

"It takes me a good while to get an idea, but when I do—" was all Dorothy would say. Presently she dressed and slipped out, as unobtrusively as she used to years ago, with skates hidden by her muff, when the river was alleged frozen.

Any one from Chiltern was sure of a hearing just then, and the name of Eades had figured picturesquely in the tale of shattered fortunes. Dorothy was admitted at once to the private office of Mr. Robert Spence, of the Spence Automobile Company. She had no idea that she was being specially favored by indulgent power, and met Mr. Spence on a cheerful equality. Her mother's complaint that she "hadn't a nerve in her body" was justified by that serene entrance into the business world.

"I'm Cyrus Eades's daughter, Mr. Spence," she began. "One of the Chiltern—hundreds," she added, with a smile for the unexpected joke. He perhaps did not get the point, for his smile was vague.

"Well, Miss Eades, what can I do for you?" He had a bluff heartiness, like a clap of hands, but it stopped short at the cool, shrewd eyes. "We businessmen have done what we could for your unlucky town, but when a pretty young lady comes after us for more—" and he threw a checkbook on the desk in mock surrender.

"Oh goodness!" Dorothy was frankly dismayed. "I didn't come for money. I only wanted some advice."

"Ho! That's easy." The checkbook vanished, and he leaned back with a fat air of joke, though the wary eyes still took no part. "What can I tell you?"

Dorothy's clear gaze met his for a full moment. Then she plunged ahead: "I've got to do something—work you know—and the one thing in this world that I really understand is a Spence car. I can take it apart and put it together in the dark. It can't play a trick on me that I can't beat. I can do the outside edge with it—I have! We own two, or did till last week. I can keep the speed laws, or I can break them, but I've never yet hurt anything bigger than a hen. Now is there any job in that?"

There evidently was something, somewhere. He had straightened up and taken a paper-knife into serious consideration. She saw him question it, reject it, try it again. At last he spoke.

"Why, as a matter of fact, Miss Eades, we are taking on some women demonstrators to show the new model—take out prospective buyers, but—" again the inner objection rose, and he laid down the paper-knife—"I don't believe it is what you would want to do," he concluded.

Dorothy considered a moment in silence, then she looked up with a boyish directness. "What is the objection to me?"

"Simply that you are a lady."

That astonished her. "Not so that you would notice it," she objected, leaning back with hands dropped into her coat pockets. "At least, not according to my mother."

He laughed out. "Perhaps I should have put it that you are a nice girl," he amended.

She was only puzzled. "Yes, I suppose I'm that, but I can run a Spence—why I've sold five cars for you already," she exclaimed, brightening. "All the Spences in Chiltern came from mine. Why don't you let me try it?"

The appraising eyes, seeing her handsome, vigorous, splendidly young, were admitting that she could indeed sell cars. "Why, my dear young lady, I would let you do anything," he protested. "Only, I couldn't guarantee that the customers would all be gentlemen."

Dorothy rode over that with no idea of what might lie under it. "Oh, that wouldn't worry me."

"Take care of yourself, huh? Well, if you want to try it—"
She rose. "Let me run you a few blocks to show you," she
offered. It was a little like asking the president of a railroad to
try out a new fireman, but he only laughed.

"I'll send my superintendent, if you don't mind. They keep
me pretty busy in here." He touched a bell. "We are paying
twenty-five a week, and—"

"Just for running cars about?"

"And selling them," he reminded her with an unsmiling emphasis that fell chillingly on her spirit.

"But, of course, I'll sell them," she protested.

"Of course you will." He gave an order to the man who
had entered. Dorothy was to go with him, but something held
her back. At the door she stopped, thought a moment, then
returned.

"Mr. Spence, do you realize that you could get any number
of young fellows at half that price?" she urged.

He could only stare. "I'm aware of it," he said finally.

"That's all right, then. I didn't want to take advantage of
you," she explained. "And I'm ever so much obliged." She
was gone before he could recover sufficient breath for his
usual manner.

The new fashion of women demonstrators had been written up in the papers, and Dorothy's first customer was a nervous gentleman who wished to see if a girl could really run
a car, as his daughters were bent on having one. Dorothy
trundled him about the streets so soothingly and safely that
he bought a Spence at once and engaged her to give lessons to
the two daughters. This brilliant beginning was followed by a
serious failure with a shriveled, stringy, horsey little man who
begged her to call him Micky, as every one did, and suggested
that they run out to the inn and "have something." Dorothy
showed off the car in bored silence and brought him back
glum and unrefreshed and muttering of "early frost." Later in
the day Mr. Spence sent for her. He was more bluffly genial
than ever.

"Sit down, Miss Eades; good of you to come up. I just want
to explain to you about the Bayberry Inn. You know it, don't
you—out on the Naugus Road? I own a half interest in the

place, so, of course, when you drop in there with a customer, nobody pays. It's on me. A bite of lunch or a glass of—oh, lemonade or something will often sell a car for you. Feed the brute, you know—there's a lot in that."

Dorothy, looking past the easy geniality, suspected that she saw beneath it a cold annoyance, and her heart sank. "I suppose that is where the nice girl in me is a drawback," she admitted. "And yet you know it helped with Mr. Fletcher. I've just given his girls their first lesson."

He edged away from her candor. "Oh you will do splendidly when you know the ropes," he said largely. "Just go ahead and try not to snub anyone. We can't all be thoroughbreds."

She was sure of the annoyance now. "But he was such a little beast," she said unhappily.

"Micky Martin?" He threw back his head for an indulgent laugh. "Micky a little beast? Why, Miss Eades, he's the best little fellow going. I've known him for twenty years. You can't expect drawing-room manners in an ex-jockey, but he's worth several million, and if he once gets the automobile craze, he'll have a new one every three months. He's got an obstinate loyalty to horses—it was a big triumph to get him in here today."

"And then I spoiled it!" She was so honest in her self-blame that a little of his artificial heartiness fell away.

"Ah, well, just try to remember that a customer needn't have had a college education," he said with a curtness that felt genuine, and so was welcome.

Dorothy lay awake for hours that night, mastering her new lesson.

"Young lady, boarding-school miss!" she flung at herself. "So aloof and fine that you lost a millionaire customer. What's the sense of hating a little man because he's common? Let him be his kind, and get some amusement out of it."

A new conception of what democracy might mean came like an inspired gospel to her ready spirit. Barriers that the fire had undermined crumbled about her. "I can know people the way a man does, good-naturedly and not judging," she thought it out. "Forget about ladies and gentlemen while you're down-town—canary-bird."

Yet, sorely humbled though she was, she did not for one minute wish herself out of it. She was only impatient for morning, that she might go back and do better.

The news that Dorothy Eades had gone to work for the Spence Automobile Company had flown about Chiltern, and she was soon receiving kind, sorry notes. "It must be so terrible for a girl who has had everything," they said. Dorothy laughed at the sympathy. Every day was an adventure, every hour she felt the pull of the harness on her strong young shoulders and rejoiced. She had a reason now for getting up in the morning. She read the papers with a new interest—for was she not a part of the business world? When she received her first week's salary, she knew, forever, that it is only the girls who have "everything" who have nothing.

It was good to rest on Sunday, but better to go back to work on Monday. Business seemed to be pouring in; she and the other demonstrators were busy all the morning. Coming in at noon, she found Nathalie Estabrook's cousin, George Estabrook, waiting for her. The big, boyish-looking fellow was so smartly equipped, so markedly the prosperous young motorist, that Dorothy, who had last seen him while he was working his difficult way through college, did not dare greet him at first. He stood waiting before her, an ingenuous grin spreading over his open countenance.

"Well, it is George!" she exclaimed, putting out her hand.

"Sure thing," he assented, and consciously looked away from and over his equipment, but Dorothy went straight to the point.

"My word, Georgie, but you've blossomed!" she said. "I didn't know you had come up in the world."

He flicked invisible dust from his sleeve with a prosperous glove. "Oh, been doing rather well," he threw off. "I've been thinking of a Spence car for some time—don't like my old car much—and Mary told me you were showing 'em. Will you really take me out?"

"Of course I will. That's my business." She led him into the showroom where the new model was posed like a great jewel in a glass case, and displayed its outer and inner perfections with a serene pride that was almost maternal. He seemed rather stupid about its mechanism for one who wore such complete motoring equipment, but then George had always had an endearing touch of stupidity.

"Well, if I tell him it's the one to get, he'll get it," she thought comfortably as she turned from her demonstration. It gave her an unpleasantly "caught" feeling to discover that Mr. Spence had been looking on.

"Mr. Estabrook wants to try the new car," she explained, wondering why she felt so guilty. George certainly had come for that. Mr. Spence greeted George—or George's clothes—with his bluffest brand of cordiality, and suggested that they run out to the inn for a bite of lunch. George, always an awkward big thing, blushed and stammered, but Dorothy, who had hitherto shirked the inn, abetted him by bringing out a car.

"'Feed the Brute' is our motto," she told George as she bore him away. "A glass of lemonade or something will often sell a car." The traffic kept her eyes engaged, but she felt a thunderous mutter at her side. When they were clear of the town, she turned to smile into his downcast face.

"Awfully good to see you," she said.

He sighed mightily. "It isn't good to see you doing this. When I think how you have always had everything—"

"Oh, I've had money. And perhaps that would have meant 'everything' if I hadn't lived in a dull hole with a family who stopped at 1880. Why, it took me years to get my car, years of solid arguing. Generally it was easier to give in. I was a prisoner, condemned to hard idleness for life—father's life. This may not be the ideal job, but it feels good!" And she put on a burst of speed that closed conversation. When she slowed down, it was to point out the beauties of the machine. George had to appreciate its every superiority before they turned in at the gates of the inn. "I want you to try it," she concluded. "You can run us back."

"Oh, I'm not on to a Spence," he said hastily.

"What is your car?" she asked, coming to a stop by other waiting motors, which the glowing autumn days had brought out everywhere by hundreds.

"A Broad," said George, stepping down.

"I don't know that make."

"It's rather old—pretty good car, though." George took her hand to help her down and gave it a hearty shake before he released it. "Fun to have you lunching with me," he said. "I shouldn't have dared suggest it myself."

"You're lunching with me," she corrected him, leading the way with a pleasant sense of adventure. "It is all on Mr. Spence," she added across their little table.

George dropped the menu. "Oh, come—I don't like that," he exclaimed.

"My good George, if I let you pay, I'd be fired. Mr. Spence would know it—he knows everything. It wouldn't be good business with a prospective customer."

Her decision quelled him, but it also swept away his appetite. She had to do the ordering.

"But suppose I don't buy his old car?" he burst out when the waiter had left them. "I am not at all sure—well, you know, what I really wanted was to see you."

"That's all right," she consoled him. "Lots of sales are made just that way. You aren't bound in the least. Only, when you do buy, you'll remember this nice run."

Speech rose in George, but sank unuttered. She tried to amuse him with the adventures of the past week, but they so palpably depressed him that she turned instead to the fire. They had a beautiful time over that. She and George had always had good times. He was her devout listener, endlessly at her service, and yet he never gave her that embarrassed, uneasy feeling that he was presently going to act like a young gentleman on a magazine cover. It was fun to see him so prosperous. Though he ate almost nothing, he gave the waiter a large tip and stopped at the desk afterward for cigarettes.

Dorothy, waiting for him on the steps, looked down with a motorist's critical patronage at a beautiful chestnut mare, then glanced at her rider, who just dismounted. He was bent over, running an inquiring hand down the mare's foreleg, but Dorothy knew him. Her first impulse was to slip past, but before Micky Martin's withered, impudent, little face could be lifted, she saw that fate had given her back her chance. She dropped her hands in her coat-pockets and stood her ground.

He knew her at once, and with a swift gesture turned up his

coat-collar about his throat, shivering. "Hello, Frostbite," he murmured.

The past hour had left Dorothy rich in gaiety. She found him funny and suddenly likeable. "Hello, Micky," she returned pleasantly.

His neck shot out of his collar. "H'h?" he grunted. "So it's Micky, is it? And what am I to call you?"

"Miss Eades, I guess," was the tranquil answer.

He liked that. His face was squeezed up into a grin. "All right. That goes. What's been changing your mind about me?"

His commonness really didn't matter. They were pleasantly man to man out there on the steps in the radiant autumn world.

"Something I heard," she said with her straight look.

He sighed, quaintly dejected. "Yep, I'm rich," he admitted.

She laughed. "Something more than that. I heard a man say that you were 'the best little fellow going.'"

"Did you, now?" He was so genuinely surprised that she laughed again. "Well, of all—I wonder now—'the best little fellow going.' Well, maybe I am, then!"

"And so I thought I'd give you another trial," she went on, made bolder by the consciousness of George's big presence at her elbow.

Micky's left eyelid drooped wisely. "Then it was me that was on trial? Now I thought it was Bob Spence's machine."

"Oh no. We try out the customers to see if they are good enough to have one."

He wheezed with amusement. "Well, now, I'll tell you, Miss Younglady, I haven't any use for an automobile. When my time comes, I'd rather be killed by an intelligent horse that knows what he's doing than by a gallon or so of cleaning fluid. But if you'll learn me to run the thing, I'll buy one. Is that a go?"

Relief on Mr. Spence's account, pride in her own sagacity, set Dorothy beaming. "Rather," she said, putting out her hand. Micky wrung it.

"Well, now, the young swell is getting restive, and you may lose a sale, so I won't keep you," he said backing the mare to let her pass. She looked up to enjoy George's amusement, but his face, usually so kind, so responsive, was stonily blank. He put her into the car in silence.

"'Smatter, Georgie?" she asked presently.

He could not at once get his lips unlocked. At last it came. "Do you mean that you are going out—alone—with a man like that?" His horror was so sincere that she felt curiously feeble before it.

"Why, that's Micky Martin," she explained. "He's the best little follow going."

"If I had known it was Martin, I should have kicked him for speaking to you."

A spark of anger came to her aid. "Don't be a goose, George! I can't drive away customers just because they aren't gentlemen."

"Nor can you go about with notoriously disreputable characters," was the answer.

Dorothy thought for a long moment, then went on more reasonably. "Look here, George, I spent a whole night thinking this thing out. The fire started it—it taught us all something about democracy. After that there wasn't anybody in Chiltern that you 'wouldn't know.' Oh, the silly little ten-cent snobs that we all were! It was worth burning up the town to see us get together. And now take Micky; he's either a vulgar, impossible little beast, or he is a shrewd, humorous ex-jockey whom I really like—while I am dealing with him. It doesn't have to go on. Don't you see?"

He was looking at her with an exasperated helplessness. "Oh, I see that you ought to be taken care of!" he burst out. "Your theory is all right, but do you believe for one minute that Micky Martin is going to understand it?"

"He'll find he has to understand. I can take care of myself." She answered sturdily.

George groaned. "I'm not afraid of actual hurt, but to have you meet vulgarity, insult, perhaps—"

"Well, they wouldn't kill me," she spoke with a defiant shrug. "I didn't know you were so much like father."

That shot ought to have finished him, but George was unmoved. "I guess all men are alike about wanting to protect the girls they care about," he said gravely, and Dorothy was smitten by a sudden amazing desire to lay her head on his big shoulder and weep. Instead, she put on speed, and they were soon threading the confusion of the city streets.

The superintendent happened to be standing in the garage, and Dorothy felt an uneasy impulse to explain that Mr. Estabrook really had wanted to try the car, but George unexpectedly played up. He thanked her formally before he hurried away.

Micky came the next afternoon, and Dorothy, confronted by his dizzying checks and his diamonds and his complacent horsey swagger, had to remember by main force that she liked him. He hunched himself down beside her with a pleased but cautious air.

"Old Bob's been telling me what a fine and fancy article you were till I don't dare lean back," he presently complained. "You may be a swell, but I guess you're a human girl too, ain't you?"

She did like him, after all. He had her own candor. "You mightn't think so," she said. "What do you mean by it?"

"Well, I'll bet you like candy, and pearls, and sitting up in the front of a theaterbox, and men crazy about you—"

Her laugh interrupted. "Wrong number, Micky," she said, turning deftly out of the congested main street into a quiet avenue. "Now I'll show you the first principles."

His little blinking eyes were questioning her with an odd concentration, but Dorothy had come out to give a lesson, and in all good faith she gave it. Micky proved less intelligent than he looked, and her patient thoroughness seemed to depress him.

"I guess I'm up against a new proposition," he said at last, so ruefully that she feared for her sale.

"It's nothing when you get the hang of it," she assured him.

Micky, for all his mechanical obtuseness, still looked mysteriously sagacious. "You see, I'm used to a different kind of critter," he said. "My kind—well, with oats and whip and stable, you can handle 'em. With your kind—I'd mean well, but I'd presently be pitched out on my head. I can see that much." His nod was significant, but Dorothy was thinking

"I'll bet," remarked Micky, "you like candy, and pearls, and sitting up in front of a theater-box, and men crazy about you—" "Wrong number, Micky," interrupted Dorothy, laughing heartily as she deftly turned a corner into a quiet street

Illustration by Hanson Booth. From "Shelter," *Good Housekeeping* 62, no. 6 (June 1916), p. 697.

only of automobiles. She recommended earnestly that he get a good chauffeur and learn gradually. Micky threw up his hands.

"You win," he said. "Run me out to the inn, and we'll call it square. I've got to have something to give me back my nerve."

The thought of driving up to the inn with her flamboyant passenger dismayed Dorothy, but it was time to make concessions. Micky clearly wasn't happy. She put the car through all its paces, to cheer him, but Micky, shriveled down into his clothes, merely blinked at the road like an indisposed monkey. They were almost at the inn before he spoke.

"You're a new one on me, and I kind of like you," he said suddenly, "but you'll never succeed at this business." He was so gravely certain that her heart sank.

"Don't I run the car well? And explain it clearly?" she protested.

Micky shrugged. "No better than forty young fellows Bob could get at half the money."

"But I told him that when he hired me," she explained with a touch of eagerness. "He said he knew it, and that he didn't mind."

"You told him—" But under her clear, anxious gaze words failed Micky. Suddenly he wheezed with laughter. "All right, all right," he murmured. "I'm for you—you're the best little girl going. I take it back—you'll get on— Now come in and have a—nut chocolate sundae."

The inn was mercifully empty at that hour, and they had the tea-room to themselves. Dorothy was wondering how quickly they could get away when Micky, setting down his glass, began to talk. He told her of his jockey days and of racetrack intrigues, of financial adventure and dark political straits, of men who had manipulated governments and made millions overnight, and committed crimes and kindnesses with equal readiness. For an hour the lawless saga flowed on, and Dorothy listened spellbound. She had not known that there was such a world. Motorists came and went, but she was not aware of them. She had a moment's chill when, glancing up, she seemed to see George in the door-way, staring at her, but it was only a big young man in George's kind of motoring clothes. Micky expanded under her listening, but never once did he lose a quaint air of caution, of looking ahead before he spoke. The tale contained nothing that a girl need have shrunk from hearing. Dusk was near when they rose.

"Oh, it's good to be out in the world!" Dorothy cried. "My grown life has been all teas—pink teas, yellow teas, engagement teas. That's a horrible world you've shown me, but it's alive."

"Yes, but there wasn't a girl in it who wouldn't have lep' to get into your world," he told her. "You've had money and safety, my girl, and don't you forget it. You've been taken care of."

The same old note—her father, George, and now Micky. Dorothy started her car in thoughtful silence. "I don't see what's so awfully dangerous, if you're sensible and clear-headed," she said at last.

A glint came into Micky's eyes, then he thrust his hands deep in his pockets, smiling inscrutably. "You're safe as in a church," he said. "You'd turn the Old Boy himself into the best little fellow going. Tell Bob you sold me the car. Perhaps you'll honor me some day by coming out to see my colts?"

"I'd love to," said Dorothy.

She put Micky down at his stable, and then went on to the garage, smiling to herself. Life opened up before her, rich with new interests. She could know and like anybody, she could earn her living, she was done with the eternal stifling of her energies in little soft amusements that didn't amuse: at last she was free to grow up!

"Good old world!" she was saying under her breath as she turned into the garage. Then, "Why, George!" she exclaimed.

He had come hurriedly to meet her. "Did you have any trouble?" he asked.

"Trouble?" Dorothy was too surprised to step down. "What about?"

George lifted her out with tightened muscles that set smartly on her feet. "Considering that you have been off most of the afternoon with a notorious scamp," he burst out, "a little anxiety—"

"Oh, don't be absurd," she interrupted impatiently. "I've had a splendid time and sold a car. Micky's all right. He's the most interesting man I ever met. How did you know?" she asked.

"Williams told me," was the answer. "He saw you out at that abominable inn. I would have gone out after you, but you had left by the time I could get away."

"Tony Williams? Your old roommate? I didn't recognize him."

"You might have recognized his clothes," said George grimly. "I had 'em on the last time. Did it for a lark, and to see you. Then, when I did see you—oh, I don't know." He kicked at the floor. "The lark all went out it. Made me sick."

Dorothy was taking in his modest attire with indignant eyes. "You told me you had a car," she accused him.

He was not in the least abashed. "I meant a trolley car," he explained differently. "Broad Street, you know. Oh, hang all that, Dorothy, I'm not rich, but I'm getting on all right. In a year or so—Well, I've always loved you, you know. Only it wasn't any use before, when you had everything and I had nothing. Now—I'm a fool to spring it yet, but I can't stand it. Since I saw you again, it's been nothing else, all night and all day. I want to take care of you, Dorothy!" His hand closed on hers. "Let me—give me the right!"

For a moment Dorothy's new vision was blurred, her new world seemed to be falling about her in confusion. Then some desperate instinct told her that if she took away her hand, she would again see clearly. She caught it back.

"That's just it," she cried, turning toward him in the dim and empty garage. "I've been taken care of and taken care of till I'm half smothered! I've just got out of my box, and you'd put me back in it, and feed me through a hole, and let a few chosen people come near enough to speak. No, George! No! I want to take care of myself!" Their eyes held them, battling; his were the first to fall.

"I won't give you up, just the same," he said, and then they went out in silence.

When they reached her door, she opened it and looked back. "I'm sorry, George," she muttered, her hands behind her.

"You don't know yet, dear, all it means," he urged. "Suppose you lost this work—it's only a fad, employing women demonstrators—what then? What could you do?"

"Something," she defied him.

"Oh, my dear girl! 'Something' is pretty hard and uncertain."

"Well, what of it? I've had enough of softness!"

He was not convinced, only patient. "When you're tired of it, I'm coming back."

"No—never! It's no use," she insisted, and closed the door on him. Alone, she was gripped again by that ridiculous, humiliating impulse to tears. She hid herself in her room. "What is it I don't know?" she made hot demand. "Why shouldn't it go on?" She sat for a long time with her face dropped on her hands. It was an older Dorothy who at last looked up.

"I'm not going to give in," she said, "but I'll tell you one thing—even if I do, my children won't! They'll know how not to! They'll have professions and—" Suddenly the hated tears rose uncontrollably. "Oh, George makes me tired!" she sobbed.

WHAT WOULD YOU
HAVE DONE IN
HER PLACE?

Edith MacVane

MILLIE May Jewett was tired. Not an ordinary dead tired, or even dog-tired, but a swimmy, marble-legs, spots-floating-before-the-eyes sort of tiredness that made it seem a matter of perfect indifference if she managed even to live to Saturday night and get her envelop. And, to cap the climax, it seemed as though everybody in New York, just this very afternoon, wanted gloves—and wanted them tried on, too—six pairs at a time.

Millie May was at the "gloves." Last spring, before she was taken down with typhoid, she had been at the "notions." Which meant that the firm, after her illness, had not only treated her square and taken her back but had promoted her as well—to seven dollars and a half a week instead of six and a half. At the hospital, too, she had received the best of treatment during her illness and the convalescence that followed. If by the time she was finally discharged as cured, her strength was a matter of theory rather than of fact, the trouble was with the wickedly destructive nature of typhoid itself, not with the provision made by society for girls in Millie May's position. She was able to work; so it was clear that her bed at the hospital must be given to some one who couldn't. And

From *Cosmopolitan* 62, no. 13 (February 1917).

Millie May, having no money and no means of supplying her defective capital, must go back to work for a living.

Which, in theory, works out like an example in the back of the arithmetic. This did not hinder, however, the fact that, at the end of a few weeks' work, what with the poor air, and the strain of standing on her feet all day, and the effort of remembering her stock and waiting on her customers, she found that her returning strength seemed to have halted at some half-way station, and her knees just got heavier and her head lighter with each busy, crowded winter day that passed by.

This afternoon, the rush was on in full force. "Yes, madam; sure they wash—dry out pliable's new— Men's gloves other side of the aisle— No, madam; those elbow suède mentioned in yest'day's ad are all sold out— Corsets? Take the elevator, second floor to the left— Yes, madam; I gotta send down to the stock-room for the other four pairs to make the dozen of thirty-button whites. They'll be here in five minutes if you'll kindly wait—"

And so on. The last order, which was for a girl in magnificent ermine furs, whose profession was written as with a finger on her beautiful dark face, caused Millie May a sudden heartburning. "*She* buys five dollar gloves by the dozen, while I, who've always lived straight as a string, gotta trot and fetch an' carry for her like I was her hired help," was Millie May's angry thought. And following a blind, implicit instinct, as though to prove to herself and to the universe that the said straightness was the result of high moral principles and not for the lack of personal attractions, she tossed her pretty little golden head with a weary coquetry as a new customer pushed into the throng on the other side of the aisle.

"Men's gloves, other side o' the aisle," she repeated, for the fifty-seventh time this afternoon.

The new customer, a sleek, fresh-colored young man in a fur-lined overcoat of marked elegance, smiled at her gaily.

"But I don't want men's gloves, this time. I want to see suèdes, elbow-length, for a lady."

A little excited color sprang into Millie May's pale face, and a little giggly tone into her voice as she demanded,

"Suède—what color?"

The customer, instead of answering, surveyed her with out-spoken pity.

"You poor kid, you're as sick and tired as a dawg, aren't you? Say, it just makes me sick, too, to see a sweet little queen like you slaving here to fit the paws of a bunch of mutts! Where you otta be is in one of these swell six-room flats, all black oak and Bokhara rugs, with some lucky fellow fetching his envelop home to you Saturday nights—"

Millie May's bloodless face flushed to a geranium red. Not that she had never heard such expressions before. In fact, the young shoe salesman from Boston, Florence's cousin, who had been Millie May's escort on the Coney Island party last June, just before the disastrous typhoid, had used almost the same words. Why was it that the picture of the little flat, which last spring had thrilled her and whose remembrance remained like a secret yearning, failed in this instant to touch any responsive chord? Was it on account of the speaker's eyes, which, belying the honest friendliness of his words, traveled from her slim form to her big blue eyes with too vividly bold an interest? At any rate, Millie May pulled him up shortly.

"What size?"

For answer, he demanded what size she wore herself, bought a pair of pale-gray suède, elbow-length, and when the parcel came, tried to crowd it on her as a belated Christmas present. And, in the same breath, he begged her for a date to go to dinner and the "movies" with him, that very evening.

Millie May's "No!" to both propositions was as prim and unbending as her careful bringing-up and her rigid little code of conduct demanded. How far was this code the result of immovable conviction, and how far the result of lack of opportunity? Swell young men offering classy invitations and expensive presents did not come Millie May's way every day. And though she had thrown the young man down, as was her duty, still, even after he had disappeared in the crowd, instinct told her that he had not gone far. When closing-time came, would she find him waiting for her near the salespeople's exit? Her heart beat fast, sending a flush of life through her dragging limbs.

But an hour later, when, buttoned up into her little imitation astrakhan jacket, Millie May stepped out into the brightly lit February night, she was too numb in mind and body even to glance about her. After the suffocating heat of the store, the icy outdoor air pierced her like a knife. Heavily she dragged herself along the slippery sidewalk.

Suddenly, a stout lady in Russian sables, sweeping out to her limousine, jostled against the slowly moving little figure. At that same instant, Millie May's foot struck a ridge of ice, and her head took a sudden dizzy turn. The next thing she knew she was flat on the icy sidewalk and content to lie there without moving, in the delicious relaxation that comes to exhausted muscles even upon frozen bricks.

Far away, as though coming to her at the bottom of a well, she heard voices—first, a throaty, important sort of woman's voice, declaring:

"There, I'm sorry; but that was her fault! She ought to have looked where she was going." Then, a younger, fresher voice that replied:

"Do you think we ought to take her into the car, mamma?"

A flutter of the eyelids told Millie May that the stout lady who had bumped into her, with a young girl, was bending above her. Other faces, too—swimming in a kind of dark confusion; she was aware of the young man in the fur overcoat lifting her head to his knee. Then her heavy lids fell to again, and in the little pin-print of consciousness that remained in her exhausted body she listened, with a perfectly detached interest, to the voices that played like waves above her.

"I suppose," boomed the throaty voice doubtfully, "we might take her into the car to some sort of institution—I know we subscribe to lots of places."

"She works in the store! I seen her, but I don't know her name!" piped up the shrill voice of a cash-girl.

Then the masculine voice spoke decidedly, falling down to Millie May as from the rim of a well where she lay hopelessly, profoundly submerged.

"I know her well. I'll take her home myself directly. Her mother keeps a delicatessen shop down on Ninth Avenue and Eleventh Street. Poor Mrs. Mulhausen! She'll be scared to pieces to see Lily like this. Come on, you poor kid!"

Away down in the dark bottom of the well where she lay, Millie May made a frantic effort to deny, to protest, to call out for aid. Her enfeebled will failed, however, to dominate the weakness of the fainting flesh. And, unable to produce any sound beyond a faint murmur, she was conscious of the growing clash of far-away voices above her head. A new voice, slightly hoarse but oddly mellow and seductive, and just now pitched to a muffled tone of indignant rage, breathed above her.

"Say, you Percy Wickman, where are you carryin' that kid off to?"

"I'm carrying her home to her mother, don't you see?"

"Oh, you black liar! *You* know where you're carryin' her off to! Here—leggo that girl!"

"And what'll happen to her?"

"I—I'll take her myself."

The young man's answering laugh was of an ugly quality which penetrated even the torpor of the prostrate girl.

"It's all over; I'm dead, and this is hell!" the horrifying thought shot through her, as the laughter's voice turned into a whisper that hissed like a snake.

"You, Goldie—you're a peach to take charge of an innocent girl! Here—leggo her hand, or I'll call the police!"

"Do you want *me* to call the police, Percy?"

There was a pause, during which the current generated by two furiously opposing human wills snapped and crackled above Millie May's motionless head with such violence as almost to galvanize her into life. She made a violent effort to call for help—opened her eyes a moment, and this time fell back fainting in good earnest. For any spark of that small vital flame known as Millie May Jewett, it might as well have been the girl's dead body that was hastily picked up and deposited tenderly on the cushions of the waiting limousine.

II

A sweet and brooding perfume, almost oppressive in its combination of sachet-powder and of cut flowers, was the first sensation which marked Millie May's return to life. Her hands, stirring feebly, were aware of the smoothness of satin below them; while her soul, streaming home with the violence of a falling star, demanded: "Is this me? What am I? Where am I?" And her blue eyes, flying wide open, found themselves staring into the smiling face of a smart, white-capped negress, bending compassionately over her.

"Fo' the Lawd's sake! Here she is wakin' up! Miss Goldie! Here she is all right at last!" cried the hearty tones of the maid, raised as though to catch the ear of some one in the next room. Then Millie May was aware of a cup of warm milk with brandy in it being held to her lips.

"Now drink dat, honey!" came the command, and she gratefully obeyed. The next moment, renewed life flowed like quicksilver through the girl's veins. She raised her head.

"What's happened? Where am I?" she cried, staring in bewilderment from the brocaded hangings of the large bed wherein she was lying to the dimly decried elegance of the half-lit room dwindling off in visions of tightly drawn red-satin window-curtains and shining plate-glass mirrors. The next instant, there was a quick step, a swish of silk, a gust of new perfume, and the tall, slim figure of a strange woman, wrapped in a pink negligée of surpassing and bewildering elegance, bent suddenly over the satin-covered bed. Poor little Millie May, feeling herself very humble and undeserving in the midst of so much gorgeousness, took in a startled breath and desperately sought for words in which to express her gratitude. The newcomer, however, spoke quickly.

"You poor kid—you're a whole lot better already, aren't you, dearie?"

The voice, slightly hoarse but oddly mellow and seductive, struck with a curiously familiar note on the ears of the prostrate girl. The beautiful dark face bending over her—where was it she had seen it before? The next instant, with an odd thrill of misgiving, Millie May perceived that the brilliant tints of the lips and cheeks at which she was staring were obviously and flagrantly artificial. And, at the same moment, as her quick eye read the impalpable, unmistakable signs which had set their tragic seal on that beautiful, painted face, remembrance flashed upon her. The girl in the splendid ermine furs, who bought long white gloves by the dozen, and who, for months past, had been the object of Millie May's mingled envy and horror—this was she! This was her house! And Millie May was here alone! With what object had she been carried here, while she lay helpless and unconscious?

In a shock of terror that almost robbed her of her breath, Millie May recalled certain stories she had read in the newspapers, various rumors and warnings wherein she and her mates, with goose-flesh running down their spines, had whis- · pered among each other of that fear which runs like a slimy undercurrent beneath their little world. And now it was her turn! Terror caught her by the throat. She began to climb out of the satin-covered bed.

"I gotta go! Where are my clothes? What was in that cup o' stuff I drank? Oh, where are my clothes? Lemme go, or I'll scream!" she cried wildly.

This time, there was no doubting the genuiness of the crimson which dyed her hostess's face. For an instant, the two girls remained glaring at each other. Then, to her infinite amazement, Millie May saw the scarlet Cupid's bow begin to twitch, and the bold, dark eyes swim and soften in a sudden glittering moisture.

"Your clothes are there, on the chair. When you're dressed, Florence'll take you to the front door. And—and thank you very much for the polite way you're behavin' to me, when I was just tryin' to treat you a little bit decent. Good-by!"

Millie May sitting unsteadily on the edge of the magnificent bed, snatched at her cheap little black-cotton stockings. But just the same, across her bewildered brain shot a new perception, fairly staggering in its novelty. Of what was owing to her, as an honest working girl, from her employers and from society at large, she had heard and thought much. That she, in her turn, had certain obligations which she must fulfil or else be branded as a quitter had never before occurred to her mind. The thought was perhaps not so fully defined, but it was there, as through Millie May's self-centered, narrow little soul, just now fiercely strung up on the defensive, there rushed the realization that this other girl had been good to her, and now in return was being made to cry.

"I beg your pardon," faltered Millie May; "you've been awful kind to me. Thank you, ma'am—miss—ma'am—" She broke off in trembling confusion, as her utter physical weakness laid its grip once more on her failing limbs. "It's time I was goin'!" she finished, and reached for her shabby white-topped boot.

The effort at stooping finished her. The next moment, she found herself once more deposited in the downy softness of the bed, with the hot-water bottle at her feet and the satin coverlet drawn up under her chin. And her hostess, bending anew over her, spoke with subdued violence.

"Don't be a darned fool! Don't kill yourself gettin' up when you're sick, and don't scream till you're hurt! An' most of all, don't treat people like rats when they're tryin' to do you a good turn. Those two swell dames that knocked you down, there outside the store—I didn't see them pickin' you up an' carryin' you home—not so's you'd notice it! For all that they'd a' stirred a little finger to help you. Percy Wickman might a' carried you off, as he'd done many another girl, spite o' the police, with his hot air about knowing your family an' takin' you home to your mother—"

"Percy—the young man that wanted to give me the gloves? Why, he don't know my family, an' I haven't any mother!" faltered Millie May.

The other girl nodded grimly.

"So he's been coughin' gloves for you, has he? Well, that's a sign he meant business, 'cause Percy's the grand little tightwad in the red-light district. And slick, too. The police have been after him for three years, an' never nailed him yet. Say, kid, instead o' yelpin' at me, I sh'd think you might own at least it was lucky I happened along to get you out o' *his* grip!"

"Thank you," murmured Millie May, completely subdued by weakness and her sense of her own ingratitude. "You've been awful good to me, and I'm just as grateful as I can be—"

Her hostess waved her thanks impatiently aside.

"I'm not one of these uplifters, out after gratitude! All I want is to be treated like a lady, an' not like a white slaver in the 'movies.' Look here. What's your real name?"

Millie May told her. The other girl laughed grimly.

"I knew Percy was lyin'! Well, no matter now. Listen! My name's Goldie Altamont—at least, that's my name here in N'York. I know—you an' your kind think I'm too rotten to touch with the tongs, and mebbe you're right. An' then again, mebbe you're not, I'm on the square, anyhow. I don't say that this house is exactly a young ladies boardin' school. But while you're in it, you'll be treated right, or I'll know the reason why. This is my chum's room. She's gone to Palm Beach for a month with—with a friend. So there's no reason you shouldn't stay, if you'd like to. I'll arrange with the madam. And if you don't feel quite as safe as you might, why Florence'll sit up with you to-night, an' tomorrow I'll have a man put steel bolts on these two doors an' the window, too, so's you can fasten them from the inside."

Goldie's voice rose urgently, full of an unconscious wistfulness. Millie May stared up at her in feeble surprise.

"You're askin' me to stay on for a visit?" she demanded suspiciously, with a sharp recurrence of her former fears. And, involuntarily, she added, "Why?"

Again Goldie's face flushed to that hot crimson.

"You think I gotta have my reasons? Well, mebbe even the toughest of us gets sick of just pluggin' on one day after another, thinkin' o' nothin' but number one. Why, even a dog don't do that, does he? An' then, mebbe you make me think of a little sister I had once—or may have now, for all I know. My family ain't written me in five years." Her painted face twitched. "Well, no matter. But as you laid there on that icy sidewalk, with your hat fallen off an' your hair all tumbled sideways, why—it's funny, but you looked just like my kid sister useta, when she was small an' I useta put her to bed. She was as fair as I'm dark—awful pretty hair she had, just like yours. Good-night."

Goldie Altamont, having locked the doors and whispered minute directions to Florence concerning the care of the sick girl through the night, tiptoed away to her adjoining room. Her lips were strangely pinched, and her beautiful dark eyes burned with a tragic fire, as with the help of the maid, she wearily made her sumptuous toilet for the evening.

III

A wet Sunday afternoon about three weeks later, Goldie came strolling into Millie May's room, with a fur-trimmed automobile bonnet dangling from her hand and a bored frown on her brilliantly tinted face.

"My gentleman friend that I was goin' automobilin' with has just called me up," she announced indifferently to the girl in the long chair beside the fire; "says he's got the toothache an' don't das' go out in this rain. Well, *I* don't care!" And, with a listless yawn, she flung herself into a little gilt chair on the other side of the hearth-rug.

Millie May stared at her with a faint smile. As was once said of another, long ago, nothing in this house of mystery seemed so strange to the girl as the fact that she still found herself in it. Though behind the steel bolts which, according to promise, had been placed on her door, and under the vigilant guardianship of Goldie Altamont, the real life of the house—whatever it was—came no nearer to the little convalescent than the actual underwater life touches the diver in his submarine armor. Occasional footsteps, a whispered conversation, a burst of laughter—this was all she ever heard. Little by little, as she became used to her environment, the shamefaced wonder, the horror, the almost physical repulsion wore away. And her unchanging intention of leaving the next morning was day after day maintained without being put into execution.

In the midst of this luxury, which she tasted for the first time in her narrow, barren little life, Millie May relaxed her weakened limbs and grew strong, without demanding too closely the sources of the comforts showered upon her or the motives for which they were offered. With the instinctive arrogance of the impeccably virtuous, she received the humbly offered kindnesses, the almost touching devotion of the gorgeous Magdalen by whom they were bestowed. The half-grudging concession which—beside the acceptance of the other girl's bounty—she made by way of a return was a recognition of Goldie's common humanity. And now, as she glanced from the streaming window-pane to the bright fire blazing on the hearth, her tightly-closed little soul opened for an instant to a thrilling perception of gratitude and of understanding.

"You're awful good to me, Goldie. I'll never forget it," she murmured shyly.

"Oh, yes, you will, as soon as you get out of *here!*" returned the other girl, with a short laugh. She was plainly pleased, however, at Millie May's tribute of gratitude. The impulse which, in the first instance, had led this queen of the half-world to pick up the little shop-girl from the icy sidewalk had been perhaps no more than the instinctive stirring of a careless good nature, and the desire, as she phrased it, to "put one over" on Percy Wickman. But now, by virtue of that human instinct which—as has been said—causes us to love even a stray dog after we have sat up with him a night or two, Goldie had begun to find a deep and unexpected pleasure in showering kindnesses on this pale waif tossed on her hands by blind accident. Her impressionable nature, starved of its natural affections, warped by exaggerated passions, had attached itself with a strange tenderness to this humble, narrowminded, reputedly spotless honest little working girl. Genuine regret was in her voice as she added, "My chum—the girl I told you about—she'll be back from Palm Beach in a day or two—"

"The one that owns this room? I gotta be goin', anyway," interrupted Millie May hastily. "I'm strong enough to go back to work, now—I sh'd think I might be, with all the chicken an' jelly an' things you've stuffed me with since I've been here spongin' on you. I wish I could pay you."

"Who wants to be paid? Don't talk like a simp!" growled the other. Then, stretching herself with a long yawn, she added, "A wet Sunday afternoon always gives me the willies."

"When I was a kid at home," rejoined Millie May pensively, "we were always let to make molasses candy on Sunday afternoons, First, we read the Bible aloud, turn an' turn about, to momma. Then—"

"My kid sister an' I used to read the Bible aloud to momma ma, too, every Sunday afternoon," interrupted Goldie, then stopped abruptly. Her richly toned, slightly hoarse voice had in it a new vibration. Half awkwardly, as though the words were forced from her, Goldie asked,

"I say, kid, do—do you ever read the Bible now?"

As awkwardly, Millie May shook her blond head.

"When I first come to N' York, I started goin' to the Baptist church on Thirty-fourth Street. Then I found I was too tired, Sundays, so I kind o' gave up. An' some one swiped my Bible—"

"I got my Bible still, the one momma gave me when I was twelve years old," broke in Goldie. Then, with that agonized, rough-spoken diffidence with which, for some reason, the Anglo-Saxon race approaches any of the inward verities of heart or of soul, she added: "Say, kid, if I go an' get it now, would you like to read a little, turn an' turn about? An' just let on we're both of us back home again—"

The other girl, equally confused, nodded brusquely. A moment later, as Goldie handed her the volume, it fell open on Millie May's lap. On the fly-leaf, in a delicate, sloping hand, her hasty eye read: "To my little Annie, on the occasion of her twelfth birthday, from her loving mother. Let your light so shine before—"

"No, not there!" cut in Goldie roughly. A moment later, in a voice rendered flat and meaningless by self-consciousness, Millie May began to gabble through the Gospel of St. John. But little by little as she read, the solemn beauty of the words, the beloved memories of home thus evoked had their effect on her careless little spirit; and her voice, gathering strength and conviction, became a very creditable imitation of her grandfather, a deacon in full standing and famous for his forceful delivery in meeting and in evenings of prayer. Goldie, with parted lips and vague, awe-struck eyes, leaned forward with a half-devout, half-bored air, like one in church. Nor did she manifest any sign that the succession of sacred tales and sayings held for her any more exact application than a holy stream of living water played, as it were, on her bruised and darkened spirit till Millie May, plunging indefatigably on, reached the eighth chapter—that which narrates the story of the woman taken in adultery. And perhaps even then the listener would not have relaxed her brooding calm had not the reader, stricken by a sudden, horrible embarrassment, stopped short on the awful word. Goldie, flushing a dark and painful red, broke the silence.

"Go on. What you stoppin' for?"

It was the first time that, even by implication, the shameful fact that lay at the basis of Goldie's life had been touched upon between the two girls. The blush was reflected on Millie May's pale cheeks, and her pompously raised tones fluttered and broke as she faltered her way through the immortal story of human sin and divine forgiveness. Might it be instrumental in converting poor Goldie? the little reader asked herself in a vaguely optimistic hope. But after the beautiful words, *"Neither do I condemn thee; go, and sin no more,"* she was rudely wakened from her pious dream by a jarring laugh from her listener.

"That's all very sweet an' lovely, if he was talkin' to a society woman, with plenty o' money to live on, an' folks glad enough to take her up anyhow, an' ask her to their houses, whether she was livin' straight or crooked. But if she was a workin' girl, where did he think she was goin' to find an honest job any more?"

The crude and ugly verity presented by these harsh words were too much for Millie May's limited intelligence to combat. She bravely presented, however, the optimistic aphorism that had been grounded into her upbringing:

"Anybody can earn an honest living when they want to work."

"Oh, *can* they?" jeered Goldie, with a laugh, which, strangely enough, made Millie May feel suddenly as though she wanted to cry. "Suppose I managed to get a job at the glove-counter— would you work alongside o' me? Would the other girls?"

"Ye-es; why, of course we would!" was Millie May's faltered response. The stern and living conviction of the Baptist deacon's tones had disappeared from her little voice. With a short, harsh laugh, Goldie rose to her feet.

"I feel kinda tired. I gotta go an' lie down. So long, kiddo!" she announced brusquely. And Millie May, left alone by the fire, meditated in bewilderment upon problems that were so much larger and more complicated and more pitiful than she had hitherto dreamed.

IV

As the day for Millie May's departure drew near, Goldie Altamont contrived to spend much time in the companionship of
her little guest. And Millie May, inexpressibly shocked by the
almost blasphemous outburst of the other day, returned indefatigably to her Bible readings. The deep religious sense of her
race, smoldering always in the depths of her skeptical little
New-Yorkized soul, blazed into sudden life. With her feeble
hands, she hoped to roll aside the great stone of circumstance.
And, with that hope, the passion of the "uplifter" seized her.
But, possessing no eloquence of her own, she fell back upon
the sacred script as upon a fetish with an infallible potency
within it, whether bearing directly upon the subject in hand
or not. And, intermingled with her readings, she gave Goldie
the benefit of scraps of her grandfather's theology.

A passage which, one snowy afternoon, provoked a spirited
discussion between the two girls was that chapter in St. Luke
relating how Peter denied his Lord. Millie May was unsparing
in her scorn of the apostle's cowardice.

"Wasn't it fierce, denying Jesus right up an' down like that!
'I know not the man!' Why, a quitter like Peter oughtn't ever to
have been forgiven!" she exclaimed vehemently. Goldie, drumming with idle finger-tips against the white-banked window,
returned slowly:

"I dunno. He was awful scared when he out an' out denied
the person he loved so much, poor Peter was. An' then—I
guess we've all got to forgive each other lots o' things, or else
the best of us couldn't get along at all."

Millie May opposed a vehement negative.

"Not for a rotten thing like that!"

"I dunno, kid," returned Goldie slowly.

Surprised at the change in the other girl's voice, Millie May
turned quickly. But Goldie's face was toward the white, falling snow without. It was as though the shadowy figure of
Tragedy had reared itself between the two girls, like a third
presence in the quiet room. Millie May, suddenly overawed,
kept silence. After a few moments, Goldie returned to the fire.

Her face, as yet unpainted for the day's work, looked oddly innocent and pale. She spoke quickly.

"Say, dearie, you're a good kid, an' I don't mind it a bit—the way you're trying to uplift me for all you're worth. I'd be a hard job, though. But listen: There's one thing you *can* do for me, when you get out o' here. I can't do it for myself, an' I ain't got anyone to ask but you."

"You've been awful good to me, Goldie, and you bet I'll do whatever I can for you. What is it?"

The answer, barely audible, was punctuated by a fluttering breath.

"Go into a church—a Roman Catholic one—an' say a prayer for the repose of the soul of Jim Lannigan—the best man I ever knew. You get that name, dearie?"

"Jim Lannigan." Millie May, overawed by the half-felt presence of a passion and a grief such as her shallow, irreproachable little life had never even glimpsed, stretched out a little hand whitened by idleness, and timidly touched the other girl's cheek. It was wet. Millie May gasped, and withdrew her hand. Goldie, unconscious of the caress, stared into the fire.

"My family an' everyone called him names enough. But it wasn't true. He was a good man, the best I ever knew. He'd a' married me if he could. But his wife wouldn't hear of a divorce. She had money an' was awful stylish—an' didn't give a flip for Jim. But she didn't want to be a divorcee. There were three kids, too. They were Catholics—oh, well, what could you do? I wasn't then what she thought me. I was just a stenog in Jim's office—Thomson & Lannigan, Real Estate, one o' the biggest in Chicago it was then. An' Jim an' I fell in love with each other. Like heaven it was for a while. Ah!"

Goldie closed her eyes, while her hard face softened to a new beauty. Her voice shook as she went on.

"Then Jim told me his wife was threatenin' to leave him. I'd been brought up right. I wasn't goin' to have it. So I ran away. I took the night train for home—a little place near Goshen, Indiana. Mother an' my kid sister were awful glad to see me, an' the kid made a little cake with candles around it, like a birthday, in honor o' my comin' home. Then I got a job in

Rosenbaum's Emporium, right there in Goshen, an hour in an' an hour out at night. Mother was awful pleased, an' said I was takin' father's place. But, somehow, I couldn't stand it. I had to give up sleepin' with the kid an' take a little room o' my own, 'cause I useta cry all night. Then, after three months of it, I just couldn't stand it an' wrote back to Chicago, to a chum o' mine in the office. She wrote back that Mr. Lannigan was like a ghost since the last three months—t.b. the doctors called it, it was said. He had a cough on him that was like a graveyard quickstep, an' now he was off for Colorado—alone, 'cause his wife was goin' to Washington to a grand convention o' women's clubs." Again silence. Goldie's warm, thrillingly raucous voice was hardly more than a thin thread of itself as she added: "He didn't go alone. He didn't die alone, either. His wife come rushin' out to the Springs by the next train to get the body. But it was *here* he died!" And she struck her beautiful bosom fiercely, as though it had been an anvil. Little Millie May shivered.

"Oh, poor Goldie! And what did you do then?"

"There wasn't anything left *to* do! His wife turned me out, o' course—after she'd had my trunk searched, an' taken away a string o' pearls Jim had given me, an' a gold-mounted dressin'-case, an' his photograph in a silver frame, an'—an' his necktie that he had on when he fell down an' died. It wasn't poor Jim's fault. He was goin' to put me in his will, all right an' regular, an' had the lawyers comin' to the hotel the very day that he was took with that last hemorrhage. Well, I didn't care much then. Nothin' seemed to matter very much, anyhow. So I didn't fight her. I just took the money that happened to be in my purse an' bought a ticket back to Chicago."

"You poor kid! So you had to go right back to work?"

Goldie made a wry face.

"I couldn't get the chance—that was the trouble. Mrs. Lannigan had talked a whole lot, you see. Everybody was onto the whole story, so the girls in the office didn't want to work 'longside o' me any more. I tried at two or three other places— I was an A-one stenog. But, somehow, that old story always leaked out. Then I wrote home. I—I wasn't feelin' very well. I wrote six times, to momma an' my kid sister, but I never got an answer." Goldie's face worked. "That was a hard winter. At last, my—my little baby was born. He was born dead, an' that was one good thing. So's soon's I was well again, I just took the train an' come to N'York to make a fresh start. But—land!—there are limiteds runnin' every day, from Chicago to N'York. So one day, down in the office of the insurance company, where I'd got a job pounding a machine, a fresh drummer from Chicago that knew me blew in. When I wouldn't go out with him, he got mad. I don't know what he said to the boss, but that evenin' *he* wanted me to go out with him. And—well, I had to leave. The next place, the other girls somehow got hold of the story, an' sent me to Coventry till I had to quit. An' then—well, what's the use? The more I got acquainted, the worse things were. So at last—well, it was a case o' sink or swim. I went into the chorus for a while, but I've no ear and made a mess of the steps. So—here I am."

She finished abruptly, and, moving over to the table, poured out a glass of water from the cut-glass carafe. Then, without turning her head, she added:

"You remember what I said to you the other day about the woman that was told to sin no more? That's the trouble with bein' a workin' girl, you see." She paused a moment, then went on reflectively: "The funny thing about it all was, though, it was the other girls that wouldn't let me come back. It's queer, you hear such a lot about the rights o' workin' girls, an' what ought to be done for them—but when it comes to some one that's a notch below them that they could give a helpin' hand to, are they there with the goods? Not much!" Again she paused. "I don't know's I can blame 'em, though, poor little kids! When I first went to work at Lannigan's, I was just the same."

Little Millie May, powerless to cope with the vast problem thus presented to her, could only murmur:

"Those girls were a lot o' mean dubs. Poor Goldie! You've been awful good to me, dearie, an' I'll never forget it!"

"Maybe not," returned Goldie, with a wistful smile, "but listen here: This is what I wanted to ask of you." She took a long breath, and, suddenly crossing the little room, flung herself on her knees beside Millie May's chair. "Listen here: I want you to go to a church—a Catholic church that was Jim's—an' say a prayer for him. I—I ain't fit to pray, myself. I went with him of my own free-will, an' he was kind to me, Jim was. Oh, he was kind! If there was anyone fit for heaven, Jim was. Say that for me, please, dearie! An' then—"

She caught her breath, and the queenly dark head went suddenly down in Millie May's lap. Half muffled by the folds of the wadded-silk wrapper, her jerky phrases came up to the young girl's ears.

"Then I want you to say another prayer—not for Jim. *To* him, this time. I ain't dared to myself, since—" She swallowed hard, then went on. "Say it plain, with his name an' everythin', so's it go up *sure* to where he is. Tell him not to be mad at Goldie for doin' what she did. It was a choice between that an' the river, an' she didn't want to be a quitter. But tell him—oh, dearie, tell him *hard* that Goldie's always true to him in her heart, an' for him to wait; she'll come to him some day, if she's let— Oh, kid, make him understand—*make* him understand!"

V

Like a dream that is told was Millie May Jewett's sojourn in the mysterious house with the red-satin curtains, when once she had left its dubious shelter and returned to the life of the store—her own life. The firm, true to its up-to-the-minute policy of building up an efficient personnel by fair treatment, took her back and put her in the Child's Ready-made Department at eight dollars a week.

The necessary explanations, after much worry and thought, she offered as follows: The gray-tweed ulster lined with squirrel, the little blue-serge dress, the muff, and the other articles of clothing with which Goldie had presented her before parting, Millie May explained as gifts of a swell married cousin up-state who had just gone into mourning, while the month's absence from the store was accounted for as having been passed with relatives out in Jersey, convalescing. The blood of youth, renewed and redoubled, coursed merrily through her veins, and, after her long imprisonment, her young spirit leaped up toward freedom like a bird to the sky.

It was just at this moment, as the first airs of early springtime began to blow over the island of Manhattan, that a wonderful thing happened. Florence, Millie May's chum, invited her to go home with her to Sunday dinner. And who should blow in afterward, to take the girls for a walk, but the wonderful cousin, Frank Simmons, the pride of the family, who traveled in shoes for a Boston firm, and who had been Millie May's escort on the famous Coney Island party the spring before.

It was quite by accident that he had happened to find himself in New York this week-end. But, before the end of the walk, he was devoutly referring to the aforesaid accident as the direct finger of Providence. By the time they parted, he had given Millie May his lodge-pin to wear, and promised to make New York again the following Sunday.

On Millie May's first Sunday of liberty, therefore, she was unable to fulfil the errand imposed on her by Goldie Altamont. Already, with her return to her normal life, the strange, secret house had faded in to something like a shadow—a dubious and growing shadow which all her instincts pushed her to forget. The following Sunday, Mr. Frank Simmons took advantage of the fine weather to arrange (by wire) a little expedition to Far Rockaway, to eat a fish dinner and angle for gudgeon off the pier.

It was just before taking the train home that Frank and Millie May, while strolling on the beach, became for a moment isolated from Florence and her family. And the young man seized this opportunity to whisper into Millie May's ear:

"Next week, if I can manage to make N' York again, you and I'll go by ourselves—just you and me. I've something to—to ask you. 'S all right, little queen?"

Millie May, quivering in a giddy and solemn rapture, nodded her little blond head. For not only was Mr. Simmons the grandest looker, and the cutest company she had ever known, but, matrimonially considered, he was far beyond the claims of a little eight-a-week kiddo. Fifty dollars a week he was earning, no less, and always on the rise, with prospects, moreover, of soon settling in New York. And, beside that, his family were so terribly classy, his father being minister in a small New England country town and his sister married to an insurance agent in Boston. And here he was choosing her—that is, if he meant what she hoped he did. Millie May's heart swelled, and her blue eyes, as she raised them in wordless assent, were lovely in an unconscious tenderness and an immortal questioning.

For Millie May, the succeeding week was passed in a kind of dream, whose blissful waking—perhaps!—was to be on Sunday. But, on Saturday afternoon, the sudden sight of Percy Wickman, jauntily twirling his cane down the aisle in front of her, shocked her back to a rude sense of reality. The hideous fate exemplified by that flashy, overdressed young man with the roving eyes—who was it that had saved her from him? Goldie Altamont!

Poor Goldie, who had asked for only one thing in return— just one tiny, weeny little favor! And Millie May, like a heartless brute, had let two Sundays slip by in selfish pleasure, and had not yet carried out her ambassadorship to the High and the Invincible with which the tragic girl in the secret house had charged her.

Accordingly, the next day, as in her fur-lined ulster and blue-velvet toque (Goldie's gifts), and side by side with Mr. Frank Simmons, Millie May tripped along in the Sunday-afternoon procession down Fifth Avenue, she suddenly stopped short before the cathedral.

"Excuse me—I gotta go in here," she murmured breathlessly. Frank Simmons, surveying her little form with frank admiration, started suddenly.

"What! You a Catholic?" he asked abruptly, thinking of his father's Congregational church and the rock-ribbed Puritanism of his home. Millie May, flushing, shook her head.

"No, I'm a Baptist myself. But I promised to say a prayer for a friend—for a person that's a Catholic. You don't mind, do you, Mr. Simmons?"

He shook his head, and, pulling off his hat, followed her in through the heavy doors and dutifully stood beside her as she knelt down to pray. And, as she knelt there, a strange thing happened.

Until now, Frank Simmons, conscious of his own value as a highly successful young business man and the son of an eminently respectable family, had regarded the little salesgirl with the eyes of an established superiority. The question that occupied him was: Shall I marry her?

But now, as Millie May knelt there in the richly tinted, consecrated dusk, her status suddenly changed. The mystic domination which the praying woman exercises over the soul of man was suddenly hers. And, in a sudden rush of tender awe, vividly translating itself into passion, the self-sufficient young man felt himself unworthy to touch so much as the skirt-hem of this fair, pure-eyed young saint before him. And, in a panic, he demanded of himself: Am I good enough for her?

As they left the church together, it was with the trembling diffidence of a school-boy addressing a princess that he asked her to be his wife. Tears of joy shone in Millie May's blue eyes as she murmured her fluttering "Yes."

This painful, horribly important matter once settled, the spirits of the two lovers rose to the level of their own joy. Like two children, they hurried down the avenue together. Suddenly, Frank exclaimed:

"Say, little lovey, we've just gotta have a celebration, right off! Here—let's go in here an' get something to eat!"

"Here" was one of the most gorgeously gilded, the most rampantly fashionable and expensive of Fifth Avenue's famous restaurants. Millie May, trembling with excitement, followed the young man through the crystal revolving door into the crowded, softly tinted fairy-land within. With difficulty, a little table was found in the brilliantly thronged palm-room. And, breathing softly, lest she should break her dream, Millie May sat gazing about her, like a happy child, at the surrounding tables, while her lover splendidly gave an order.

Suddenly Millie May caught her breath. Her eyes had met a pair of burning black eyes gazing straight into hers. Goldie Altamont, seated among a hilarious group at a near-by table, was looking straight over at her and Frank.

The familiar ermine furs, the big solitaire earrings, the beautiful painted face, the dark, lustrous eyes with their touch of tragedy—there they were! There was Goldie. And Goldie's shining gaze was bent full into hers, while the tinted lips beneath were parted in a bright smile of greeting.

"Millie May, do you *know* that woman?"

The harsh, horrified tones were beyond Millie May's recognition as those of her lover. But the change in the voice was only faintly expressive of the agonizing revulsion in Frank Simons' soul. In choosing as his wife a nameless little waif of the great city, he had flown straight in the face of the severe traditions of his family's rigid, middle-class New England respectability. What, after all, beside the bewitching sweetness of her pretty blue eyes, did he know of Millie May Jewett? And now, if it was to a friend of that rouged and overdressed creature opposite, whose profession was stamped as with a die on her lovely, slightly haggard face, that he was offering his name and his life—if it was a girl of such associates that he was purposing to bring home and present to his mother as her new daughter!

Millie May shuddered. With a long gasp she dragged her eyes away from Goldie's without a sign of recognition, and turned her head back to the man she loved.

"No," she answered slowly and clearly: "I don't know the woman."

That was all. There was nothing else for her to do, of course. What would *you* have done in her place?

When Millie May turned back her head, painfully and timidly, about ten minutes later, Goldie had disappeared. What had she felt as she went away? What was it that she had said, that rainy afternoon when the two girls had talked together? "The funny thing about it all was, though, it was the other girls that wouldn't let me come back."

Remembrance of the past rushed upon Millie May, and the salted walnuts turned to dust upon her tongue. Bright as in a mirror, an unforgettable picture filmed itself upon her mind— the heavy red-satin curtains with the white, snow-covered pane beyond, and her own voice saying,

"Why, a quitter like Peter oughtn't ever to have been forgiven—not a rotten thing like that!"

"Millie May! Little love! What's the matter? Feelin' sick?"
Millie May leaped at the excuse, lest her rising tears disgrace
her in public.
"A little. I guess it's the heat in here. Would it—would it be
all right for me to go out to the dressin' room an' bathe my
forehead a little?"
"All right, sweetheart. Don't be long!"
So Millie May, like the unhappy apostle nineteen hundred
years ago, went out and wept bitterly.

THE LOTUS EATER

Grace Sartwell Mason

THE first time I saw her she was swinging down Fifth Avenue with a huge dilapidated portfolio under her arm. It was not the portfolio alone that made her conspicuous in the five o'clock parade; nor the casual sort of way she did her hair—in a loose knot on her neck with the hairpins sliding out and a nut-brown lock blowing across her cheek; nor her suit of rough tweeds, with the belt of the Norfolk jacket unbuttoned; nor her sensible boots, when every other woman was teetering on two-inch heels; nor the delicious tan of her skin that had so evidently never known a flick of powder. No, it was none of these details that made her stand out from the conformity of the crowd; rather it was the expression in her eyes.

They were the sea-gray eyes of the poet's phrase, and they held a light that startled one, met in that avenue so worldly with all the magnificent things of the flesh. They did not gaze into shop-windows, nor into the faces of her fellow pedestrians, nor at the long lines of crawling motor-cars. It wasn't that she didn't see these things, but that they didn't matter—to her. The shop-windows, full of everything to make women desirable, did not matter; the glittering motor-cars, that con-

From *Good Housekeeping* 66, no. 1 (January 1918).

vey women luxuriously hither and yon, did not matter; the women themselves, so different from her in the grooming of their bodies and in the expression of their eyes, did not matter. For she was watching the blue-gray shadows creeping up to the knees of the tall buildings down the avenue, the sky making itself into a background of ashes of roses, against which the skyline bloomed all at once into medieval castles, mysterious and romantic. That was what mattered to Mary—Beauty. She had the artist's eye, a touch of the genuine thing.

In the cheapest room in the cheapest street of the only part of Manhattan that is able to get away with dirt and discomfort and noise, that casts a glamour over them with the word "atmosphere" and turns them to commercial profit, Mary lived. She had gravitated to Greenwich Village direct from a fruit-ranch in California, leaving behind her a pair of concerned, resentful parents. But, inasmuch as she was twenty-one, and had earned the money to bring her within touch of her heart's desire, she was legitimately mistress of her own destiny. So she wrote cheerful and tender letters home, counted her money over every night, and was most amazingly happy and scared. And she had scarcely learned her way to the art schools when she fell in love with Courtney Cabot.

Courtney Cabot looked a good deal like his name. He was tall, with a high, thin nose, dark eyes, a tossing mane of hair, slender hands and feet, and a world-weary air. Just then, he was going to be either an essayist, a novelist, or a poet. So he lived in Greenwich Village, where he was learning life. He spent a great many hours in the bad air of studios, with a tea-cup in one hand and a cigaret in the other, talking to women old enough, almost, to be his mother. But there their resemblance to his mother ceased.

For Mrs. Cabot was New England, deepdyed, rock-bound. Her life was as orderly as the calendar. She was an instinctive preserver of the traditions of her family and section. And so was Courtney's father. Their fetish was education. The result was that Courtney from the beginning was cultivated almost to the limit. He grew up in awe of his own mental endowment; and in his third year at college he decided that the role of a great Universalist preacher was not going to afford sufficient scope for his powers. The world of art suddenly opened up to him. Overnight, so to speak, and to the bewilderment of his parents, he shook the dry dust of college from his feet and came to New York. He took to Greenwich Village as a duck to water; he became in an amazingly short time one of the nearest Bohemians that ever scattered cigaret ashes over the long, greasy tables at Polly's. And it was at Polly's that he met Mary.

I can imagine her feeling her way for the first time up the steps and along the dingy hall that is postered with announcements of undressed balls, strikers' meetings, and cartoons from propagandist papers. I can see her hesitating in the doorway of the long dining-room, trying to see her way through the smoke from cigarets and broiling steaks. She had not been in the Village long enough to lose her spontaneity, and her sea-gray eyes were still very wide with the wonder of everything, her skin was still tanned from the western sun; and she stood in that doorway very slim and boyish in her brown tweeds, her wonderful eyes shining and eager.

Courtney, looking up from a volume of Mallarmé's poems, met her glance squarely. He was so startled that he half stood up. And then she moved straight across the room to him.

"May I sit here?" she indicated the chair opposite him.

"Oh, will you?" he answered eagerly, forgetting to be world-weary.

Now it happened that I was having an after-theater bite with Courtney's cousin, Nancy Garrettson, when Courtney burst in upon us with an account of this meeting. He had become acquainted, so he declared, with the most wonderful girl in the wide world. Ever since supper at Polly's they had been walking, walking, he didn't know where, but their talk had been amazing. They had discussed, so it appeared, every known subject; they had compared their philosophies of life, their likes and dislikes, and had got at the inner meaning of almost everything. And they were Comrades of the Soul.

"Humph!" snorted Nancy, who was a very plain-spoken direct-seeing person, "what's become of that Russian sculptress you were going about with?"

"That was merely a phase I was passing though," replied

Courtney, with dignity. "The trouble with you, Nancy, is that you're hard. You have the odious Broadway flippancy—"

Nancy gave him one of the clear looks. "You've got something that's worse than anything Broadway can produce in the way of flippancy, Courtney. It's worse, because it pretends to be something else."

"I don't understand you, Nancy!" And Courtney left us with his handsome head in the air.

"Understands me perfectly well," chuckled Nancy, as the outer door slammed. Then she elevated her feet to the divan where they had been when Courtney burst in, ran a hand through her outrageous, flaming hair, and sighed, "Wish he hadn't told me about that girl," she said presently. "Somehow, I have a hunch she's different. The others—it doesn't matter if they *do* eat the soap and lick the blacking—does 'em good. Makes 'em less cocky, more fit for human uses. But the talented ones—it's such a waste of their divine energy, the things they do when they come here and find themselves what they call 'free.' Courtney's going to be very bad for that girl, something tells me." She relapsed into thoughtful silence for a few minutes. Then she grinned, suddenly and hopefully. "Unless I decide to take a hand in the game myself," she added.

With her usual energy she began at once by getting acquainted with Mary. And the first thing she knew she was liking the girl tremendously. But this was not surprising, for so did we all. Mary had brought with her an unspoiled naturalness that was most refreshing in a community where poseurs flourish like weeds. She was so young, and so in earnest, so receptive, and so happy. And besides, there was that touch of the real thing. At the schools they began to speak of her almost from the first as having possibilities. They said that if she worked hard and kept her head cool and her eyes fixed straight ahead, they'd be able to liberate that tiny flame in her, that divine tongue of fire that is worth dying for, if you happen to be built that way. Of course it would take long months, months that would stretch into years; and in the meantime, here was life, demanding to be taken notice of, life hungry, bewildering, and sweet.

"The days aren't nearly long enough," Mary said. "I should

like to work twelve hours, and then play twelve. There are such heaps and heaps of things to do and see and learn. I wish there were three of me."

But she did not say why she wished there were three of her. Nancy knew. She knew that when Mary had finished the allotted hours of work at the schools she had to toil several hours at designs and sketches she carried uptown to dressmakers and an "art card" concern. For she had to earn money to stay in the Village. She, unlike Courtney Cabot, had no snug little allowance from home. The fruit-ranch had had several bad years, and besides, Mary's was an independent spirit. To study and to make a comfortable living at the same time was as much as two Mary's could have managed; and for Courtney Cabot there should have been a third.

For Courtney's idea of a comrade of the soul was one that should be available at any hour of the day or night. He himself despised fixed hours; they shackled his spirit, he said. So, after the day had got well aired and the wheels for ordinary persons had been going round for some five hours, Courtney rose, breakfasted, toyed with the thought of work, generally rejected it, dressed with careful carelessness, and went out. From this time on until midnight he was a busy person. Many and many a studio tea he graced with his good-looking world-weary self, many a rehearsal at the amateur playhouses he watched, many of his friend's pictures, poems, and plays he criticized, many hours he spent at table talking, often quite brilliantly about the novel he was just beginning or the essay he had half done.

This was all very well for Courtney, but from the moment he and Mary became soul comrades he could not let her alone. She was the most fascinating raw material he had ever come across. In the first place, there was that touch of the real thing, which gave her a fineness and a fire; and then there were the freshness of her mind and imagination, and her young veneration for everything that Courtney seemed to her to represent. The way she listened to him was wine to Courtney. For to her he was the authentic voice of all she had come here to learn. She was humble before his erudition, his ancestors, and his old New England background, a background he scorned even as he painted it for her. The fruit-ranch became very raw and crude, although she was too real ever to be really disloyal to it. When he talked to her about modern art and literature, she worshiped him; and when he talked about his essays, she burned with indignation at thought of the editors who couldn't see their way to publishing them. And finally when they had been soul comrades for a month, and he told her that he was falling in love with her, the whole world became a flame-colored incredulity.

"Well, what are you going to do about it?" Nancy asked them that night. They had formed the habit of discussing themselves before her with the astounding frankness of the section.

"You're so crude, Nancy," sighed Courtney. "What does one do when the great passion comes to one?"

"One generally gets married," replied Nancy dryly, looking at Courtney.

Mary blushed vividly, and Courtney looked pained. "That's the bourgeois solution," he said, "but you know the size of my allowance. It's the best the poor old pater can do."

"You might get a job," suggested Nancy.

But at this Mary flared. "And give up his wonderful work? Just to support me! No, a thousand times, no! I should feel as if I had deprived the world of something precious."

Courtney caught her hand and kissed it. "Isn't she the most understanding child? No, Nancy, Mary and I have discussed this question of marriage, and we're perfectly agreed. I have no inclination to become anyone's keeper, and Mary doesn't wish to become a parasite. We shall show the world what it is to love unselfishly, greatly, without a taint of obligation on either side. It's obligation that crushes the wings of Love, you see," he added.

"I see," responded Nancy.

She admitted to me that the affair didn't worry her as much as it might, for, after all, Courtney couldn't get rid of all the family traditions. He could be relied on not to hurt Mary in any gross way—he was a gentleman of sorts; and besides, his white corpuscles far outnumbered his red, so Nancy averred. In one sense Mary was safe with him.

This began what was one of the most idyllic and decorative affairs of the Village. Every evening they could be seen dining together at the Purple Dog, or the Red Sarafan, or Bill and Mike's, or Fizzrolli's, Courtney talking and Mary listening with her starry eyes shining happily. Later they swung their feet from the hard benches of the latest amateur theater; still later they ate deadly things in front of somebody's studio fire. Afternoons they often walked up Fifth Avenue to tea at a little French place in the Forties, Courtney very striking in a soft black hat pulled low on one side, a heavy stick, a care-free tie, black-rimmed glasses, and his world-weary air. The difference between them in these promenades was that Courtney never missed one of the many glances sent after them, and Mary never saw one. She was generally thinking, as she walked with her chin eagerly lifted and that expression so different in her eyes, what a place of lovely miracles the world was, and could she ever hope to get those shadows that were creeping up to the knees of the Flatiron Building, and what had she done to deserve Courtney? They were very frank indeed about their feeling for each other, for that was part of their creed.

"The frankness of little children," said Courtney, "that is what we have. We want every one to see how simply beautiful love can be, on how high a plane, how free from prudery or the taint of self-consciousness." And he kissed Mary before a whole studio full of persons, who murmured with delight at the unexpected naiveté.

But in spite of the high note to which his devotion was pitched Courtney prepared to flee from the city at the first hint of summer.

"Why don't you take Mary up to spend the summer with your mother, Courtney?" Nancy suggested. "The city is beginning to tell on her."

Courtney looked alarmed. "You know my mother— and East Bradford, Nancy. They'd never understand Mary."

"But how about the propaganda of self-unconsciousness? You're always preaching it—why not carry it up to New England? Do 'em good. And really, the summer is going to be hard on Mary here all alone."

But Courtney merely looked irritated, and by the middle of

June he was off. Nancy put off her own vacation a month in order to help Mary become better acquainted with those of us who were to swelter through the summer in the Village. She introduced men to her in shoals, with the malicious hope that in one of them Mary might find an antidote for Courtney. But Mary looked through and beyond the most charming of them, politely, but without interest.

All through that summer Mary went about the Village a jaded, rather lonely little figure. Courtney had absorbed her so completely that she had never made many friends, and she had now the appearance of a person who is marking time while waiting for some longed-for event to occur. She painted doggedly in Nancy's studio, and wrote every day to Courtney, whose replies were scant and infrequent, for he hated letter writing. Knowing Courtney, and figuring on Mary's youth and artist's temperament, Nancy often expressed the hopeful conviction that three months apart would cure them.

But one night, in the autumn, when we were all seated about the round table at the Samovar, the door opened quietly, and Courtney walked in. Mary, who was eating alone at a little table against the wall, looked up at our exclamation of surprise. Such a light of triumphant radiance came into her face that I for one could not bear to look at her. Courtney, nodding nonchalantly to the rest of us, walked over to her table, took her two hands impressively, held the picture for an instant, and then sat down opposite her and ordered his dinner.

Nancy gave them one glance of disgust, despair, and rage. "I wash my hands," she growled. "She's got to eat the soap and lick the blacking like the rest of 'em, Lord help her!"

But Nancy's heart is always kinder than her words. And when, a few months later, a crisis came in the affairs of Mary and Courtney she could no more hold aloof than the most sentimental one of us. Soon after his return Courtney had become what Nancy called a "sediment worker," having decided that the world was not yet ready for either his essays or his vers libre. So he took to talking to groups of bewildered but admiring garment-shop girls on what to read to acquire cultivated minds, and he planned for them a Greek Pageant, which was to teach them simpler ideals of beauty. Of course, in all these activities, Mary had to take part, for it was important that she should see him against this new background. He needed the stimulus of her beautiful understanding. So between Courtney's settlement activities, her own work, and the necessity of earning her daily bread, Mary often toiled until past midnight and rose at dawn. By Christmas time she had lost her outdoor look, her eyes were a bit too bright, and her joyousness was sometimes a bit feverish. There were small hollows in her cheeks and deep shadows under her eyes.

Then, just when Nancy had decided she really must speak her mind about Mary's health, Courtney got himself into the limelight by contracting scarlet fever in one of his slums. Through Nancy's influence he was taken to a private hospital where Mary was allowed to come and gaze at him from a distance. Every day through a month of abominable winter weather she performed the long and dreary pilgrimage to the hospital. Without fail, every day she carried him delicacies, flowers, and the news of the Village. We could only speculate as to how she managed to get the time and the money for her devotion. But we were to comprehend how much that month took out of her for the day Courtney left the hospital Mary fainted in the studio at school. The doctor whom Nancy promptly fetched said a good deal about over-strain and under-feeding; and with that, Nancy bore her off to a convalescent home.

Every one of her friends in the Village rallied to cheer her with flowers and messages and visits. Every one, that is, save Courtney. He had the legitimate excuse at first that he wasn't strong enough. Then, one day, Nancy called a taxicab, coerced him up to the home with her, and waited for him outside. He came tottering back at the end of fifteen minutes.

"Never, never ask me to visit another hospital!" he cried as he fell into the cab. "It makes me feel ill!"

"But do you mean to say that you won't go to see Mary, after the heroic way she behaved when you were ill?"

"I will not," he declared doggedly. "I tell you it *bores* me, Nancy!"

And he looked bewildered and hurt when Nancy opened

the cab door, ordered him out, and left him standing on the curb.

"I never want to speak to you again," she said, as she drove off.

Mary's recovery was slow, but at the last it was all too quick for Nancy, who, in spite of her repudiation of Courtney, was obliged to perform one more task for him. The day that Mary left the home Nancy had to break to her the news that Courtney had thrown her over. He had confided to Nancy that little Mary was no longer sufficient for his soul's growth. She was a phase, and he'd passed through it. He had decided to write plays, Eugene Walter plays with a Dostoyevsky flavor, and he must live, live intensely, even brutally. His relation with Mary was too idealistic to give him what he needed for his plays. Therefore, Nancy must tell Mary that their chapter was finished and closed.

"Lord help me!" groaned Nancy. Then she chuckled. "He says he is now the Goethe-man, and he's going about with two Broadway fluffs with yellow curls and a Pomeranian. Two of 'em! If life wasn't so funny it would be awful."

The night Mary came back to the Village from the convalescent home Nancy told her. Mary listened in a white silence.

"I don't believe you," she said when Nancy had finished.

"All right," said Nancy. "But you will, sooner or later. And when you do I want you to come and tell me."

It was only a week later that Mary crept up to Nancy's apartment. "I believe you, now," was all she said. "I've seen him."

From that time on we all watched her. We were like persons standing on the bank of a stream helplessly observing an inexpert swimmer trying to make the shore.

At first Mary went about the Village white-faced and silent. She avoided her friends—Courtney she was spared the trouble of avoiding, for he had betaken himself somewhere north of Forty-second Street; she was rarely ever seen in any of the restaurants or tea-shops where she and Courtney had been so well known; and she re-entered her classes at the school so listlessly that her teachers declared she might as well not be there at all. This was the first stage. Then overnight she entered upon the second. She stalked in upon Nancy and me one

evening at twilight with just a hint in her face of the old ecstatic radiance.

"You should have seen the light in the Avenue just now,"
she cried. "Saffron and mauve—I wonder if I can ever get it?"

"Not unless you buck up considerably, my dear," retorted
Nancy bluntly.

Mary went and stood looking out at the old Square. All at
once she threw back her shoulders. "I've been an awful fool,"
she said bitterly; "there's nothing in the world worth thinking
about but work. From this time on there isn't going to be anything else for me, nothing else, ever."

Nancy puckered her brow thoughtfully after Mary had left
us. "Not natural," she sighed. "The soap and blacking have
given her an awful indigestion. I'm afraid that by the time she
gets over it she'll be one of those scornful spinsters who wear
a man's derby and think they're emancipated from men when
they're merely rude to them. She'll cut off her hair and smoke
cigarets between the soup and the roast at table'd'hôte dinners, and her work'll get jerky and eccentric. And sooner or
later she'll break out in some way that may not be wholesome.
No, she'll never get over Courtney till she meets some man
that is capable of showing her the difference between the real
thing and the shadow."

After that she relapsed into a long silence, frowning and
running her hand up through her flaming hair. "There must be
a man like that somewhere!" she cried finally.

She stood thoughtfully at the window for a few minutes,
tapping at it, and whistling softly under her breath. Then she
threw up her head and glared at me challengingly. "I've never
missed a thing I've gone after yet, and I'm not going to fall
down now. You wait!" It was not so long after this that Nancy
surprised us by introducing into our artistic midst a plain
American business man. She appeared in the Square with him
one afternoon in his beautiful car, piloted him up the stairs to
the Samovar, introduced him casually all around, and then ap-
propriated him at a small table for two. From the way she
laughed and from the few remarks of his we caught we knew
he was no bore. He was certainly nice to look at. Clean, well-
tailored, spare, with a slow, pleasant smile, and the keenest

eyes the Samovar had seen in many a day, he was immensely likeable. He exhibited a boyish interest in us and our doings, and didn't make the mistake of crass jokes about us. He admitted that, like most New Yorkers, he didn't know much about our part of town, but hoped, now that he had made a start, he should be allowed to know more.

When later I questioned Nancy about John Briscombe, she gave me scant satisfaction. She said that he was prosperous, the general manager for a big automobile concern, and a gentleman. She liked him better than any man she had met in ages, and if she weren't already married to the *very best*, she would make a frank angle for John Briscombe. When I asked her where she had met him, who had introduced them, she became uncommunicative. Peeved, I twitted her with having picked him up at the corner of Broadway and Fifty-seventh. Whereupon she laughed so hilariously that I almost felt my suspicion confirmed.

"Do you think I'm going to gum the game by issuing bulletins?" she asked. "Perhaps you noticed that I merely introduced Mary as one of the bunch? And possibly you observed that he looked twice at her to every glance he gave the rest of my female friends? That was due to very, very subtle press-agenting on my part. But do you think I'm going to give away the source of my supply? Indeed, no—I may want to marry you off some day."

After that I was not surprised to see the Briscombe car in the Square quite frequently. And my admiration for Nancy's skill was only confirmed when one day I saw Mary going up the Avenue, not walking this time with a rapt expression in her eyes, but riding beside John Briscombe with a healthy enjoyment in her face. I repaired at once to Nancy's apartment.

"Oh, that's nothing new," she said complacently. "He frequently takes her out for air, after she's finished work. It's almost pathetic, the pleasure he takes in bringing a little color into her cheeks. He's never known any one like her. Her talent, her frailness, both appeal to him. I almost believe the miracle is going to happen."

"But you expected it to when you introduced them, didn't you?"

She shook her head. "Knowing how queer the chemistry of human souls is, I didn't expect anything. I just let them come together very, very casually. I told him just enough of her story to give her piquancy, but I never mentioned him to her. I'm just sitting tight now, and waiting."

But our waiting stretched into weeks and the weeks into months. As spring came on the car had a regular parking place in the Square. Of a fine afternoon after five John Briscombe was always waiting to give Mary her hour of fresh air before dinner. If there was work to be taken to her uptown customers Mary never had to carry it under her arm. Fruits, flowers, even lamb-chops and beef-extracts, flowed into her shabby room. When the house was torn down and Mary had to move, it was John Briscombe who found her a better location, and it was in the car that she made her removal. On her precious time he never made a demand. He told Nancy that it was enough for him just to see her growing stronger. He had a feeling for Mary's talent that was next door to reverence. He admitted to Nancy that he was very much in love and getting in deeper every day, but he would never ask Mary to give him a thought or an hour of her time if doing so would spoil her chances for success.

"Have you told her how you feel?" Nancy asked.

"Somehow, I can't," he returned. "I don't know what it is, but there is a kind of wall between us. She's as sweet and friendly to me as possible, but I've got a hunch that half the time she's thinking about some one else."

"That's exactly what she's doing," Nancy said, not to him, but, later, to me. "She's still holding on to a little shred of Courtney. And it's a shred of her girlish idealism, too. She's afraid to let go of it, and she's built it up into a wall between herself and John Briscombe. I'd be willing to bet my new hat that in that last interview of theirs Courtney managed to make a romantic and impressive exit. He'd leave the way open behind him; trust his kind for that."

Then spring came. The trees in the old Square budded, and under them a soft lavender-gray haze hung tenderly in the long-twilights. On one such evening Nancy, Mary, and I sat in front of the open windows in Nancy's apartment overlooking the Square, when suddenly Mary made a low sound and leaned forward, staring down at the street. We, too, leaned forward and looked. Like a romantic ghost revisiting old haunts and somewhat conscious of the sensation he was about to create, Courtney Cabot was crossing the Square.

Nancy glanced at me with a panic-stricken eye. Then like a good general she gathered herself together. "Will you go into the other room a few minutes, Mary? Courtney's coming up, I believe, and we want to see him alone."

I knew that what she wanted was to prevent their meeting, and Mary evidently understood, for she hesitated an instant. But she went into Nancy's room and closed the door just as Courtney tapped.

He came in, and we saw at once that his attitude of the moment was to be a dignified lassitude.

"Hello, Courtney," Nancy greeted him. "Has Broadway turned you out? How's the play?"

"Dear Nancy, don't speak of it," he replied languidly, "I'm fed up with it. In fact, I'm through with the theater, at least the uptown theater. It's too gross, their commercialism. I've practically decided to come back to the Village. I shall probably go on the *Masses*."

"Have they invited you?" Nancy queried brutally.

But Courtney apparently did not hear her, for he had come in his languid promenade of the room to the chair in which Mary had been seated. Suddenly he bent over it and appeared to inhale a perfume from its upholstery.

"Mary—she's here!" he cried.

At first it was uncanny. Mary had not left behind her a trace, not so much as a handkerchief, or a hairpin. It was rather thrilling. But later Nancy and I agreed that he had seen her from the street. Courtney advanced to the middle of the room, fine head in the air, every muscle tense.

"She is here!" he repeated.

"No such thing!" stammered Nancy weakly.

For an instant Courtney stood there in silence. Then in his resonant, dominating, slightly theatrical voice he called.

"Mary!"

Silence from beyond the door. Nancy and I both sat there,

helplessly staring at that door. I think in that moment we both prayed that the door would not open. I, for one, hated him in that instant. But he did not see either of us. When the door remained closed, he stiffened, his head went back with the familiar domineering gesture, and once more he cried, this time with a dramatic mixture of longing and command:

"Mary!"

And this time the door opened. She came across the threshold with slow feet, but Nancy and I knew we had lost, for her eyes flew to meet his. Her face, which she was trying hard to keep stern and calm, was beginning to flush, the radiance was coming back to it.

"Mary, Mary, I've come back," Courtney cried. "I could not live away from you any longer. Little comrade; little comrade!"

He took her hands and bent his face to them. A quiver ran through Mary, a kind of fatal softening; and yet, she drew her hands away and caught at a new command she had learned during the months of her loneliness. Nancy made a queer sound that was the beginning of an authentic swear-word. She got up, gently but firmly, led Mary to the chair by the window, and with a gesture waved Courtney to a seat.

"We're going to talk this thing over now, quietly, thoroughly, and honestly," she said, "without sentiment or stage tricks. Sit still, Courtney. If you mean what you've just said to Mary, then you'll stand talking it over. And Mary, if you mean what you've been talking all winter, then you'll welcome honest discussion. Now—"

There was a small table in the center of the room. Behind this Nancy took her seat, sweeping aside the books that cluttered it. From this position she was able to keep them both under her glittering, judicial eye. There was something calmly exultant about her, as if now she had got the situation where she wanted it.

"To begin at the present moment, I understand you to say, Courtney, that you have come back because you can no longer live without Mary. What, then, is your proposition?"

"Really, Nancy, can one reduce a feeling like mine for Mary

to what you call a proposition? I dislike that word very much, Nancy. It is a typical Broadway word."

"It's a good word," said Nancy calmly. "What is your proposition?"

Courtney rose with dignity. "I refuse to be badgered, Nancy, by you or any one. I am certain that Mary doesn't wish it either. Mary—"

But unexpectedly Mary interrupted. "I think Nancy is right," she said in a low voice. "If a thing won't stand discussion, it's not worth much."

Courtney stared at her incredulously. Then he showed his mental agility. For he walked across the room, took Mary's hand with a kind of sad dignity, and said: "I came back, Mary, to ask if you will marry me. *That* is my proposition."

Even Nancy was staggered. And across Mary's face there swept a queer mixture of radiance, incredulity, and fear. She had risen to her feet, and she and Courtney stood looking at each other intently. There was in Mary's eyes a very agony of questioning. Then slowly Courtney took her other hand. We saw the desire to yield warring in her face with some new shrewdness. Nancy leaned forward across her table with a sharp dismay in her face.

"Mary! Wait! Don't answer him yet. Give yourself time to think."

Mary turned and looked at her slowly. "But, Nancy, I think I love him," she said as simply as a child.

Courtney lifted his head triumphantly. "You're answered, Nancy. There's nothing more to be said. Mary—"

Nancy suddenly brought her fist down upon the table. "But there is something more to be said. And I'm going to say it. Sit down, both of you. You're going to hear the truth about yourselves, and then you can go out of here and do what you like. I shall be through. But I've stood you both for a year and a half, and for that I deserve a little satisfaction."

"If it's any satisfaction to you to be malicious, Nancy, go ahead." Courtney seated himself defiantly.

"No malice in this, Courtney, I assure you. Just the truth. Mary, let's go back over the last year and a half. You left a comfortable home and came here with one ambition, to learn to paint. You had to make your living at the same time. You were like a person starting out to row for shore against a heavy tide: you could just make it if you didn't carry too much freight, or if nobody rocked the boat. We all knew that. We see those conditions repeated time and again down here, in the case of some talented girl. Courtney knew it. But all the same, he climbed on board—and rocked the boat. Wait! How much, last winter, did he actually help you in your work? Oh, I know he gave you the benefit of his ideas of culture—most of them spurious, not one of them that would make you in the end a better artist or a bigger woman. And in exchange for his ideas he took from you time and thought that should have gone into your work, he took your sympathy and adoration. He made out of the very breath of your life an atmosphere of adulation he craved. And now he comes back and tells you he can't live without you. God save any woman from a man that can't live without her! But that doesn't matter; the point I'm asking you to consider is this: you've given him a year of your life. How has he repaid you?"

"You don't understand!" broke in Mary. "I've never asked for anything. I've never wanted—"

"Exactly! You're the kind of woman that makes Courtney's kind of man possible—your instinct to give fits in so well with his instinct to take. And he has always the grand excuse of life for art's sake. Life! What does a man like Courtney know about life? Look about you. Is the work of the world done by men who dodge responsibility? Is any real thing ever done by a man who is such a coward he won't acknowledge obligation? What kind of a thinker is a man who's so muddled that he declares the world is being made better by the spectacle of two people philandering together without ever having the courage to marry or the conviction to live together without marriage. I tell you, Mary, you've been a sentimentalist; but Courtney—"

"But I tell you, I'm asking Mary to marry me!" Courtney cried, with an hysterical note in his voice. He was white to the lips and the hand he had dug into the cushion beside him was trembling.

Nancy gave him a clear, straight look. "When you came up

here, Courtney, you had no intention of asking Mary to marry you. You had got tired of your Broadway adventure, and you were coming back to an atmosphere more congenial to you. When challenged, you did the thing that suddenly appealed to you as dramatic. Deep in your heart you don't want to marry her, or any one. You want to get out from under the burdens of life. You talk about freedom and self-expression, and it all means one thing; you want to live soft, to gratify yourself without paying. You don't want to sweat or grind or deny yourself. If all the men in the world were like you, courage would die and the race with it. But, thank God, they're not. And some day Mary's going to marry one of them. He'll protect her and her gift, he'll make her happy and give her a place in the procession of the world."

Courtney was on his feet now. "I won't stand another word of this!" he cried, his voice shaking. "Mary, can you sit there without a word and let her make light of the love you and I have had for each other?"

"Love!" broke in Nancy. "If you'd loved her like a man, wouldn't you have wanted long ago to give her your name and protect her and cherish her?"

"The bourgeois ideal of a parasite!" Courtney sneered.

Nancy let herself go, then. All of her several years of shrewd observation of Courtney's kind she gathered up and made into a bundle of stinging rods which she applied without mercy. She reminded him of the number of years he had lived on his father's bounty, of the way he had failed Mary when she was ill, of his failure to produce anything but talk, of his general likeness to that organism he had just mentioned so scornfully. She was eloquent and quite reckless in her use of adjectives and similes. And Mary said not a word.

She had risen to her feet, and she stood during the whole of Nancy's invective, leaning against the side of the window-frame, with her eyes fixed on Courtney's face. She looked shocked and horrified. But in her face there was something I had never seen there before—the beginning of thought that had nothing to do with sentiments or emotions. She looked away only once, and that was when John Briscombe drove under the Arch and parked his car in the usual place.

The evening light was lovely now with dusty blues, and the Square was as peaceful as an old garden. But inside the room Nancy's voice was implacable.

"When it comes right down to bed-rock, Courtney," she was saying, "you're just one thing. You can make your phrases, and dodge life ever so deftly, and live like the lotus-eater you are, but that doesn't change the fact that there are two common, vulgar words for you, Courtney; you're a piker and a slacker."

"Oh, Nancy—don't!" Mary's face quivered.

"Let her go on," Courtney cried. "Let her—let her—"

Then, to our amazement and horror, his voice broke, he put his head in the sofa cushion, and sobbed.

I have always believed that up to that instant Mary's decision hung by a thread. And Courtney, in spite of his agitation, must have believed that he had only to make one last appeal to sweep her over to his side. But there was one bit of feminine psychology Courtney had never learned: a woman will take a man in her arms for a tear of her own causing, but she'll despise him for letting another woman make him weep. She stood there very quietly looking at him, curiously and intently, and across her eyes there flitted and was gone a quick, keen hint of distaste.

In that instant I knew that Mary had gained the shore. Never again would she know the wild spring-flavor of youth; but never again would she know its disproportions, its fever, and its pain that is so absurd and so poignant. She was becoming under our eyes a woman, with at last a soul and a cool judgment of her own. She crossed the room and lightly put her hand on Courtney's hair with a gesture of farewell.

"Don't, my dear," she said gently. "Tomorrow you will have forgotten. You mustn't think of me as hard, or Nancy, either. It's just that we know something so—so much more real."

Her eyes met Nancy's in a long glance of understanding. Then she caught up her hat and was gone. We heard her running down the stairs, heard her voice under the window and another voice answering before Courtney had begun to take in the fact that at last he too had become merely a phase.

THE AMAZING GENERATION

Josephine Daskam Bacon

"YOU were very good to come all this way to see an old lady," said Mother Fellowes, knitting.

"Oh, good!" her guest repeated reproachfully. "How can you, Mrs. Fellowes? It was good of you to have me."

Mother Fellowes smiled whimsically. "Aren't most people glad to have you, my dear?" she asked.

Betty's flexible mouth twisted into the humorous little curves that gave her face that surprisingly girlish look; it was incredible that she could never be forty again. Where did all her experience hide when she looked that way at you? Where were her two grown children, her years of celebrity, her disillusions?

"Oh, I know. . . " she said, poking out her lower lip, "I know what you mean, of course. People are always glad to have people, when they're not too plain or too badly dressed or too stupid or too disagreeable. And as I'm not exactly any of those—"

"No, I shouldn't say you were any of those," Mother Fellowes agreed quietly.

It was scarcely an enthusiastic remark, but it had its distinct effect upon the handsome woman on the opposite side of the

From *McCall's* 45, no. 11 (July 1918).

little fire. With the easy movement of a young girl, she drew herself out of the deep, comfortable, faded old chair and patted Mother Fellowes' shoulder.

"You're very dear to be so clever, too," she said, and slipped back into the comfortable faded chair.

"Bob sometimes tells me I'm clever," smiled Mother Fellowes, "and then I tell him he's silly. But I wouldn't dare tell that to a celebrated artist, of course," she added mischievously.

"No," said the celebrated artist, with mock solemnity, "no, I suppose not"; and she smiled at the little old lady in her rocking-chair.

Not that Mother Fellowes ever was known to rock in it. She sat as straight and as still as Whistler's Mother, and never even crossed her ankles. But the atmosphere of the rocking-chair was there, and it was this, as Betty said afterward, that made some of her remarks so surprising.

"It's Bob I've come to talk about," Betty began abruptly.

"So I judged," Mother Fellowes replied, slipping her needles expertly among her veined, slightly knotted fingers.

"You don't mind?"

"No, indeed, my dear—why should I? My son is very fond of you, I've always known. Both he and Phyllis are fond of you. She has often told me how kind you were to them when they moved out to the country. And you're the baby's godmother, aren't you?"

"Yes: The Filly and I are great pals," Betty answered absently.

The quiet old sitting-room was very restful. It had been Bob's grandfather's house, and the chairs and tables all knew it. Any furniture, Bob used to say, that had withstood three generations of Fellowes' spring-cleaning had earned the right to stay where it was; and the walnut bookcases with the queer old china urns painted with marine subjects reflected the twisty brass andirons from precisely the angle of his boyhood. One would as soon have suggested altering the position of the Pyramids, with a view to bringing out the effect of a new sky-line.

"I'm ten years older than Phyl," Betty began.

"You don't look it, my dear."

"No. Phyl's aging quicker than I like. Isn't it funny about all this executive work for women, Mrs. Fellowes? I think it makes them look five years older than they used to be. The newspapers are always telling them what youthful grandmothers they are, and then they go on to explain how it must be all this work that's keeping them so young—but I don't see it. I've been painting their portraits for eighteen years now, and I'm blessed if I see it! Their figures are younger, yes; but their faces, no."

"That's interesting," said Mother Fellowes placidly. "How do you account for it, Mrs. Girard?"

"I'll tell you, if you won't call me that," Betty replied, smiling one of her famous, warm smiles straight into Mother Fellowes' shrewd eyes. "You won't, any more, will you?"

"Why, no—Betty. Not if you'd rather."

"I would rather. I think it's this way. Of course, they're slimmer. Twenty years ago—ten years ago—they didn't exercise enough and they ate too much. We've always eaten too much starch over here. They got stiff and they took little short, old steps, and they looked dumpy. Then they didn't know how to do their hair: they simply wadded up a great lump at the top of their heads on the back, and dragged it away from their faces. Now, only a very handsome woman can afford to do that—a woman with a good profile."

"But this bores you, perhaps, and I didn't really come to lecture on American women's looks—"

"It interests me very much," said Mother Fellowes. "People don't talk to me about these things: they ask me for my rule for pickled peaches."

"You're a brick," said Betty, "an honest-and-truly brick."

"Bob tells me that Phyllis is working too hard," Mother Fellowes suggested, with the effect of merely adding to her guest's remarks.

"Oh, yes, I suppose she is," Betty answered vaguely.

"You see, she seems to have this real gift for working with children. I heard her telling what she calls an 'acting-story' to forty kiddies yesterday, and the way she got them interested in it, and half telling it themselves, and learning so much history out of it—really, Mrs. Fellowes, it was a very pretty little performance. She's not a bit shy about it now; she has developed a real technique, and she's learning lots and lots herself.

And then, it's practically a new profession, you know, and she's proud of doing so well in it. You really can't expect that a woman who can earn a very decent little income by doing work that she likes, should stop it, simply because her husband doesn't like the idea of her earning money? When it's only his idea! It isn't a law of nature, you know, nor in the Bible, even, that she should give up her life."

"Bob feels that there are others who might need the money more, perhaps . . ."

"Oh! That is certainly too bad of Bob!" Betty's baffling eyes turned suddenly as clearly, coldly gray as Bob Fellowes' own. "I must say!"

She stared severely at the golf stockings tangled among Mother Fellowes' needles.

"I suppose that's for Bob?" she asked.

"Yes. Since he's grown so interested in his Boy Scout work, he likes these heavy stockings, and he likes me to do them for him."

"And I suppose it doesn't occur to him that you're taking the bread out of the mouth of some worthy poor person who ought to have the knitting of them?"

Mother Fellowes smiled. "You're much too clever for me, my dear," she said. "What do you want me to say?"

"Well," said Betty, "I'll tell you what I want you to say. I want you to tell me what to do."

"What to do?" Mother Fellowes repeated, gazing with her clear, wrinkled brown eyes into Betty's smooth, troubled hazel ones.

Betty nodded her quick, whimsical little schoolgirl nod. It was a very endearing nod, and many people had found themselves much influenced by it, first and last.

"You see," she began, "I'm not worrying about the economy of the Fellowes' ménage, so to speak. That's their own affair—they'll have to work it out themselves, just like all the other husbands and wives to-day. I've seen too many of my friends go through it: if it isn't one thing, it's another.

"Well, here's Phyllis. She can't make as much money as I, but she has discovered—quite by chance—a very nice little talent of her own; and it takes her out into the big game and makes her independent and gives her a feeling of power— Oh, I see perfectly how little Phyl feels, Mrs. Fellowes—don't you?" Both women were quiet a while, thoughtful.

"Of course, I never thought about these things quite in this way before," Mother Fellowes explained.

"I'm nervous," Betty admitted. "I always chatter this foolish way when I'm nervous. Of course, it's not that we're talking about at all, anyway."

"What are we talking about?" Mother Fellowes inquired mildly.

"We're talking about whether Bob is going to let Phyllis get interested in another man," Betty answered simply.

"Oh," said Mother Fellowes. "Oh, I see."

"If there's one thing I detest," Betty burst out violently, "it's meddling. In the first place, I'm too lazy and selfish to bother about people's affairs . . . But it was really on my account that they moved out to Westchester."

"I know."

"I was quite surprised to find they were really going to be neighbors, and naturally I introduced Phyl to the people around."

She sighed, and her mouth grew childish.

"Well, my dear, I don't know as I'd call that meddling, exactly; that was only friendly," Mother Fellowes reminded her.

"Ye-es, of course. Perhaps if I'd let her alone after that . . . Oh, I don't know! But I hated to see her settling down into such a ridiculous little young, middle-aged woman. You see, it's a sporting neighborhood, up there, Mrs. Fellowes. If you don't play tennis or golf or ride or dance, you don't meet anybody of your own age. And Phyl was really getting lonely, I thought, with Bob stodging at home every night—she was so attractive and clever, we all thought it was a shame."

"The Felloweses aren't much for company," Mother Fellowes agreed.

"Well, I suppose you know how it went on," Betty continued, a little listlessly.

"Phyl completely changed, and Bob refused to change at all, and at first people talked a little, and then they gave it up, and there are always people to play with, you . . ."

She paused a moment, but Mother Fellowes was silent, knitting.

"So then, when Phyl took up this story-telling business, and began to get these invitations from clubs and schools and educational conventions, I thought it was just as well, perhaps, because she was getting interested in one of the men there—"

"What man?" Mother Fellowes asked bluntly.

"Does it make any difference?" Betty fenced.

"Is he a tall, dark man with white teeth?"

"Yes, Turkey Turkington. What made you think so? Did you hear anybody say anything? But, of course, you understand, that means nothing at all. Nobody takes Turkey very seriously, anyway. And the funny thing about it is, that I think Phyl has been very good for him, in lots of ways. She's so serious, you know, and so interested, once she gets started. And he takes her seriously, and is interested in her work, which Bob simply refuses to be. Oh, dear, Mrs. Fellowes, you didn't have all these mix-ups, did you?" she said wistfully.

Mother Fellowes lifted her wrinkled eyelids and looked strangely at her guest.

"Of course not," she answered briskly, "human nature was an entirely different thing forty years ago!"

"Wh-what?"

"Women and men," Mother Fellowes pursued her theme gently, "have altered entirely since I was twenty-five, my dear, and, anyway, how could a Connecticut woman pretend to understand a woman who lived in Westchester County?"

Betty gave a gurgle of sudden laughter.

"You are a dear," she said, "and I am a stupid woman, in spite of what they all say! Now, tell me—shall we do anything, or mind our own business?"

Mother Fellowes patted her shoulder. "Phyllis will never do anything that's not right, you may be sure of that."

"Of course, she won't," Betty replied, "but Bob may do something that's not wise—you can't be sure of that, you know."

"I know," said Bob's mother.

"You see," Betty went on softly, "it's not as if it all just simply happened, Mother Fellowes. I asked Turkey to Phyl's first dance at the Country Club. And I encouraged the tennis."

"You meant to be kind, I'm sure."

"I not only meant to be—I was kind," the younger woman returned shortly. "Phyl would have had a very stupid, lonely time, without friends of her own age. She was beginning to feel it—and show it."

Silence, and knitting.

"Phyl had to develop—there wasn't one chance in—in a hundred, it seems to me, that a healthy, handsome young woman who attracts friends as easily as Phyl, should settle down at thirty as—as—as women used to settle down. Don't you agree with me?"

"It may be so, my dear."

"Only, as I happened to be the one . . ." Her voice trailed off.

"As you happened to be the one?"

Betty shrugged her shoulders helplessly.

"Tell me, Mother Fellowes, for goodness' sake, is the only way to keep out of all this sort of thing, to have no leisure at all? Was it because you didn't play golf that you didn't get interested?"

"Nobody played golf, of course," she observed, "then. Certainly not young married women with three boys growing up, like me. The boys played baseball, and I was too busy darning their stockings."

"But did you really need to? Couldn't Father Fellowes have had it done for you?"

"I suppose he could have, but it would have been thought extravagant."

"Then what it amounts to is that women were too busy to have time to get interested in anybody else?"

Mother Fellowes considered carefully.

"They seem to be pretty busy now, don't they?" she suggested.

"Yes, indeed," Betty assured her, "that's just it. They're doing other things."

"Other things," Mother Fellowes repeated, "so if they could do what you call the 'pottering things,' themselves, again, they wouldn't need to pay anybody else the high prices labor costs? I mean they'd be saving money."

Betty blinked rapidly, drew in a deep breath, and then burst into a short laugh.

"I don't believe," she said solemnly, "we'll talk about this any more, Mother Fellowes! I'll have to send you down a suffragist or a professor of economics or something—you're too deep for me."

Mother Fellowes smiled. There was a long silence, and across it the old clock ticked out its halting, uneven rhythm.

"Listen, Mother Fellowes," said Betty at last. "Phyllis won't do anything, of course. But if it occurs to Bob, as it may any moment, to lay down the law about Turkey, I don't think she will accept his orders."

She paused, and Mother Fellowes obeyed the pause. "I—I know," she said gently.

"And Phyl, who only knows that she gets a great deal of comfort and interest out of a real friend, isn't going to submit without more concessions, in return, than Bob is likely to make. It's a pity Turkey shouldn't be interested in somebody else—Phyl is so busy, now, that, really, I think she might get along perfectly well without just the kind of friend he's turned out to be. Another thing," and Betty's smile was rueful, "Turkey seems more constant than we've seen him for years! It wouldn't be so easy for him to change now. You see, he feels responsible in a way, for Phyl; he's taught her so much. And that's pretty fatal, you see."

She allowed a dimple to occur in the cheek nearest Mother Fellowes.

"I suppose that held good even in the early eighties?" she suggested gravely.

"Yes. As far back as the Centennial year, I guess," Mother Fellowes agreed.

"I'm afraid it would take an exceptionally clever woman to get Turkey now," Betty pursued thoughtfully. "Nothing could be nicer than Phyl, in her way, and I think it would have to be some one who 'really understood him,' probably. I'm afraid you find it all rather shocking, don't you?"

"I don't think you mean to be shocking," Mother Fellowes

answered. "But, does Mr.—Mr. Turkey like exceptionally clever women?"

"Of course not," Betty agreed. "No man does—unless they're also exceptionally attractive. And there aren't many of that kind."

"There's you," said Mother Fellowes simply, "isn't there?"

Elizabeth Naldreth Girard, gold-medalist in many countries, stared up blankly at the little woman before her. "Wh-what did you say?"

"I said there was you," Mother Fellowes repeated placidly. "It seems to me that's just what you are, isn't it, my dear?"

"Just what I am?"

"Yes. Exceptionally clever and exceptionally attractive."

"Oh, I see. You mean that I am to get Turkey away?"

"Why not?" said Mother Fellowes.

A vivid wave of deep crimson washed over the brilliant face below her.

"Oh, Mother Fellowes! Oh—Oh!" she murmured, and dropped her modish head forward into the quiet black lap.

"You—you've done it," she said softly, wiping her eyes, "you've accomplished something Paris never did. Mother Fellowes—you—you've shocked me!"

"I'm sorry. I didn't mean to. I only thought you would be the best one," the erect little woman explained. "You seemed to think some one could manage it."

"But what about me? You don't seem to be bothering about me!"

"I didn't think I needed to," said Mother Fellowes, gravely.

"I suppose that's fair," she said softly. "You seem to understand the case. Probably you don't need to bother. Oh, well . . . I suppose there were women like me, that one needn't worry about—even in the Centennial year?" she suggested.

"I think there are always women like you, my dear," Mother Fellowes answered.

"Wouldn't it be embarrassing, Mother Fellows, if Turkey should refuse to see what was good for him, after all?" she suggested "Suppose he'd rather . . ."

Mother Fellowes looked up swiftly.

"I don't believe he'd rather," she said. "I'm very fond of

Phyllis, of course, and I know she's got a head of her own; but if anybody had the chance to talk to you—why, I guess he'd rather, my dear."

"Thanks," said Betty dryly, "—and never mind what happens, I suppose?"

Mother Fellowes was silent.

"I'm sorry," Betty murmured repentantly, kneeling swiftly by the rocking-chair. "I always was a pig."

"You've always been a good friend to Phyllis and Bob," answered Mother Fellowes smoothly. "I'm sure of that. And I don't believe anything will happen."

"It never did, in Connecticut—in the Centennial year?"

Mother Fellowes dropped her stocking and laid her hands on the firm shoulders.

"Oh, my dear," she said, "you know that everything has always happened!"

And Betty, sitting beside the silent chauffeur, pondered on this for the two hours that carried her to New York.

She was dining with Turkey at one of the big hotels. Before the third course came, she had turned the conversation to Phyllis and her work.

"That was a jolly idea of Phyl's—a story-telling class based on the great pictures, wasn't it?" Betty asked.

"I'll bet it was your idea," he ventured quickly. "Come now, wasn't it?"

"Maybe," she answered indifferently.

"You've done a lot for Phyl, Betty."

"Have I? Sometimes I wonder . . ."

"Oh, nonsense! You've made the girl over. Everybody knows that."

"I had a little help, hadn't I, Turkey?"

"For goodness' sake, Betty, don't you begin that, too! Phyllis and I happen to have a very strong friendship. A perfectly sensible—"

"Oh, don't go into all that with me!"

"All I can say is, Phyl and I have decided to go calmly along and not let it make any difference. That's all."

"Oh! That's all?"

"Don't you think so? You're a sensible woman, Betty."

Betty looked ahead of her. Then—

"Jess told me last week that your father wanted you to take charge of the Cleveland plant for a year," she said at last.

"Yes. But I'm not keen about it."

"Turkey," she began suddenly, "here is my hand—I lay all my cards on the table. You're free, and here are Walter and I. As far as he's concerned, I'm free."

"I'm hanged if I understand how a man who had the amazing luck to get you—you—!"

"We needn't go into that," she interrupted. "Then, here are Phyllis and Bob. They're not free—yet."

"He doesn't deserve . . . A man who won't even take an interest—"

"They'll have to work it out," she put in, wearily, "like the rest of us, Turkey. Anyway, it's my belief that Phyl doesn't need anything but her work, for a while. Apparently, you do. Bob won't stand much more of this. If he puts an ultimatum to Phyllis, she's pretty edgy, just now, and she may refuse it."

"All right. Then let him see—"

"He won't see," said Betty quietly.

He studied her white profile against the window of the taxi. "Just what do you mean, Betty?"

"I mean—hadn't we better let them alone, you and I?" she answered.

"We? You and I? Do you mean . . . "

"If you like," she said.

He drew a sharp breath. "You mean that you'd be willing to be bothered by my tiresome talk . . . and me hanging around . . . Of course, I'm the most ordinary cuss, you know, and you're so wonderful!"

"You seem to need some kind of nurse," she said.

Suddenly, Turkey laughed; a curious, sharp little laugh that was half a sob.

"George!" he cried, "That's about it! A nurse! And all for Phyl! For that's the whole reason—I see that well enough.

"Look here—you'd rather I went to Cleveland, wouldn't you? Now, be honest?"

"Much rather," she said simply.

"Shake hands!" he blurted. "I'll go. If you can do as much

as that for her—" he gulped with a wry sort of mirth, "I'll go you one better! I'll clear you out."

"Good for you, Turkey!" she said, and put both her hands into his.

To Mother Fellowes she telegraphed the next morning. "Everything all right. Nothing will happen."

It was the receipt of the answering yellow slip that moved her to her announcement, on the occasion of the farewell dinner to Turkey Turkington at the Club.

"I didn't think anything would," Mother Fellowes had actually wired!

"I'm going to paint a portrait of a member of your family, Bob," she called out across the big round table to him.

Bob Fellowes looked up, more like his old self than he had been for some time.

"Phyl, I suppose?" he asked.

Every one looked curiously at Phyllis.

"I shall call it 'The Amazing Generation,'" Betty continued, flashing a wonderful, deep smile at Turkey, who raised his glass to her, proud of the smile.

"Of course that will be Phyl," somebody said. "Women are amazing today."

"I don't think they've changed much, really," said Betty. "It will be a portrait of Phyl's mother-in-law."

"My mother? Not really!" Bob exclaimed. "Dear me! We shall be flattered, I'm sure, but I'm afraid you don't understand her, Betty. She's not amazing at all. Quite of the old school, thank God. You'll have to change the title of that picture."

And the artist smiled to herself.

THE CAT AND THE KING

Jennette Lee

SHE had been up this morning at four o'clock, and had crept out through the gate, almost guiltily, and off across the fields for a long walk. There might be nothing wrong in taking a walk at four o'clock in the morning; perhaps no one would have stayed her in her flight through the college gates, munching her bit of crackers and cheese, had they known. But no one knew. She had carefully *not* inquired. . . .

She had had her walk, with the freshness of the spring luring her on, up Redmond Hill, down the slope by Boardman's and along home by the road, gathering from the bushes on either side the great masses of trailing vines that draped her head and shoulders and hung swaying from her arms. It had been a wonderful walk—pulling the vines from the bushes, shaking the dew from the clustering blossoms and drenching herself in freshness.

The blossoms were a faint, greenish white and, with her green-and-white striped skirt and white blouse as she stood in the gateway looking in on the college halls, the flowers and the twisting stalks of leaves twined about her and framing her

From *Ladies' Home Journal* 36, no. 10 (October 1919).

in, she might have been the very spirit of the outdoor world peeping shyly in at the halls of learning, curious, wistful and tiptoe for flight.

She stood a moment gazing up at the great masses of brick and stone that made up her college world. The side of the buildings nearest the lodge gate was in shadow and the vines and the dull red of the bricks seemed to hold for her something mysterious and strange. She went slowly up the brick walk, holding in check a sudden longing to turn back, to flee once more to the fields and the little brook that ran gurgling by Boardman's and make a day of it, out in the free world.

It was mysterious and wonderful—this college where her name was enrolled: "Flora Bailey, 1920." But there was something overpowering about it. The great walls that looked so gracious in the fresh morning light had a way of shutting one in, of hampering and binding the movements of freshmen. There were so many things one must and must not do within the gracious walls! Her eye glanced up to a tower of South Parker, high up to a window where silken curtains hung in even folds, and a sigh escaped her lips. One must not make friends with seniors, for instance, except by invitation—and a senior was very high up!

The curtains parted a little. A girl's eyes glanced quickly. A firm hand pushed back the curtains and a figure stood between them looking out on the morning. The lifted head bore a mass of reddish hair gathered carelessly, and the light that fell on the tallest peaks and gables of the college touched it with gold. To the freshman, gazing from her walk, it was as if a goddess, high-enshrined and touched by the rising sun, stood revealed. She gave a gasp of pleasure.

It had been a glorious walk out in the dew and sunrise, and now Annette Osler was gazing from her tower window—not on the girl on the college walk, to be sure, but on the world of wonder.

She looked up adoringly at the figure in the tower of South Parker. And the girl high in the window turned a little and looked down. There was no one in sight—only the quiet light of morning on the campus and the wind rippling shadowy waves in the ivy leaves on brick walls. A little rippling wave seemed to run from the walk to the high tower window, and with a gesture of happiness the girl on the walk turned toward the entrance of Gordon Hall. Her pulses sang as she went, her step danced a little, hurrying up the stairs and along the corridor to her room. She opened the door quickly.

Across the room by the window, her roommate, surrounded by books, was taking notes, dipping in here and there with alert pencil. She looked up in swift surprise. "Why, where have you— Oh, how lovely!" Her eyes caught the green-and-white blossoms and she sprang up. "Here—I'll get the pitcher!"

She brought a pitcher from the bedroom, and Flora placed the vines in water, standing back to survey them. They trailed down over the window sill and onto the seat below. She touched them with quick fingers. "That will do. We'll arrange them after breakfast."

Her companion had gone back to her task of scooping up notes with flying pencil. She suspended it a minute and looked up. "Do you remember Bainnuter?" she asked absently.

"Bainnuter?" repeated Flora. "I don't seem to remember— Was he on the Yale Team?"

Her roommate stared. Then she chuckled. "He's ancient history, Flora dear! Early Egyptian. I was wondering if Doxey would ask us about him. Do you suppose he will?"

Flora wheeled. She regarded her with startled eyes. "History exam! This morning!" she gasped, "I forgot—oh, I forgot!" She seized her books from the table, hunting out a stub of pencil in haste. "I hate 'em all—everybody that's had any history done about 'em. I hate 'em!"she said savagely.

"Why, I thought you liked history! You did splendidly in the February exam. You're such a clever thing! I wish I were!" She sighed deeply and returned to her scooping and dredging.

The roommate's name was Aspasia—Aspasia Elton. That was another of the perplexing things about college, living night and day with a girl named Aspasia. It made life topsy-turvy. No one at home had names out of history books.

Aspasia glanced at her casually. "Better cram on Rameses II," she said kindly. "They say he's dippy on Rameses!"

The room was quiet. No sound came from the corridors or from the rooms above or below.

The two girls turned leaves and crammed notes. Now and then one of them sighed. Sounds began to come from the corridor—hurried feet in slippers, and splashings and calls from the bathrooms, and bits of conversation floating over transoms.

Flora closed her book with a little shrug. She put a pencil carefully in the place. "Doxey gave me warning last week," she said.

Aspasia looked up. "What a shame!"

"No-o. It's all right. *I* knew I wasn't doing anything; only I hoped *he* didn't know. I thought the February exam had fooled him—maybe."

"Anyway, you don't need to worry. Your February mark will carry you through."

"Yes; but it won't put me on the team. That's all I care about, all I've ever cared about," she said slowly.

Aspasia nodded. It was sympathetic and vague. "Well—you can live if you don't make the team. Other folks do."

"*I* can't!" said Flora.

Her roommate looked at her reflectively. "It's Annette Osler," she announced. "Just because she's captain, you want—"

Flora's face was scarlet. "I don't care if it is!" she murmured.

"Be a sport, Flora! *You* can't have a crush on a senior—"

"It is not a crush!" said Flora vehemently. "I just want to know Annette because she's the kind of girl I like. And if I get on the team, she'll notice me; she'll *have* to notice me! There isn't any other way to get to know a senior, is there?" she demanded.

"You're too aspiring," said Aspasia. She gathered up her books and notes. "Come on to breakfast. There's the bell."

"I'm not going to breakfast," said Flora firmly. "I've got to study."

Her roommate reappeared from the bedroom. "You're a weak, sentimental freshman!" she remarked casually.

"I am *not* sentimental! I want to know Annette Osler because she's a great, glorious creature! So, there! Let be teasing, Aspasia."

"'Let be teasing'! I must save that for Professor Goodwin. Funny English! Did you get it from your grandmother, honey? He'll be sure to ask the 'source,' you know."

"Go along!" said Flora crossly.

She was left alone, and there was only the sunlight falling on the green-and-white vines in the window and traveling to the scattered books on the table. She looked at them a minute; then her arms dropped to the table with a little gesture of defeat, and her face dropped to her arms. . . .

A bumblebee hummed in the window and went away. It may have been the blossoms.

She lifted her face and looked at them balefully. If only she had known enough to get up at four o'clock to study instead of going off for the miserable walk! And suddenly the sunrise as it came over Redmond Hill flashed back to her; it brought the song of a bird that trilled softly out of the woods.

Her face seemed to listen to the fluttering call. Then it grew thoughtful. If there were some way, some legitimate way, of attracting the attention of a senior! Annette liked the things she liked. Often she watched her setting off alone over the hill that let to the fields. And because she was a freshman she might not hurry after her and say: "Come on for a walk with me!" . . . And suddenly she looked at it. Why not? Why not go to her, this very morning, lay the case before her and *ask* her to go for a walk? Why not . . . The history exam might as well be cut; she was bound to flunk anyway! She pushed the books aside with a look of distaste. She would do it—and do it now!

There was a sound in the hall. She picked up her book and opened it swiftly to Rameses II.

The door swung open on Aspasia, one elbow holding careful guard over a glass of milk and two large slices of bread and butter.

Flora sprang up. "You dear!"

Aspasia set the milk on the table and turned, a little breathless. "What do you think? Annette Osler has sprained her ankle! They're taking her up to the infirmary now!"

And Flora looked at her with a foolish, half-startled smile.

"Now isn't that a stupid thing to do!" she said slowly. "How long do you suppose she will have to stay in the infirmary?" "Oh—ages!" said Aspasia carelessly. "A sprained ankle isn't a thing you get over in a day, you know. She'll be there weeks maybe."

And Flora looked down at Rameses II. "How stupid!" she said to him softly.

It had seemed so simple this morning to go to Annette. And now she might have been a thousand miles away, for any chance there was of getting at her.

The history examinations came and went in a maze of gloom. She had flunked of course. She did not care particularly about the flunking, but it was embarrassing to meet Professor Dockery on the campus next day; and she made a little skillful detour to evade him—only to see him coming toward her along the path by the elms.

He stopped as she came up and looked down at her consideringly: "You wrote a good paper yesterday; a very good paper indeed!"

"I did!" cried Flora.

"I shall withdraw my opposition to your being on the team," he said kindly.

Flora gazed at him mutely. "Now isn't that a shame!" she said swiftly. And she hurried on to the fields, leaving him to extract what sense he could from the wail.

She tramped far that afternoon. A new bird lured her on; and she found a curious hummocky nest on the ground, with a breakfast of shining roots spread out before it. She went down on her knees—a field mouse probably—or a mole perhaps. She wished there were someone to share it with—the delicately lined dome that her fingers explored and the shining roots at the door. . . . Her thoughts traveled rebelliously to the infirmary— "weeks perhaps," Aspasia said.

And then, as she knelt by the hummocky nest, the idea came to her. She got up from her knees, smiling down on the little brown dome and the breakfast of roots and nodded to it slowly and happily.

"I'll do it," she said softly. "I'll do it—right off."

When she came in from her walk she went directly to the

library and asked for medical books. The librarian bent a keen, spectacled inquiry on her.

"I want them for fiction purposes," explained Flora, "for local color."

But when the musty books were laid before her, she had a period of depression. She attacked them in a little gust of discouragement, selecting the most modern-looking one with colored plates and diagrams and opening it at random. The charts and plates held her. Next to outdoors could there be anything more fascinating and mysterious than the human body? Why had no one ever told her about these things!

She looked down curiously at her own hand resting on the book. It seemed to her a new hand, one that she had never seen before. The network of blue veins fascinated her; they were little branching trees or the delicate veining of leaves. She had not guessed people were like that, as wonderful as trees!—like trees really, with all those branches of muscles and nerves and veins.

Perhaps they *were* trees once.

Her mind dreamed on happily. She knew how it felt to be a tree, swaying in the wind, with the rain on your leaves. Perhaps she *was* a tree once, and grew on a hillside, and the squirrels ran up and down and nibbled at branches. She gave a little chuckling laugh in the silence of the library, and the librarian looked over reprovingly from her platform.

Flora made a gesture of apology and plunged again into her search. But it had changed now from seeking to dallying enjoyment. Why had no one told her? And she read on till the librarian touched her on the shoulder and she looked up, blinking.

"The bell has rung," said the librarian reprovingly.

"Oh-h!" breathed Flora. "Yes; I want them again, please!" And she hurried off blithely.

It was only as she was making ready for dinner that it occurred to her she had not found what she started out to seek.

But in the evening, in the library again, she came on it. She had almost given up her search and was only looking idly at the oldest of the brown books when her eye fell on "The Curious Case of Prudence Small."

She began to read. And as she read her cheeks glowed and her eyes danced. She looked speculatively at the librarian. The librarian was a small woman, and there were only two other girls in the room. Better wait? She shook her head. She would never have the courage if she waited! She opened the book again to "The Curious Case of Prudence Small" and read the details once more—and looked up.

The green-shaded reading lights in the dim room made little ghastly circles about the two girls bending over their books; and the librarian, mounted on her platform, seemed like some priestess of knowledge waiting for mystic rites to begin. The librarian went on counting out cards. Flora scraped her chair a little on the floor; and then, as no one paid attention, she gave it a shove that upset it with a clatter and brought the spectacled glance full upon her and a look of annoyance from the girls across the room.

Flora lifted her arms slowly. She gave a long, low moan and subsided gently to the floor.

There was a flurry of green-shaded lights, a glimpse of the librarian's startled face; then the sound of running feet, and the two girls were bending over a rigid figure and lifting it from the floor.

Five minutes later, in the consulting room of the infirmary, the college physician, summoned from a comfortable game of whist, bent above the rigid figure.

Flora's eyes rested trustfully on the physician's face. She had recovered consciousness almost as soon as they had deposited her on the infirmary couch. Five minutes the book said; she judged it must be about five minutes—and she opened her eyes and gazed pensively at the perturbed faces that surrounded her.

The physician dismissed them all with a curt gesture. She brought a basin of water, with a bit of ice tinkling in it, and began to bathe the girl's forehead with swift, sopping strokes.

"I fell," murmured Flora dreamily.

Doctor Worcester nodded. "You will have a good-sized lump, I'm afraid." She went on sopping with skillful strokes.

Flora's eyes closed meekly. She felt a little thankful for the bump. She had never seen Doctor Worcester before, near to, and there was something in the face bent above her that made her wonder how "The Curious Case of Prudence Small" would come out. "There!" The doctor put aside the basin. "I don't think it will be discolored now. How do you feel?" She was looking down at her critically.

Flora's face flushed. She recalled hastily how she felt—and stretched out her arms and rubbed them a little. "I feel better," she said slowly, "only there is a little buzzing in the top of my head, and the soles of my feet are slightly paralyzed, I think." She said it neatly and glibly and lay with closed eyes, waiting for what might happen.

The doctor's swift eyes studied the passive countenance. "I think we will keep you here to-night," she said quietly.

She touched a bell and gave directions to the nurse. Her fingers rested lightly on Flora's wrist. "We will put her in the ward," she said, "next to Miss Osler." She started and glanced sharply down at the wrist under her fingers, and then at the girl's placid face.

She held the wrist a minute and dropped it slowly, her eyes on the face. "I shall look in again before I go to bed. She may need a quieting draft to make her sleep."

From her desk on her platform, the librarian peered over at the doctor, who was standing looking down the green-shaded, quiet room.

"Tell me just what happened," said the doctor briskly.

And while the librarian recounted the meager details of the story, the doctor's thoughtful face surveyed the vacant room and the table where the brown books lay.

"It might have been studying to soon after eating—don't you think?" inquired the librarian helpfully.

"I don't think anything," said the doctor. "I'm puzzled." She walked across to the table and picked up one of the books. "What was she reading?" she asked.

The librarian flushed. "She said she wanted them for fiction purposes; 'English A,' I suppose, don't you?"

But the physician did not reply. She was looking at a page that had fallen open in her hand, perhaps because an energetic elbow had held it pressed back for half an hour. "The patient said, on inquiry, that her head still buzzed a little, and the soles of her feet were slightly paralyzed."

She shut the book with a laugh. "I'll take this along with me. No, I don't think it's serious—a case of nerves maybe." Her face wore a thoughtful look as she gave directions to the night nurse in the infirmary and looked over charts. She did not go to the ward, and she left no directions for a sleeping draft for the new patient.

The nurse wondered afterward if the doctor could have forgotten. But there was no sign of restlessness in the ward when she went in a little later. The new patient was asleep. There was only one other patient in the ward, a senior who had sprained her ankle a few days ago. She had been asleep when the new patient was brought in. The nurse stepped very softly and passed out of the shaded ward, drawing the door to behind her.

Flora opened her eyes. Through the chink of door a light burned dimly. And through the open window beside her the moonlight streamed in. The infirmary was at the top of the building, and she could look down on the sleeping world and off at the great clouds drifting and swinging against a blue-black sky. She turned her head a little. The senior was asleep, one hand tucked under her cheek, the reddish hair gathered into a quaint cap; the moonlight, touching the quiet face, made it seem like a child's. Flora gazed with devoted, happy eyes. The little pricks of conscience that had stirred in her under the doctor's inquiring gaze subsided. She felt happy and at home for the first time in her college life.

Something flew across the window, shutting out the moon, with great flapping wings. She turned quickly; a bat maybe— no, too large for a bat! . . . The doctor's keen eyes flitted before her, and she sighed a little and moved restlessly and caught a glimpse of her hand lying on the coverlet. How pale it was in the moonlight! She lifted it curiously and gazed at the delicate strangeness of it—all the little veins and bones and tissues. They were made of moonlight! Charts and diagrams floated before her—filmy lungs, delicate branching nerves, all the mysterious network of wonder.

Then her mind flashed to the mole's nest and shining roots. And she gazed again at the pillowed head in its cap. Tomorrow she would tell Annette! Tomorrow—and a whole week to come! She was not sentimental. She only wanted to know Annette—and take long walks—with Annette. Her eyelids drooped a little. She tried to prop them open, to gaze at the beloved face. She wanted to show Annette the mole's nest and the breakfast—of—roots. . . . And she trailed away into a dream world, carrying the mole's nest and the little roots with her far down into her sleep. . . .

When she opened her eyes they were gazing straight into a pair of gray ones framed in a curious cap. The gray eyes smiled.

"Hello!" said the senior. "Did you drift in in the night?" And Flora smiled back shyly. No need to talk or make advances now. There would be a week—a whole week—

The senior sat up and reached for a purple robe that hung at the head of the bed and drew it about her. It was a gorgeous robe with tracings of gold running over it; and, as she gathered it about her shoulders, a lock of the reddish hair escaped from her cap and fell across it. She made a royal picture for watching eyes.

She tucked in the escaped lock with half-apologetic fingers. "Stupid, to wear a cap! But my hair tangles so!"

"I like it," said Flora promptly. "I think it looks—quaint!"

"Thank you!" said the senior. She turned a smiling glance. A little look of surprise touched it. "Why, you're the wood nymph—green and white!" she exclaimed. "I saw you the other morning, didn't I, coming in, before breakfast!"

"I'd been for a walk," said Flora.

"You were a little bit of all outdoors!" said the senior laughing. She stretched her arms in a restful gesture and looked about the sun-filled room. "Glorious day, isn't it? Perfect—for the game!" She glanced at Flora kindly. "Too bad you'll miss it. Are you in for long?"

"I don't know," said Flora happily. "They haven't found out yet what's the matter with me." She stopped short.

The senior had thrown back the covers and was sitting on the edge of the bed, gathering her robe about her.

Flora's startled gaze held her. "You'll hurt your foot!"

"My foot?" She glanced down at it and thrust it into a purple slipper by the bed, and stood upright—on both feet. "I didn't hurt it at all—not really. But they thought I'd better be careful. Rest for a day or two—on account of the game. Too bad you can't come!"

She had knotted her girdle about her and was moving toward the door with a vigorous stride.

"Oh—ah!" gasped Flora. She waved her hands in a helpless gesture.

The senior glanced back. "Yes?" she said.

"Did you—did you ever happen to see—a mole's nest?" asked Flora. It came in a little jerk, almost a cry of pain.

"A mole's—nest?" The senior paused doubtfully. "I don't think so. It sounds interesting!" But there was a laughing note in the voice that brought a quick flush to the freshman face.

"It might have been a field mouse," said Flora weakly.

The senior's eyes were laughing now and she nodded kindly "I hope you won't have to stay long. But they're awfully good to you here—take the best care of you!" And she nodded again and was gone.

And Flora gazed for a moment where the purple cloud of glory had been. It vanished into a misty blur; and she subsided, a bundle of sobs, under the tumbled clothes.

Doctor Worcester appeared in the doorway. The hunched-up figure in the bed by the window was very quiet. Only a damp handkerchief pressed tight over two eyes was visible, and a tumbled mop of hair.

The doctor came in, glancing about the sun-filled room with a look of pleasure. The infirmary ward was always a cheerful place, but never so attractive as when all the beds were vacant—or nearly all. The fewer heads on pillows the better, to Doctor Worcester. She was a tall, motherly woman, with snow-white hair and a little stoop of the broad shoulders that seemed to take something from the keenness of the straight-glancing dark eyes. She wore a white dress of soft material and in her hand she carried a book, an oldish-looking book in brown covers.

She sat down by the bed and the brown book rested unob-

"'They thought I'd better be careful . . . on account of the game. Too bad you can't come!'" Illustration by Ralph Pallen Coleman. From "The Cat and the King," *Ladies' Home Journal* 36, no. 10 (October 1919), p. 10.

trusively on her lap. For a time there was silence in the room. The doctor's chair creaked a little as she rocked. Outside the window great white clouds were floating; the sunshine in the room had something of the same cloudlike quality of ethereal lightness. Only the huddled figure on the bed was darkened with grief.

"They tell me you didn't eat your breakfast," said the doctor tranquilly.

"I didn't want any." It was muffled and subdued.

"It would have been better to eat it," said the doctor.

"How long do I have to stay here?" asked the voice from the clothes.

The doctor's chair creaked. "Well, it depends. I have to find out just what's the matter with you. It seems to be—a curious—case."

The words came slowly, and one small ear emerged above the bedclothes and cocked itself with almost startling alertness. "If you get on all right, of course you will not have to stay long, not more than a week or so—"

There was a movement of the clothes and a muffled sound from beneath.

"But of course if you are foolish and cry—"

The handkerchief moved briskly and drew back from one eye, and the eye gazed out at the doctor intelligently. After a moment it dropped and traveled downward and reached—the brown book. "Oh-h-h!" said Flora. She sat up swiftly and wiped both eyes and gazed at the book.

The doctor's hand rested on it. She nodded quietly. "Wouldn't you better tell me all about it?" she asked.

Flora gazed from the window at the great clouds traveling by. Her short upper lip trembled. "I just read about her—in the book." She waved her hand. "And so I—I did it."

"Yes, I'd got as far as that myself," said the doctor. "But why?"

The two souls were silent. The doctor had brought up three daughters. There was something about this alert-eyed freshman that touched her interest—and her sense of humor.

"You didn't do it because you wanted to meet me, did

you?" the shot was closer than she knew, and Flora cast a quick glance at her.

"I didn't know about you. If I had, I'd have done it maybe." Her eyes had a look of shy pleasure.

The doctor laughed out. "Pretty good—for a freshman!" She held up the book. "Was it reading this put it into your head?"

"I thought of it first, and then I hunted in the library. I didn't know she was there. I was just looking for a disease—a disease that was quick and easy to have, you know—and I came on Prudence."

"I thought so," said the doctor with a look of satisfaction. "Go on, please."

So, little by little, the story came out, sometimes in bold sweeps and sometimes with Flora's back half turned and her eyes following shyly the great white clouds that went billowing by in the sky. She told it all—even to the catastrophe of the mole's nest, Annette's laughing exit and her own tragic grief.

But a little smile touched the words as she ended. "And that's all," she said.

"You're not looking at it sentimentally any more," said the doctor practically.

The face flushed. "I wasn't sentimental," swiftly; "not exactly sentimental, I guess. Only it's hard sometimes to tell. Your feelings get mixed up so."

She glanced inquiringly at the doctor, who nodded with amused face. "That is one of the discoveries of science," she replied.

Flora looked at it. She shook her head. "You're not making fun of me?" she inquired timidly.

"Not in the least!" said the doctor.

"Anyway—that's the way it was. I wanted to know her. She's so beautiful! Don't you think she's beautiful?"

"Yes," said the doctor gravely.

Flora nodded. "And she likes walks, the way I do. But it was the mole's nest. Maybe it was a field mouse," she said reflectively. "Anyway, I wanted to show it to her. It was so wonderful!" She sighed softly. "It seemed as if I couldn't stand it not to have her see it. And I was lonely, looking at it all alone! You see it's all mixed up." She looked appealingly at the doctor.

"I see," said the doctor.

"The roots were shiny and laid out for breakfast, as if somebody was coming back in a minute. And it was all still around, and the light in the sky just growing pink. It almost hurts you when things are like that. You can't help being lonely" She had forgotten the doctor and the infirmary. She seemed to see only the shining roots and the little nest on the ground. "I guess it's because it's like me, inside," she was saying softly "the way I am inside—all little branches and bones and shining things."

The doctor leaned forward to catch the words. Perhaps she asked a question or two. Her steady eyes watched the girl's face as the story went on—the discovery of the charts and diagrams, and the swift response and delight in them.

The doctor sat very quiet. This was the sort of thing one sometimes came on, once in an age! And the child had supposed she was playing a prank—getting to know a senior! And the books she opened were life! The doctor had watched girls come and go, reaching out to choose some nothing. And now and then it seemed to her a gentle hand reached down and touched the chosen nothing and it became shining, a crystal ball holding life in its roundness.

The doctor was a scientist. To her also the human body was mysterious and wonderful, and often she seemed to graze the edge of truth and catch a glimpse of the unity that binds life in one. She looked at the girl, who had finished speaking and was lying back watching the sky and the clouds moving it. "Which of your studies do you like best?" she asked gently.

The girl turned. "I hate 'em all," swiftly. "History's worst, I think—studying about Rameses II and mummy things!" She threw out her hands. "It's wicked—when there's all outdoors and all the beautiful things inside of us!"

She had spread both her hands across her chest, as if to cover as much territory as possible; and to the doctor there was something almost tragic in the gesture. Her eyes dwelt on the small figure—the disheveled hair and round eyes and reddish lids.

"You'd like to study biology, I suppose," she said reflectively. "Everything that's alive," said Flora promptly.

"Perhaps you'd better have your breakfast now—and keep alive yourself."

And Flora ate it, propped against the pillows, the brown book lying on the foot of the bed. Now and then she cast a swift, resentful look at the book. But she was hungry and the marmalade was good and it was a wonderful day.

And then she glanced at the window and remembered suddenly the game that she was not to see!

The doctor had returned and was standing by the bed, looking down and smiling. "All through?" she asked serenely.

Flora nodded. "I was pretty hungry," she acknowledged.

"I thought so." The doctor removed the tray.

"How long do I have to stay here?" meekly.

The doctor sat down. She seemed to ignore the question. "I've been thinking about a biology course for you. There isn't any class you could go into just now."

"No," Flora sighed. "I didn't suppose there would be. Perhaps I can do it after I'm through being educated." She said it with a gleam of mischief, and the doctor laughed out.

"How would you like• to work in my laboratory, once a week?"

Flora leaned forward, breathless. "To study—with you!"

"Well—study, or call it what you like. I am working there Saturdays, and I generally have a student with me to help and look on. Sometimes she experiments a little herself."

"Oh!" It was a sigh of pure joy.

"It's usually a senior of course. In fact, I have a senior now." She was watching the glowing face. "Annette Osler is helping me this year."

Flora's face flushed; then the joy in it laughed out. "I don't deserve that, do I?" she said softly.

The telephone sounded in the next room and the doctor left her a moment. When she returned she glanced at her with a little smile. "Do you think you are feeling well enough to get up?"

The girl sat up with a swift glance of hope.

The doctor nodded. "It's from the team. Someone has given out; they are calling for the next reserve. I thought of you"—she looked teasingly and dubiously. Then she smiled. "Well, go along! And remember you're to come to me Saturday."

She went toward the door. She turned and looked back. "I forgot. You are to report at once to the captain—in her room."

Ten minutes later, in the morning of clouds and wind, a small figure in knickerbockers and blouse, with hair in a braid down its back, was scudding along the walk that led to South Parker. The braid of hair was tied with green-and-white ribbon and it swung gayly behind as the figure scudded on.

THE SLEEPER WAKES

Jessie Fauset

The Crisis *published three installments of "The Sleeper Wakes" from August through September 1920; this selection is taken from parts two and three. Amy Kildare has been adopted by a black family in Trenton, New Jersey, at the age of five but has no memory of her past beyond the day she was brought to the Boldin home by a white woman. The story opens when Amy is seventeen, enamored of the movies, and—though she loves her family—anxious to get out into the world. She has earned enough money by sewing to get to New York, where she passes for white and finds work as a waitress in a bakery on the edge of Greenwich Village. After two years there, Amy becomes friends with one of her customers, Zora Harrisson, a divorcée who aspires to be a painter and lives off of her alimony. Zora invites Amy to share her apartment, taking her under her wing, and advising that she marry a wealthy man in order to pursue her own interest in art. Among Zora's many male callers, Amy is attracted to an older man, a retired broker of considerable wealth, who is twice divorced as a result of his overbearing manner. Stuart Wynne is also a member of one of the South's oldest families and has no inkling that Amy is part African-American or has been raised by the Boldins. Amy marries him out of a desire for financial security and naive belief in the romance of Hollywood movies. She has just taken up residence as a white, suburban housewife outside Richmond, Virginia, when this episode opens.*

FROM the very beginning *he* was different from what she had supposed. To start with he was far, far wealthier, and he had,

From *The Crisis* 20, nos. 5–6 (September–October 1920).

too, a tradition, a family-pride which to Amy was inexplicable. Still more inexplicably he had a race-pride. To his wife this was not only strange but foolish. She was as Zora had once suggested, the true democrat. Not that she preferred the company of her maids, though the reason for this did not lie *per se* in the fact that they were maids. There was simply no common ground. But she was uniformly kind, a trait which had she been older would have irritated her husband. As it was, he saw in it only an additional indication of her freshness, her lack of worldliness which seemed to him the attributes of an inherent refinement and goodness untouched by experience.

He, himself, was intolerant of all people of inferior birth or standing and looked with contempt on foreigners, except the French and English. All the rest were variously "guineys," "niggers," and "wops," and all of them he genuinely despised and hated, and talked of them with the huge intolerant carelessness characteristic of occidental civilization. Amy was never able to understand it. People were always, first and last, just people to her. Growing up as the average colored American girl does grow up, surrounded by types of every hue, color and facial configuration she had had no absolute ideal. She was not even aware that there was one. Wynne, who in his grim way had a keen sense of humor, used to be vastly amused at the artlessness with which she let him know that she did not consider him good-looking. She never wanted him to wear anything but dark blue, or somber mixtures always.

"They take away from that awful whiteness of your skin," she used to tell him, "and deepen the blue of your eyes."

In the main she made no attempt to understand him, as indeed she made no attempt to understand anything. The result, of course, was that such ideas as seeped into her mind stayed there, took growth and later bore fruit. But just at this period she was like a well-cared for, sleek, house-pet, delicately nurtured, velvety, content to let her days pass by. She thought almost nothing of her art just now, except as her sensibilities were jarred by an occasional disharmony. Likewise, even to herself, she never criticized Wynne, except when some act or attitude of his stung. She could never understand why he, so fastidious, so versed in elegance of word and speech, so careful in his surroundings, even down to the last detail of glass and napery, should take such evident pleasure in literature of a certain prurient type. He fairly revelled in the realistic novels which to her depicted sheer badness. He would get her to read to him, partly because he enjoyed the realism and in a slighter degree because he enjoyed seeing her shocked. Her point of view amused him.

"What funny people," she would say naively, "to do such things." She could not understand the liaisons and intrigues of women in the society novels, such infamy was stupid and silly. If one starved, it was conceivable that one might steal; if one were intentionally injured, one might hit back, even murder; but deliberate nastiness she could not envisage. The stories, after she had read them to him, passed out of her mind as completely as though they had never existed.

Picture the two of them spending three years together with practically no friction. To his dominance and intolerance she opposed a soft and unobtrusive indifference. What she wanted she had, ease, wealth, adoration, love, too, passionate and imperious, but she had never known any other kind. She was growing cleverer also, her knowledge of French was increasing, she was acquiring a knowledge of politics, of commerce and of the big social questions, for Wynne's interests were exhaustive and she did most of his reading for him. Another woman might have yearned for a more youthful companion, but her native coldness kept her content. She did not love him, she had never really loved anybody, but little Cornelius Boldin—he had been such an enchanting, such a darling baby, she remembered,—her heart contracted painfully when she thought as she did very often of his warm softness.

"He must be a big boy now," she would think almost maternally, wondering—once she had been so sure!—if she would ever see him again. But she was very fond of Wynne, and he was crazy over her just as Zora had predicted. He loaded her with gifts, dresses, flowers, jewels—she amused him because none but colored stones appealed to her.

"Diamonds are so hard, so cold, and pearls are dead," she told him.

Nothing ever came between them, but his ugliness, his hatefulness to dependents. It hurt her so, for she was naturally kind in her careless, uncomprehending way. True, she had left Mrs. Boldin without a word, but she did not guess how completely Mrs. Boldin loved her. She would have been aghast had she realized how stricken her flight had left them. At twenty-two, Amy was still as good, as unspoiled, as pure as a child. Of course with all this she was too unquestioning, too selfish, too vain, but they were all faults of her lovely, lovely flesh. Wynne's intolerance finally got on her nerves. She used to blush for his unkindness. All the servants were colored, but she had long since ceased to think that perhaps she, too, was colored, except when he, by insult toward an employee, overt or always at least implied, made her realize his contemptuous dislike and disregard for a dark skin or Negro blood.

"Stuart, how can you say such things?" she would expostulate. "You can't expect a man to stand such language as that." And Wynne would sneer, "A man—you don't consider a nigger a man, do you? Oh, Amy, don't be such a fool. You've got to keep them in their places."

Some innate sense of the fitness of things kept her from condoling outspokenly with the servants, but they knew she was ashamed of her husband's ways. Of course, they left—it seemed to Amy that Peter, the butler, was always getting new "help,"—but most of the upper servants stayed, for Wynne paid handsomely and although his orders were meticulous and insistent, the retinue of employees was so large that the individual's work was light.

Most of the servants who did stay on in spite of Wynne's occasional insults had a purpose in view. Callie, the cook, Amy found out, had two children at Howard University—of course she never came in contact with Wynne—the chauffeur had a crippled sister. Rosa, Amy's maid and purveyor of much outside information, was the chief support of her family. About Peter, Amy knew nothing; he was a striking, taciturn man, very competent, who had left the Wynnes' service years before and had returned in Amy's third year. Wynne treated him with comparative respect. But Stephen, the new valet, met with entirely different treatment. Amy's heart yearned toward him; he was like Cornelius, with short-sighted, patient eyes, always willing, a little over-eager. Amy recognized him for what he was: a boy of respectable, ambitious parentage, striving for the means for an education; naturally far above his present calling, yet willing to pass through all this as a means to an end. She questioned Rosa about him.

"Oh, Stephen," Rosa told her, "yes'm, he's workin' for fair. He's got a brother at the Howard's and a sister at Smith's. Yes'm, it do seem a little hard on him, but Stephen, he say, they're both goin' to turn roun' and help him when they get through. That blue silk has a rip in it, Miss Amy, if you was thinkin' of wearin' that. Yes'm, somehow I don't think Steve's very strong, kinda worries like. I guess he's sorta nervous."

Amy told Wynne. "He's such a nice boy, Stuart," she pleaded, "it hurts me to have you so cross with him. Anyway don't call him names." She was both surprised and frightened at the feeling in her that prompted her to interfere. She had held so aloof from other people's interests all these years.

"I *am* colored," she told herself that night. "I feel it inside of me. I must be or I couldn't care so about Stephen. Poor boy, I suppose Cornelius is just like him. I wish Stuart would let him alone. I wonder if all white people are like that. Zora was hard, too, on unfortunate people." She pondered over it a bit. "I wonder what Stuart would say if he knew I was colored?" She lay perfectly still, her smooth brow knitted, thinking hard. "But he loves me," she said to herself still silently. "He'll always love my looks," and she fell to thinking that all the wonderful happenings in her sheltered, pampered life had come to her through her beauty. She reached out an exquisite arm, switched on a light, and picking up a hand-mirror from a dressing-table, fell to studying her face. She forgot Stephen and fell asleep.

But in the morning her husband's voice issuing from his dressing-room across the hall, awakened her. She listened drowsily. Stephen, leaving the house the day before, had been met by a boy with a telegram. He had taken it, slipped it into his pocket, (he was just going to the mail-box) and had forgotten to deliver it until now, nearly twenty-four hours later. She could hear Stuart's storm of abuse—it was terrible, made up as it was of oaths and insults to the boy's ancestry. There was a moment's lull. Then she heard him again.

"If your brains are a fair sample of that black wench of a sister of yours—"

She sprang up then thrusting her arms as she ran into her pink dressing-gown. She got there just in time. Stephen, his face quivering, was standing looking straight into Wynne's smoldering eyes. In spite of herself, Amy was glad to see the boy's bearing. But he did not notice her.

"You devil!" he was saying. "You white-faced devil! I'll make you pay for that!" He raised his arm. Wynne did not flinch.

With a scream she was between them. "Go, Stephen, go, —get out of the house. Where do you think you are? Don't you know you'll be hanged, lynched, tortured?" Her voice shrilled at him.

Wynne tried to thrust aside her arms that clung and twisted. But she held fast till the door slammed behind the fleeing boy.

"God, let me by, Amy!" As suddenly as she had clasped him she let him go, ran to the door, fastened it and threw the key out the window.

He took her by the arms and shook her. "Are you mad? Didn't you hear him threaten me, me,—a nigger threaten me?" His voice broke with anger, "And you're letting him get away! Why, I'll get him. I'll set bloodhounds on him, I'll have every white man in this town after him! He'll be hanging so high by midnight—" he made for the other door, cursing, half-insane.

How, *how* could she keep him back! She hated her weak arms with their futile beauty! She sprang toward him. "Stuart, wait," she was breathless and sobbing. She said the first thing that came into her head. "Wait, Stuart, you cannot do this thing." She thought of Cornelius—suppose it had been he— "Stephen,—that boy,—he is my brother."

He turned on her. "What!" he said fiercely, then laughed a short laugh of disdain. "You are crazy," he said roughly, "My God, Amy! How can you even in jest associate yourself with these people? Don't you suppose I know a white girl when I see one? There's no use telling a lie like that."

Well, there was no help for it. There was only one way. He had turned back for a moment, but she must keep him many moments—an hour. Stephen must get out of town. She caught his arm again. "Yes," she told him, "I did lie. Stephen is not my brother, I never saw him before." The light of relief that crept into his eyes did not escape her, it only nerved her. "But I am colored," she ended.

Before he could stop her she had told him all about the tall white woman. "She took me to Mrs. Boldin's and gave me to her to keep. She would never have taken me to her if I had been white. If you lynch this boy, I'll let the world, your world know that your wife is a colored woman."

He sat down like a man suddenly stricken old, his face ashen. "Tell me about it again," he commanded. And she obeyed, going mercilessly into every damning detail.

. . . .

Amazingly her beauty availed her nothing. If she had been an older woman, if she had had Zora's age and experience, she would have been able to gauge exactly her influence over Wynne. Though even then in similar circumstances she would have taken the risk and acted in just the same manner. But she was a little bewildered at her utter miscalculation. She had thought he might not want his friends—his world by which he set such store—to know that she was colored, but she had not dreamed it could make any real difference to him. He had chosen her, poor and ignorant, out of a host of women, and had told her countless times of his love. To herself Amy Wynne was in comparison with Zora for instance, stupid and uninteresting. But his constant, unsolicited iterations had made her accept his idea.

She was just the same woman she told herself, she had not changed, she was still beautiful, still charming, still "different." Perhaps that very difference had its being in the fact of her mixed blood. She had been his wife—there were memories—she could not see how he could give her up. The suddenness of the divorce carried her off her feet. Dazedly she left him—though almost without a pang for she had only liked him. She had been perfectly honest about this, and he, although consumed by the fierceness of his emotion toward her, had gradually forced himself to be content, for at least she had never made him jealous.

She was to live in a small house of his in New York, up town in the Eighties. Peter was in charge and there were a new maid and a cook. The servants, of course, knew of the separation, but nobody guessed why. She was living on a much smaller basis than the one to which she had become so accustomed in the last three years. But she was very comfortable. She felt, at any rate she manifested, no qualms at receiving alimony from Wynne. That was the way things happened, she supposed when she thought of it at all. Moreover, it seemed to her perfectly in keeping with Wynne's former attitude toward her; she did not see how he could do less. She expected people to be consistent. That was why she was so amazed that he in spite of his oft iterated love, could let her go. If she had felt half the love for him which he had professed for her, she would not have sent him away if he had been a leper.

"Why I'd stay with him," she told herself, "if he were one, even as I felt now."

She was lonely in New York. Perhaps it was the first time in her life that she had felt so. Zora had gone to Paris the first year of her marriage and had not come back.

The days dragged on emptily. One thing helped her. She had gone one day to the modiste from whom she had bought her trousseau. The woman remembered her perfectly— "The lady with the exquisite taste for colors—ah, madame, but you have the rare gift." Amy was grateful to be taken out of her thoughts. She bought one or two daring but altogether lovely creations and let fall a few suggestions:

"That brown frock, Madame,—you say it has been on your hands a long time? Yes? But no wonder. See, instead of that dead white you should have a shade of ivory, that white cheapens it." Deftly she caught up a bit of ivory satin and worked out her idea. Madame was ravished.

"But yes, Madame Ween is correct—as always. Oh, what a pity that the Madame is so wealthy. If she were only a poor girl—Mlle. Antoine with the best eye for color in the place has just left, gone back to France to nurse her brother—this

World War is of such a horror! If someone like Madame, now, could be found, to take the little Antoine's place!"

Some obscure impulse drove Amy to accept the half proposal: "Oh! I don't know, I have nothing to do just now. My husband is abroad." Wynne had left her with that impression. "I could contribute the money to the Red Cross or to charity."

The work was the best thing in the world for her. It kept her from becoming too introspective, though even then she did more serious, connected thinking than she had done in all the years of her varied life.

She missed Wynne definitely, chiefly as a guiding influence for she had rarely planned even her own amusements. Her dependence on him had been absolute. She used to picture him to herself as he was before the trouble—and his changing expressions as he looked at her, of amusement, interest, pride, a certain little teasing quality that used to come into his eyes, which always made her adopt her "spoiled child air," as he used to call it. It was the way he liked her best. Then last, there was that look he had given her the morning she had told him she was colored—it had depicted so many emotions, various and yet distinct. There were dismay, disbelief, coldness, a final aloofness.

There was another expression, too, that she thought of sometimes—the look on the face of Mr. Packard, Wynne's lawyer. She, herself, had attempted no defense. "For God's sake why did you tell him, Mrs. Wynne?" Packard asked her. His curiosity got the better of him. "You couldn't have been in love with that yellow rascal," he blurted out. "She's too cold really, to love anybody," he told himself. "If you didn't care about the boy why should you have told?"

She defended herself feebly. "He looked so like little Cornelius Boldin," she replied vaguely, "and he couldn't help being colored." A clerk came in then and Packard said no more. But into his eyes had crept a certain reluctant respect. She remembered the look, but could not define it.

She was so sorry about the trouble now, she wished it had never happened. Still if she had it to repeat she would act in the same way again. "There was nothing else for me to do," she used to tell herself.

But she missed Wynne unbelievably.

If it had not been for Peter, her life would have been almost that of a nun. But Peter, who read the papers and kept abreast of the times, constantly called her attention, with all due respect, to the meetings, the plays, the sights which she ought to attend or see. She was truly grateful to him. She was very kind to all three of the servants. They had the easiest "places" in New York, the maids used to tell their friends. As she never entertained, and frequently dined out, they had a great deal of time off.

She had been separated from Wynne for ten months before she began to make any definite plans for her future. Of course, she could not go on like this always. It came to her suddenly that probably she would go to Paris and live there—why or how she did not know. Only Zora was there and lately she had begun to think that her life was to be like Zora's. They had been amazingly parallel up to this time. Of course she would have to wait until after the war.

She sat musing about it one day in the big sitting-room which she had had fitted over into a luxurious studio. There was a sewing-room off to the side from which Peter used to wheel into the room waxen figures of all colorings and contours so that she could drape the various fabrics about them to be sure of the best results. But today she was working out a scheme for one of Madame's customers, who was of her own color and size and she was her own lay-figure. She sat in front of the huge pier glass, a wonderful soft yellow silk draped about her radiant loveliness.

"I could do some serious work in Paris," she said half aloud to herself. "I suppose if I really wanted to, I could be very successful along this line."

Somewhere downstairs an electric bell buzzed, at first softly, then after a slight pause, louder, and more insistently.

"If Madame sends me that lace today," she was thinking, idly, "I could finish this and start on the pink. I wonder why Peter doesn't answer the bell."

She remembered then that Peter had gone to New Rochelle on business and she had sent Ellen to Altman's to find a certain rare velvet and had allowed Mary to go with her. She would dine out, she told them, so they need not hurry. Evidently she was alone in the house.

Well she could answer the bell. She had done it often enough in the old days at Mrs. Boldin's. Of course it was the lace. She smiled a bit as she went down stairs thinking how surprised the delivery-boy would be to see her arrayed thus early in the afternoon. She hoped he wouldn't go. She could see him through the long, thick panels of glass in the vestibule and front door. He was just turning about as she opened the door.

This was no delivery-boy, this man whose gaze fell on her hungry and avid. This was Wynne. She stood for a second leaning against the door-jamb, a strange figure surely in the sharp November weather. Some leaves—brown, skeleton shapes— rose and swirled unnoticed about her head. A passing letter-carrier looked at them curiously.

"What are you doing answering the door?" Wynne asked her roughly. "Where is Peter? Go in, you'll catch cold."

She was glad to see him. She took him into the drawing room—a wonderful study in browns—and looked at him and looked at him.

"Well," he asked her, his voice eager in spite of the commonplace words, "are you glad to see me? Tell me what do you do with yourself."

She could not talk fast enough, her eyes clinging to his face. Once it struck her that he had changed in some indefinable way. Was it a slight coarsening of that refined aristocratic aspect? Even in her subconsciousness she denied it.

He had come back to her.

"So I design for Madame when I feel like it, and send the money to the Red Cross and wonder when you are coming back to me." For the first time in their acquaintanceship she was conscious deliberately of trying to attract, to hold him. She put on her spoiled child air which had once been so successful.

"It took you long enough to get here," she pouted. She was certain of him now. His mere presence assured her.

They sat silent a moment, the late November sun bathing her head in an austere glow of chilly gold. As she sat there in the big brown chair she was, in her yellow dress, like some mysterious emanation, some wraith-like aura developed from the tone of her surroundings.

He rose and came toward her, still silent. She grew nervous, and talked incessantly with sudden unusual gestures. "Oh, Stuart, let me give you tea. It's right there in the pantry off the dining-room. I can wheel the table in." She rose, a lovely creature in her yellow robe. He watched her intently.

"Wait," he bade her.

She paused almost on tiptoe, a dainty golden butterfly.

"You are coming back to live with me?" he asked her hoarsely.

For the first time in her life she loved him.

"Of course I am coming back," she told him softly. "Aren't you glad? Haven't you missed me? I didn't see how you *could* stay away. Oh! Stuart, what a wonderful ring."

For he had slipped on her finger a heavy dull gold band, with an immense sapphire in an oval setting—a beautiful thing of Italian workmanship.

"It is so like you to remember," she told him gratefully. "I love colored stones." She admired it, turning it around and around on her slender finger.

How silent he was, standing there watching her with his somber yet eager gaze. It made her troubled, uneasy. She cast about for something to say.

"You can't think how I've improved since I saw you, Stuart. I've read all sorts of books—Oh! I'm learned," she smiled at him. "And Stuart," she went a little closer to him, twisting the button on his perfect coat, "I'm so sorry about it all,—about Stephen, that boy you know. I just couldn't help interfering. But when we're married again, if you'll just remember how it hurts me to have you so cross—"

He interrupted her. "I wasn't aware that I spoke of our marrying again," he told her, his voice steady, his blue eyes cold.

She thought he was teasing. "Why you just asked me to. You said, 'Aren't you coming back to live with me?'"

"Yes," he acquiesced, "I said just that—'to live with me.'"

Still she didn't comprehend. "But what do you mean?" she asked bewildered.

"What do you suppose a man means," he returned deliberately, "when he asks a woman to live with him, but not to marry him?"

She sat down heavily in the brown chair, all glowing ivory and yellow against its somber depths.

"Like the women in those awful novels?" she whispered. "Not like those women!—Oh, Stuart! you don't mean it!" Her very heart was numb.

"But you must care a little—" she was amazed at her own depth of feeling. "Why I care—there all are those memories back of us—you must want me really—"

"I do want you," he told her tensely. "I want you damnably. But—well—I might as well out with it—A white man like me simply doesn't marry a colored woman. After all what difference need it make to you? We'll live abroad—you'll travel, have all the things you love. Many a white woman would envy you." He stretched out an eager hand.

She evaded it, holding herself aloof as though his touch were contaminating. Her movement angered him.

Like a rending veil suddenly the veneer of his high polish cracked and the man stood revealed.

"Oh, hell!" he snarled at her roughly. "Why don't you stop posing? What do you think you are anyway? Do you suppose I'd take you for my wife—what do you think can happen to you? What man of your own race could give you what you want? You don't suppose I am going to support you this way forever, do you? The court imposed no alimony. You've got to come to it sooner or later—you're bound to fall to some white man. What's the matter—I'm not rich enough?"

Her face flamed at that—"As though it were *that* that mattered!"

He gave her a deadly look. "Well, isn't it? Ah, my girl, you forget you told me you didn't love me when you married me. You sold yourself to me then. Haven't I reason to suppose you are waiting for a higher bidder?"

At these words something in her died forever, her youth, her illusions, her happy, happy blindness. She saw life leering mercilessly in her face. It seemed to her that she would give all her future to stamp out, to kill the contempt in his frosty insolent eyes. In a sudden rush of savagery she struck him, struck him across his hateful sneering mouth with the hand which wore his ring. As *she* fell, reeling under the fearful impact of his brutal but involuntary blow, her mind caught at, registered two things. A little thin stream of blood was trickling across his chin. She had cut him with the ring, she realized with a certain savage satisfaction. And there was something else which she must remember, which she *would* remember if only she could fight her way out of this dreadful clinging blackness, which was bearing down upon her—closing her in.

When she came to she sat up holding her bruised, aching head in her palms, trying to recall what it was that had impressed her so.

Oh, yes, her very mind ached with the realization. She lay back again on the floor, prone, anything to relieve that intolerable pain. But her memory, her thoughts went on.

"Nigger," he had called her as she fell, "nigger, nigger," and again, "nigger."

"He despised me absolutely," she said to herself wonderingly, "because I was colored. And yet he wanted me."

....

Somehow she reached her room. Long after the servants had come in, she lay face downward across her bed, thinking. How she hated Wynne, how she hated herself! And for ten months she had been living off his money although in no way had she a claim on him. Her whole body burned with the shame of it.

In the morning she rang for Peter. She faced him, white and haggard, but if the man noticed her condition, he made no sign. He was, if possible, more imperturbable than ever.

"Peter," she told him, her eyes and voice very steady. "I am leaving this house today and shall never come back."

"Yes, Miss."

"I shall want you to see to the packing and storing of the goods and send the keys and the receipts for the jewelry and valuables, to Mr. Packard in Baltimore."

"Yes, Miss."

"And, Peter, I am very poor now and shall have no money besides what I can make for myself."

"Yes, Miss."

Would nothing surprise him, she wondered dully. She went on, "I don't know whether you knew it or not, Peter, but I am colored, and hereafter I mean to live among my own people. Do you think you could find me a little house or a little cottage not too far from New York?"

He had a little place in New Rochelle, he told her, his manner altering not one whit, or better yet his sister had a four-room house in Orange, with a garden, if he remembered correctly. Yes, he was sure there was a garden. It would be just the thing for Mrs. Wynne.

She had four hundred dollars of her very own which she had earned by designing for Madame. She paid the maids a month in advance—they were to stay as long as Peter needed them. She, herself, went to a small hotel on Twenty-eighth Street, and here Peter came for her at the end of ten days, with the acknowledgement of the keys and receipts from Mr. Packard. Then he accompanied her to Orange and installed her in her new home.

"I wish I could afford to keep you, Peter," she said a little wistfully, "but I am very poor. I am heavily in debt and I must get that off my shoulders at once."

Mrs. Wynne was very kind, he was sure; he could think of no one with whom he would prefer to work. Furthermore, he often ran down from New Rochelle to see his sister; he would come in from time to time, and in the spring would plant the garden if she wished.

She hated to see him go, but she did not dwell long on that. Her only thought was to work and work and work and save until she could pay Wynne back. She had not lived very extravagantly during those ten months and Peter was a perfect manager—in spite of her remonstrances he had given her every month an account of his expenses. She had made arrangements with Madame to be her regular designer. The French woman guessing that more than whim was behind this move drove a very shrewd bargain, but even then the pay was excellent. With care, she told herself, she could be free within two years, three at most.

She lived a dull enough existence now, going to work steadily every morning and getting home at night. Almost it

was like those early days when she had no high sense of adventure, no expectation of great things to come, which might
buoy her up. She no longer thought of phases and the proper
setting for her beauty. Once indeed catching sight of her face
late one night in the mirror in her tiny work-room in Orange,
she stopped and scanned herself, loathing what she saw there.

"You *thing!*" she said to the image in the glass, "if you hadn't
been so vain, so shallow!" And she had struck herself violently again and again across the face until her head ached.

But such fits of passion were rare. She had a curious sense
of freedom in these days, a feeling that at last her brain, her
senses were liberated from some hateful clinging thralldom.
Her thoughts were always busy. She used to go over that last
scene with Wynne again and again trying to probe the inscru-
table mystery which she felt was at the bottom of the affair.
She groped her way toward a solution, but always something
stopped her. Her impulse to strike, she realized, and his brutal
rejoinder had been actuated by something more than mere sex
antagonism, there was *race* antagonism there—two elements
clashing. That much she could fathom. But that he despising
her, hating her for not being white should yet desire her! It
seemed to her that his attitude toward her—hate and yet desire, was the attitude in microcosm of the whole white world
toward her own, toward that world to which those few possible strains of black blood so tenuously and yet so tena-
ciously linked her.

Once she got hold of a big thought. Perhaps there *was* some
root, some racial distinction woven in with the stuff of which
she was formed which made her persistently kind and unex-
acting. And perhaps in the same way this difference, helplessly, inevitably operated in making Wynne and his kind,
cruel or at best indifferent. Her reading for Wynne reacted to
her thought—she remembered the grating insolence of white
exploiters of foreign lands, the wrecking of African villages,
the destruction of homes in Tasmania. She couldn't imagine
where Tasmania was, but wherever it was, it had been the
realest thing in the world to its crude inhabitants.

Gradually she reached a decision. There were two divisions
of people in the world—on the one hand insatiable desire for

power; keenness, mentality; a vast and cruel pride. On the other there was ambition, it is true, but modified, a certain humble sweetness, too much inclination to trust, an unthinking, unswerving loyalty. All the advantages in the world accrued to the first division. But without bitterness she chose the second. She wanted to be colored, she hoped she was colored. She wished even that she did not have to take advantage of her appearance to make her living. But that was to meet an end. After all she had contracted her debt with a white man, she would pay him with a white man's money.

The years slipped by—four of them. One day a letter came from Mr. Packard. Mrs. Wynne had sent him the last penny of the sum received from Mr. Wynne from February to November, 1914. Mr. Wynne had refused to touch the money, it was and would be indefinitely at Mrs. Wynne's disposal.

She never even answered the letter. Instead she dismissed the whole incident,—Wynne and all,—from her mind and began to plan for her future. She was free, free! She had paid back her sorry debt with labor, money and anguish. From now on she could do as she pleased. Almost she caught herself saying "something is going to happen." But she checked herself, she hated her old attitude.

But something *was* happening. Insensibly from the moment she knew of her deliverance, her thoughts turned back to a stifled hidden longing, which had lain, it seemed to her, an eternity in her heart. Those days with Mrs. Boldin! At night, —on her way to New York,—in the workrooms,—her mind was busy with little intimate pictures of that happy, wholesome, unpretentious life. She could see Mrs. Boldin, clean and portly, in a lilac chambray dress, upbraiding her for some trifling, yet exasperating fault. And Mr. Boldin, immaculate and slender, with his noticeably polished air—how kind he had always been, she remembered. And lastly, Cornelius; Cornelius in a thousand attitudes and engaged in a thousand occupations, brown and near-sighted and sweet—devoted to his pretty sister, as he used to call her; Cornelius, who used to come to her as a baby as willingly as to his mother; Cornelius spelling out colored letters on his blocks, pointing to them stickily with a brown, perfect finger; Cornelius singing like an

angel in his breathy, sexless voice and later murdering everything possible on his terrible cornet. How had she ever been
able to leave them all and the dear shabbiness of that home!
Nothing, she realized in all these years had touched her in-
most being, had penetrated to the core of her cold heart like
the memories of those early, misty scenes.

One day she wrote a letter to Mrs. Boldin. She, the writer,
Madame A. Wynne, had come across a young woman, Amy
Kildare, who said that as a girl she had run away from home
and now she would like to come back. But she was ashamed
to write. Madame Wynne had questioned the girl closely and
she was quite sure that this Miss Kildare had in no way in-
curred shame or disgrace. It had been some time since Madame Wynne had seen the girl but if Mrs. Boldin wished, she
would try to find her again—perhaps Mrs. Boldin would like
to get in touch with her. The letter ended on a tentative note.

The answer came at once.

My dear Madame Wynne:
   My mother told me to write you this letter. She said even if
Amy Kildare had done something terrible, she would want her
to come home again. My father says so too. My mother says,
please find her as soon as you can and tell her to come back.
She still misses her. We all miss her. I was a little boy when she
left, but though I am in High School now and play in the
school orchestra, I would rather see her than do anything I
know. If you see her, be sure to tell her to come right away. My
mother says thank you.

                    Yours respectfully,
                    CORNELIUS BOLDIN

The letter came to the modiste's establishment in New York.
Amy read it and went with it to Madame. "I have had wonderful news," she told her. "I must go away immediately, I
can't come back—you may have these last two weeks for
nothing." Madame, who had surmised long since the separation, looked curiously at the girl's flushed cheeks, and decided
that "Monsieur Ween" had returned. She gave her fatalistic
shrug. All Americans were crazy.

"But, yes, Madame,—if you must go—*absolument.*"

When she reached the ferry, Amy looked about her searchingly. "I hope I'm seeing you for the last time—I'm going home, home!" Oh, the unbelievable kindness! She had left them without a word and they still wanted her back!

Eventually she got to Orange and to the little house. She sent a letter to Peter's sister and set about her packing. But first she sat down in the little house and looked about her. She would go home, home—how she loved the word, she would stay there a while, but always there was life, still beckoning. It would beckon forever she realized to her adventurousness. Afterwards she would set up an establishment of her own,—she reviewed possibilities—in a rich suburb, where white women would pay and pay for her expertness, caring nothing for realities, only for externals.

"As I myself used to care," she sighed. Her thoughts flashed on. "Then some day I'll work and help with colored people—the only ones who have really cared for and wanted me." Her eyes blurred.

She would never make any attempt to find out who or what she was. If she were white, there would always be people urging her to keep up the silliness of racial prestige. How she hated it all!

"Citizen of the world, that's what I'll be. And now I'll go home."

Peter's sister's little girl came over to be with the pretty lady whom she adored.

"You sit here, Angel, and watch me pack," Amy said, placing her in a little arm-chair. And the baby sat there in silent observation, one tiny leg crossed over the other, surely the quaintest, gravest bit of bronze, Amy thought, that ever lived.

"Miss Amy cried," the child told her mother afterwards. Perhaps Amy did cry, but if so she was unaware. Certainly she laughed more happily, more spontaneously than she had done for years. Once she got down on her knees in front of the little arm-chair and buried her face in the baby's tiny bosom.

"Oh Angel, Angel," she whispered, "do you suppose Cornelius still plays on that cornet?"

CALL OF THE HOUSE

Ruth Comfort Mitchell

This excerpt is from the first installment of a three-part serial that ran in Woman's Home Companion *from December 1926 through February 1927. In subsequent episodes, after Doria Dean Yale is elected to the California State Legislature as its first woman senator, she engages in a stiff battle over reapportionment of state representatives according to population rather than region. As the daughter of a northern rancher, Dean initially opposes the move in order to keep power away from the urban centers and the more populous south, which she perceives as alien territory. While exploring the ramifications of this hot political issue, Dean discovers a new feeling of independence in the state capital and loves it so much that she envisions herself a permanent member of the assembly. Interrupting her career plans is a romantic attraction to Malcolm Douglas, a "land baron" who has financed the campaign against her election but who inexplicably draws her to him with his ardent interest. Although she has turned down a marriage proposal from Kenneth Conway and intends to follow in the footsteps of other single career women, Dean is moved by Malcolm's advances. Ultimately, he assures her that marriage to him would mean freedom for both of them and that he would never chain her to the house as a conventional wife. Malcolm demonstrates the sincerity of his egalitarianism by driving her to the capitol just in time for the roll call on reapportionment. Dean, too, evidences strength of character by casting the tie-breaking vote in favor of population-based representation because she has decided that it is the right thing to do.*

From *Woman's Home Companion* 53, no. 22 (December 1926).

"WELL, now, I s'pose the next thing," said her Uncle Joe Dobie, with the big booming laugh which always struck his niece
and guest of honor as curiously immature for a gentleman of
his years and his girth and his guile, "I s'pose the *next* thing,
we'll be runn' you for state senator!"

Dean herself was obligingly amused. It was a family tradition to be indulgent with the Colonel's rather simple wit. "Oh,
not Governor, Uncle Joe? I'd rather set my heart—"

"There's never been a woman senator in California, has
there?" someone well down the table wanted to know.

"No," said the Colonel, "but—"

"And I sincerely trust there never will be," said Dean Yale's
mother earnestly. She was a blonde, beautiful, ample lady, and
she bent upon her brother-in-law a look of mild disapproval.
"I have hardly seen my daughter for two months, Joseph, and
I'll thank you not to put any more wild ideas in her head."

Everyone laughed at that, but into Uncle Joe's small round
eyes there came the dilation of sudden thought.

"I mean it, by golly!" he ejaculated, clearly surprised to find
that he did. "I *mean* it!"

For an appreciable instant his emphasis seemed to hang and
pulsate in the warm and odorous air above the dinner table.
Then the light talk went comfortably forward again, duets and
trios, side by side and across, but a gray silent man, three
places removed from his host, looked at him consideringly
between narrowed lids.

The Colonel, catching his look, leaned forward and addressed him directly. "I'm serious, Henry. Why not? Never
struck me till this minute, I'm free to confess, but—why isn't
it a whale of an idea?"

"Talk to you later," said the gray man, hardly moving his lips.
It was Henry Flint's most salient peculiarity—almost a ventrilo-
quist's power of conversing with an immobile countenance.

"Now listen," Uncle Joe's enthusiasm was mounting, "isn't
it just what we've been looking for without knowing it? And
right now, after her community chest campaign—why, she's
got ten thousand dollars' worth of paid-up publicity already!
And she—"

"Later," the other repeated, his thin lips never vibrating.

The girl, in her guest of honor's place on her uncle's right, had not missed a look nor a syllable and there was a faint quickened beat in her blood, but she kept a convincing semblance of attention for the man on the other side who was giving her his heated convictions on the subject of college athletes going over to professional football.

Kenneth Conway was a full-blooded, high-colored, entirely objective youth with whom sport was creed and code. He was something less than fourteen months Dean Yale's junior, and he had been ardently trying to marry her for the last five years, rather obviously aided and abetted by her mother and her aunt.

....

[Dean] settled herself to listen amiably to her suitor with the top layer of her mind, and to accept the congratulations of the people who came up to her, managing their fragile little cups rather more handily, on the whole, than Mrs. Joseph Elston Dobie had expected, but her whole preoccupation was with the two absent gentlemen. If, not as a compliment to her, but for some canny reason of their own, they might consider the possibility . . .

Dean had surprised everyone, including her family and herself, by her success with the community chest drive. It was by long odds the hardest thing she had ever attempted. It was one thing to bring back a medal for standing gamely steady in a bombed hospital; it was likewise one thing to give most of her post-war days to base hospitals and her more recent years to Camp Fire Girls and tubercular preventoriums; it was quite another to extract large sums of money from a community not at all thoroughly sold on the community chest idea, from people who sentimentally or cannily "liked to do their own giving."

That she could do it, pleasantly and painlessly, was soon an acknowledged fact. Her campaign was surprisingly brief, surprisingly free from internecine inharmonies. Santa Clara County went over the top with a tidy margin of surplus, and the Colonel gave himself only less credit for putting her in power than he gave the young woman for her achievement.

The Colonel was immensely fond of his niece and increasingly proud of her and he resented the efforts of his wife and his sister-in-law to marry her off to young Conway. Ken was a good boy; he liked him. But—good lord—why rush the girl? She had all her life before her.

....

Kenneth Conway, talking sulkily to his hostess, kept a constant watch upon Dean. Presently, she knew, he would dash over during a lull and beg her to come out on the porch or down to the billiard room, and he would ask her once more, ardently, breathlessly, to marry him, and she would refuse him. Very well. And then what should she do? She was a singularly serene young woman on the surface and for a considerable depth beneath the surface, but there was deep down, she admitted to herself and to nobody else, a restlessness.

Dean saw her suitor coming eagerly toward her, colliding perilously with a delicate table en route.

"Say, Dean, aren't you fed up with this show? Say, do we have to stick any longer?"

"I'm afraid guests of honor stand by till the bitter end, in the front families, Kennie." She was tired she discovered suddenly.

"Well, then, after tonight—going to have some time?"

She sighed. "Nothing but, I fear. Whole calendars full of it!"

"Time for some riding? Some golf? Time for—me?"

"Always time for you, old thing." She grappled with an overpowering yawn. "Rick was talking about a week-end at the ranch. I want some stiff riding. Will you come?"

His face darkened. "That's not what I meant. And you know darn well it isn't." He always became vehemently angry at her just before proposing. "I don't mean Rick or Coby or anybody else. I mean—us. Deanie—" he softened swiftly—"gee, it's hot in here! Come on out on the porch for a minute!" His color rose hotly and he put a persuasive hand under her elbow.

It was astonishing, the way all the accumulated weariness of the community chest campaign seemed to descend upon her at once with Ken. . . .

Ken was a dear; she would be as free as she was now, and

perhaps she would be satisfied. It was possible that the feeling of being up on her toes, waiting for the crack of the pistol, would be over. She looked at him wistfully and consideringly, with an expression so at variance with her usual comradely frankness that the young man's candid blue eyes dimmed for an instant.

"Come on!" he muttered thickly.

....

She was to wonder afterward whether the Colonel's message coming ten minutes later would have found her, in the sentimental shadows of the porch, young Conway's reluctantly promised wife.

"Sorry, Ken! I won't be long." She was at once remorseful and thankful.

"What does he want?"

She shrugged. "Some loose end of the community chest business, I dare say."

He continued to scowl.

"Good heavens," she inquired of herself as she went down the hall, "what was the matter with me a moment ago? That's the closest I ever came to it! I must have been more than half asleep." She stopped by an open window, raised it higher and stood for three or four minutes resolutely freshening herself with deep breaths. There was an old-fashioned full-length mirror in a gorgeous gilt frame close by, and she halted again for a deliberate scrutiny, as if to make certain that the spell had actually lifted.

The reflection was reassuring; there was nothing in the look of the young woman before her to indicate weakness. Tall enough, slim, hard-muscled; clear-skinned, dark-eyed; hair which, as even a sharp-tongued sister-in-law admitted, was born to be bobbed. ("Even the back of her neck is nice!"sighed Mrs. Rickford Yale.) Her nose was distinctly good and her mouth was wide, sweet and generous, with a whimsical lift at one corner which people liked and remembered and looked for. She had a good deal of color of her own and used very little to supplement it, and while she knew that she was not nearly so beautiful as Kenneth Conway believed her to be, she considered herself decidedly better-looking than Rick's mother thought her. Not a ship-launching face at all, she realized, but a good durable sort for all wears and weathers.

The walls of the Colonel's office were lined with the books Mrs. Dobie didn't want in the library, and now as always in occupancy it was thickly blurred with smoke.

"'Lo, Deanie! S'down!" Her Uncle Joe gave the nearest chair a shove in her direction and she saw that his round little eyes were dancing in spite of his solemnly portentous expression. "Well, girlie, glad to slam down the lid of the chest and get back to your knittin'?"

"If any," she answered him amiably and in kind. Certainly something was coming when Uncle Joe looked like that. It was the exact duplicate of the expression he had worn when he offered her the chest campaign.

"S'pose you wouldn't feel like tacklin' another job for me?"

"That depends, of course. An interesting one—" She saw that Henry Flint was watching her closely.

"Well, now Henry and I, we've been having a little talk. Just a little discussion, you understand; nothing settled. Nothing definite at all. But we were just figuring on the possibility—"

The gray man cut in smoothly. "Let me analyze the situation for you, Miss Yale. The Colonel here, and many other men of his stamp who have the best interest of Santa Clara County at heart, are concerned over the present political outlook. They are, and with good reason, anxious about the outcome of the next election, at which time a new state senator will be sent to the legislature. Dr. Howard, the present senator from this district, is in poor health, as you may have heard."

Dean nodded. They had—they *were* considering it! She kept her eyes on his almost motionless lips.

Henry Flint put the tips of his long thin fingers together. "He has made the positive statement that he is not a candidate for reelection, and we readily admit that the good doctor has already done his generous share of public service. Down to date, there has not been found a logical successor, for any one of the candidates drew upon strictly individual groups, and would lay himself open to the danger of a strong opposition candidate. The Progressives, we are reliably informed, have a man who—"

"Henry! Tell the girl!" the Colonel exploded, his fat face mottling with hot color. "Deanie, honey, we're goin' to run you!" . . .

"And so, my dear Miss Dean," Henry Flint concluded after a discussion that covered all the pros and cons, "to sum up the matter briefly, you are exceptionally fortunate in that you should have the backing of the cattlemen, not a large group perhaps, but an important unit in the district; of the fruit men, which is more vital; and of the towns. Added to which, you personally should be able to swing the churches and the women's clubs. I need not tell you that this matter still requires a great deal of careful analytical thought; a great deal of weighing and balancing; a great deal of threshing out, before we—"

"Yeah, but we want to move quick just the same," Uncle Joe Dobie objected. "We won't be any surer tomorrow or next week or next month than we are now, and the first thing we know, the other crowd'll get the drop on us! What say, girlie? How's it strike you?"

"Well, Uncle Joe, I agree with Mr. Flint. It needs a lot of talking over and thinking over. In the first place, frankly, I feel very inadequate.

"I can appreciate your reaction to the suddenness of the proposal, Miss Yale," the gray man conceded, "and your modesty does you credit, but I don't mind telling you that I personally, without mentioning it to my good friend the Colonel here, have had my eye on you for some time as possible senatorial timber."

She nodded gravely. "I see. That is of course very reassuring. Then, the next thing, Uncle Joe—I can't even consider it until I know what the boys would think."

"Well, good lord—there's two of 'em here tonight, and you can call Coby up at the ranch! Wes' is the only one you can't reach immediately, and he's the one of the four you can be certain would be for it, for it a million!"

The Colonel pulled his desk telephone toward him and put in a call for Coburn Yale at the home ranch in the San Felipe Valley, in spite of Henry Flint's precautionary protest against undue haste. "No, Deanie, the only member of your family that's going to throw a fit will be your mother and, poor Ella, lord knows she's been doing that ever since you were out of your cradle."

....

Doria Dean Yale, whose healthy habit it was to sleep the night through without a break, woke at four the next morning with a sense of chill disaster. It was an instant before she could collect her thoughts and marshal them in order, and she sat upright in her narrow bed on the sleeping porch. It wasn't a nightmare, then?

She was going to run for state senator?

Under the black velvet sky, the soft darkness enfolding her on every side, the thing took on the semblance of a distorted dream.

How had it happened—been allowed to happen? How had she been managed, manipulated so? She drove her bewildered thoughts backward, step by step . . .

She had been carried along on a relentless current. There was time only to hold her two brothers back for a hasty word in the hall as they followed the county leader. Sitting up in the darkness, her arms gripped about her knees, shivering, she re-created for herself their startled, delighted, rapidly consenting faces. Of course! *Of course* she could—if she wanted to? She mustn't let Uncle Joe and old Frozen face Flint rush her into anything she wasn't keen for! But if she was for it they were, for it a million, ready to get out and get under, and put it over. The dear, foolish, loyal old things—Rick, solid, dependable old Rick, and the bonny brilliant, adorable Don. But how much, stripped of the clan spirit, was their opinion worth? Even though Coburn, the eldest and canniest of them all, had given an unqualified approval by long distance from the San Felipe ranch, put his bride in the car and started, at ten o'clock, the thirty-mile drive to the old home; even though they had all sat up, talking, scrambling eggs, talking until after one? After all, they were family—*Family.* The Yale family; the Yales of Yale Acres; the Santa Clara County Yales, whose clannishness was a legend.

Henry Flint! There was the one rock in a soft sea of foamy praises. If the cool, imponderable politician from Ohio thought she had a chance, she must have!

But granted that she was elected, could she carry on? Good heavens, what had she been thinking of? She couldn't. She didn't want to go!

Where was she in the night's review? The bomb from Uncle Joe, the rallying round of the dinner guests, her beautiful mother dissolved in pretty, becoming tears, Donald Yale's aside to Kenneth Conway, and Ken's red rage.

Suddenly, one voice above the other voices: "Say, listen! Wait a minute! Now then, all together, everybody! Three cheers for the little lady! Three cheers for Senator Yale."

The drive home, with Rick and his wife, and the mother, after all, since Kenneth Conway had flung himself into his car and started the engine furiously, without a word of farewell. Don had leaped upon the running board and gone with him, and succeeded presently in heading him toward Yale Acres.

....

One of the dogs, the oldest of the Chesapeakes, slept on Dean's porch and he roused now, yawning mightily, stretching, and thudded to her on his thickly cushioned feet. "Hullo, Beaver King!" Companionship was welcome. He seated himself and rested his chin on the bed's edge, pressing down, and she heard the swish of his tail across the floor and put a welcoming hand on his broad, dome-like forehead.

The panic was coming back. Merry memories could not rout it.

Three clocks, with a slight difference of opinion, struck five . . . five-thirty . . . Beaver King had let himself down again and gone to sleep with a long gusty sigh and Dean had gone under the covers again for warmth, but she had not closed her eyes, and at six o'clock she put on her slippers, pulled on an orange-colored robe of padded Chinese silk and slipped downstairs.

She was going to telephone to her Uncle Joe Dobie and tell him—as he doubtless already knew—that they had been out of their heads, all of them, the night before. Now she was in her right mind again, and she was not going to attempt that mad enterprise.

A boy on a bicycle darted by with a lifting sweep of his

arm, and there was the thump of tightly twisted newspaper on the porch steps, startling in the new day's silence.

Dean stood still, staring at it. There had been no reporters at the Colonel's dinner, but—

She ran out and picked it up and carried it indoors, unfolding it and straightening it out with shaking hands. Nothing on the front page. Of course not. It had been too late, and Henry Flint wouldn't permit—nothing on the—

DEAN YALE TO RUN FOR STATE SENATOR
POPULAR VALLEY GIRL'S HAT IN RING
COLONEL JOE DOBIE ANNOUNCES CANDIDACY AT BIG DINNER

A picture in uniform, a picture on horseback, three headlines, almost a column.

"Oo-li-loo!" Don's mocking voice, his prankish face at the top of the stairs; he slid swiftly down the banisters. He looked like a heroic-size little boy in his pale blue pajamas, his fair hair mussed. "If you're waking, call me early, call me early, Mother dear! Who's going to be the lil' ol' Queen of the May?" He took the paper from her limp hand. "Lapping up the publicity already, huh?"

"I came down to telephone Uncle Joe," said his sister faintly, "to say I couldn't possibly—"

"Nix on that 'couldn't possibly' stuff, old gal!" the youngest Yale rallied her, his eyes racing through the print. "We're aboard!"

. . . .

Presently the others came in howling for tea. Donald stirred up the fire, and Naka brought in tea with amazing promptness. The little boys and the puppies divided themselves between Dean and the uncles, and Dean made toast on an electric grill near the hearth.

Prue, looking from one to another, thought they seemed, all of them, rather grave under their banter. Dean's face bent over the toaster was distinctly wistful.

"Any more toast?" She gave a sharp sigh. "Well, family? I suppose there's no good pretending to myself that I dreamed last night, or today!"

The brothers shook their heads.

"We're aboard, Sis," Donald said again as he had said in the morning.

They had spent hours, Prue gathered, with the Colonel and Henry Flint, and there had been conferences with prominent fruit and cattlemen, bankers, merchants; interviews with newspapers.

Naka came in to call Dean to the telephone and she came back in a moment, looking rather rueful. "It was Hester McGlurk. She wants me to go to her office tomorrow and have a talk with her."

"The Pro-hi? An old Antisaloon bird? You tell her," Donald counseled cheerfully, "to take a run and jump on herself."

"Out for that line, Don," Rick shook his head.

"You weren't there when Henry Flint was talking about it. 'It isn't a question of whether you're wet or dry,' says Henry. 'It's a question of whether you're going to make the race. Unless you're bone-dry, there's no use even weighing in!'"

"I can't figure it all," Coburn said. "I don't know anybody, with the possible exception of Hester herself, who doesn't have what he wants when he wants it but—"

"But when it comes to an issue, the county is dry as dust, five to one!" the candidate for senatorial honors cut in sharply. "It's absurd and inconsistent but it's a fact to be faced. I don't understand the psychology of it."

"Here comes a telegram for the candidate!" Coburn announced. He took the message at the door and Dean tore it open and read it.

"Listen to this, family! It's from San Francisco and it's signed Belinda Buell, and—"

"Of course, Thee, there aren't any names, really, like Hester McGlurk and Belinda Buell," Hilda drawled from the couch. "She makes 'em up as she goes along."

"—and she says," Dean went on, "'Don't sign up for publicity until you have seen me stop coming two-fifty train tomorrow Friday.'"

"Well, that's easy," Don yawned. "Fair enough. Till you've seen her stop coming. Wire her as follows: 'Yours of the 18th ult. received, and contents noted and in reply would say stop so's your old man!'"

But the girl from Philadelphia saw that Doria Dean Yale stood with the yellow slip in her fingers, her back to her bantering clan, staring gravely out into the gathering dusk,"I believe she *is* scared," the bride [of Coburn Yale] reflected.

Henry Flint and the Colonel failed to see any comedy in the advances of Hester McGlurk and Belinda Buell, and insisted that both be taken very seriously.

"No two women, I should say," Flint stated, "can do as much for—or against—you."

"Henry's right, Deanie. Old Hester's the Carrie Nation of the county. If she's for you, the Drys are for you, solid, and if she comes out against you we'll have the deuce of a time putting you over. You go see her, Deanie, like a nice girl, anytime and anywhere she says. You tell her—"

"I shall tell her the truth, Uncle Joe. I shall—"

"Of course, of course," the veteran from Ohio said soothingly, "but as tactfully as possible, Miss Yale. Tactful and frank, that's the combination for Mrs. McGlurk, eh, Colonel?"

"Yeah," Uncle Joe admitted cautiously, "but easy on the tact and bear down on the straight-from-the-shoulder stuff, is my guess. She didn't drop off last year's Christmas tree. Can't put anything over on her. But at that, she's a good old scout. You'll make a hit with her allright, Deanie."

"But this other woman, the Belinda person?" The candidate registered distaste.

"See her by all means," Flint urged.

"Lord, yes," Uncle Joe contributed. "I've known Belinda since she was knee-high to a hydrant, and that's quite a piece out of the calendar, I'll say!"

"But—good heavens—Uncle Joe, Mr. Flint! I don't want a publicity writer! There'll be enough—too much—publicity in any case, and I certainly don't want it manufactured!" Dean was emphatic.

"Well, I'm not suggesting that we retain her on salary," the Ohioan said hastily. "That would not be necessary or advisable. But it is decidedly necessary to know her, and to—

to register with her: to make the right impression. With a person of her sort, publicity exudes. With her good will, she can be of tremendous service to us even in the most casual mentionings."

She left her two counselors in the Colonel's office and drove herself to call on Mrs. Hester McGlurk.

Mrs. McGlurk was a familiar figure to her by name, in print and by word of mouth, but she had never happened to meet her, in spite of their joint public activities. She ran more slowly, looking for numbers. This must be the place; a frowsy lawn, a mangy, ungroomed palm towering before the house, shutting out the sun. Perfect! She stopped the car.

She was annoyed, and amused to note that she was annoyed, to find that the reformer lived in the one modern and prosperous-looking place in the neighborhood—a bungalow of creamy plaster with an apron of brilliant green grass, and little beds and window boxes of bright flowers. A hysterical fox-terrier, milkily clean, tore down the walk to meet her and went with her to the door.

It opened before she rang, and a large woman in rosy gingham almost filled up the aperture. "Hello!" she said happily. "On time, aren't you? You don't know me, but I know you, Doria Dean Yale, you and your pretty name! Come right in! How'd you like to be Hester McGlurk?" She gave a deep rumbling chuckle. "'Pester,' that's what some of 'em call me, and I guess I do. Sit down. Now, Bootsie (that's short for Bootlegger. My bad children named him!), don't jump up on the company! Like dogs? He always knows." It was a gay, high-colored room with a lived-in look. "He minds about as my children do! Sit there, where I can look at you, my dear."

She pushed Dean briskly into a very comfortable chair where her face would be in the light. "There!" She studied her frankly. "Yes! You're even nicer at close range than you are across a hall. I'm pretty happy about this thing, Dean Yale! I've watched you for years, and I think you're the leaven that's going to leaven the lump for us up at Sacramento."

Mrs. McGlurk herself had taken the largest of all the chairs and was filling it snugly. She consulted a watch which looked like a young alarm clock, strapped to her thick pink wrist. "I've got just ten minutes, but two'll do me for what I've got to say." She smiled at her confidently.

Dean, a little bewildered by the size and speed of the Anti-saloon League lady, marshaled her quietly defiant remarks and began mentally to rearrange and modify them: they need not, it appeared, be quite so truculent. She began to speak in her pleasant, richly cadenced voice, but her hostess held up a plump hand.

"I'll wager I know just exactly what you're going to say! You come from a family of very sincere drinkers!" She twinkled apologetically. "I pick up a lot of slangy talk from the young ones. I knew your father; George Yale drank what and when he liked, but he was a fine man. You're the image of him, aren't you? I hope you've got his grit! And your brothers—well, I expect they're no worse and no better than lots of other nice boys in this county. And you—say, wait a minute!" She consulted the mammoth watch again. "I'm not going to have time for lunch, and you probably won't either! Wait a shake!" She got up out of her chair, left the room with heavy swiftness and came back very quickly with a tray. "Gingerbread, just out of the oven, and milk. Say, wouldn't that be a publicity picture for your life? 'Senatorial candidate, accused of being a Wet, drinks milk with Hester McGlurk!'" She heaved with mirth. "Well, now I think you were going to tell me that you think prohibition, as is, is pretty foolish and futile, but if you run on a dry ticket you're going to *be* dry while you're in politics! Wasn't that about it? Take another piece, they're little!"

"That is, in substance, exactly what I was going to say, Mrs. McGlurk. You evidently know how my family stands in this matter and I myself, while I—"

"While you've never been in the gutter," the other chuckled, "you do honestly think it helps a dinner along. Well, I guess it does, sure enough. If that was all—" For the first time the watcher saw a sudden tensity in the round merry face, a quick contraction of the light hazel eyes. "Well, now you eat another hunk of gingerbread and drink up your milk while I get on my hat—it's parent-teachers meeting, and I'm not going to be late if I have to run all the way. The rushing 'round I do, wouldn't

you think it'd reduce me? But say, I thrive on it like a tonic!"
She came back presently with a long cloak over her gingham
dress and a stern helmet-like hat on her head.

At the door Dean paused. The interview had not gone according to form at all. "I am amazed that you don't want to
ask me anything, to have me promise—"

Mrs. McGlurk gave her deep comfortable chuckle. "Land,
child, I think more of people than I do of promises!" She put
her hands on the young woman's shoulders and gave her a
slight intimate shake. "You don't have to tell me what you'll
do when I can read, like coarse print, what you *are*. You just
run and play with your blue dishes, and if anybody asks you,
you say you're Hester McGlurk's favorite senator."

"But I should like to ask you one question, then." Dean was
a little sharp about it. The calm assumptions of the great pink
creature! "Do you honestly think you're getting anywhere with
this prohibition business—with bootlegging and rum-running,
with bribery and corruption everywhere and your own agents
failing you every day? Do you think even in the future, that
you're going to succeed?"

"*I'm* not! No. Not me. Not Hester McGlurk. But what does
that matter." Again that curious look, the tensity, the narrowing of the eyes, the distant gaze. "Somebody will. Some day."

Dean found the large lady, for all her blind and stubborn
believing, oddly pathetic and appealing. "That's a stunning
spirit, of course, but look about you! Listen to people! Read
the paper! Consider—"

"Wait a minute! I guess you can see Mount Tamalpais from
your ranch, can't you?"

"On clear days, yes."

"Well, then, in hazy weather do you say it isn't there, just
because you can't see it? There's a lot of haze and fog on the
landscape, first and last, but it's never melted any mountains
that I know of! . . . I must run!" She leaned down swiftly, took
the candidate's face between her hands and dropped a quick
kiss on her forehead. "God bless you! And watch out, will
you, that Bootlegger doesn't follow your car?"

When Dean met the publicity woman, later in the day,

she learned that she had already been interviewed by Uncle
Joe Dobie and Henry Flint. Miss Buell was frankly disappointed at not landing a definite job, but entirely good-humored
about it.

"I think you're overlooking a bet, dearie, but it's your funeral. And it's a darn sight more apt to *be* your funeral, too,
without my distinguished services." She was in sharp contrast
to the reformer, thin to the point of emaciation where the
other was opulently plump, haggard instead of rosy, saggingly
weary rather than brisk. "I'm a dying woman," she apologized
for the rending yawn which escaped her. "Lot of nice morgue
stuff at three this morning. Well, coming down on the train I
doped out hot stuff for you—a series, short and snappy—
domestic stuff, sob stuff. Say, it's a crime to miss it! At that,"
she admitted, rueful, honest. "I'll probably run some of it anyway, just because it'll be darn good reading."

Dean had driven her to Yale Acres, and they were sitting
now before the big fireplace, and Naka [the family servant]
brought in a tray. "You take tea, Miss Buell?"

"I can. I have," she sighed. "But the way I'm feeling now—I
suppose you haven't got a drink on the premises?"

"Miss Buell, I had an interview with the head of the Anti-
saloon League this morning, and—"

"Check!" said Belinda Buell. "I got you. But she isn't hiding
anywhere around here now, is she? Sweet Patootie! You mean
it, don't you? Pure as the heart of a lily. Well, I'm for that. It'll
make you good copy too." She leaned back very limply with
such an air of battered exhaustion that Dean was alarmed.

"I'm afraid you're frightfully tired!"

"I was born tired . . . and I've never had a chance to get
rested. But there's zip in me yet, let me tell you, and when you
need something in the line of limelight . . . you ask your uncle.
He'll tell you. I know my canned goods!"

She looked, indeed, as if she knew everything and had known
it always.

Dean took her to the train and as she turned from seeing
her aboard she found herself facing Kenneth Conway. "Well,
Ken," she said gayly, "greetings! I've just been seeing off the

publicity woman I'm not engaging. But she's delicious! I wish you'd come in time to meet her, but you'll have other chances, because—"

"No, I won't have any other chances," said young Conway thickly, "because I'm going away tomorrow."

"Ken! Where? And for how long?"

"Just as far as I can go and forever, I hope!" He had been drinking, she saw. His candid blue eyes were bloodshot and his high-colored face even ruddier than usual. "Who wants to know?"

Dean slipped an arm through his and walked him toward her car. "Get in and come home to supper with us, Ken, and let's talk this thing over. Why, the boys are counting on your working with them in the campaign, and so am I, of course. Surely you'll be back in time?"

"Yeah, I'll be back in time to vote for you for President," he gulped, furrily ironic. "I'm going to Africa, that's where I'm going, to shoot lions with a bow and arrow, with those birds that wrote the book."

"But—Ken *dear,* you don't know how!" Dean wailed.

"So much the better, then. Less chance of having to come home." He jerked his arm away.

"Look here, Kenneth, you're being absurd," she said sharply. "I'm counting on you, as I'm counting on all my best friends, to stand by me and help me in my fight."

"Yeah? Say, listen, Deanie, you know what this thing means to me. Well, I'd be doing myself a good turn, wouldn't I, helping to put you in the Senate. Out! When they're going to hang a feller, they can't ask him to tie the rope himself!" He swallowed hard, winking. "Oh, Deanie, *Deanie,* I—" In the soft winter dusk, scantily screened by her car, he caught her in a crushing embrace. "Deanie, give up this fool thing and marry me!"

With a good deal of guile she got him into her little machine, leaving his own at the station, and drove him to Yale Acres where Don took capable and matter-of-fact charge of him.

Her campaign, in its earlier stages, was very calm and comfortable, and she surprised herself by enjoying it keenly. It was a heartening thing to be liked! The opposition candidate was an obscure little rancher, negligible as a personality, and the principles of his party were not acceptable to the solid rank and file of the community. He was an earnest inarticulate creature, and Dean, who was a facile speaker, had him at a cruel disadvantage in debate.

She was wholesomely aware of the fact that much of her strength was in her opponent's weakness; nevertheless there was deep satisfaction in the discovery of how amazingly many friends she had.

Dean and her brother Rickford sat on the porch at Yale Acres on a mild and moonlit night of midsummer, checking up on their joint activities.

"Uncle Joe and the Chief seem to feel things are running nicely," she told him. Henry Flint, managing her, had been labeled Chief.

"Yeah. Just got to keep riding your fences." He nodded his big blond head. "Doing clubs this week?"

"Yes, funny little ones 'way off in the country."

"Get a great kick out of 'em, don't you?" he grinned sympathetically.

"Oh, I do! Much more than the sleek town clubs. These lean, workworn, sun-burned ranch women! Their eyes shine, even if their noses do too, and their fingernails don't! If you get me!"

He got her, Rick said.

"And keen and eager! 'Atlantic Monthlies' under their arms, and what do I think of 'The Peasants'? I don't know; they've got something which the city clubs miss. I suppose it's because they don't see so much that—"

"That they see more?"

"Yes! I lunched with a tiny brand-new one today, high in the mountains above Alma—wicked road. 'The Women's Improvement Club of Eucalyptus Point.' Seven members. Isn't that priceless? And the president, Mrs. T. Lulie Jessop—Rick, I wish you could see her!"

"Yeah."

"Oh, not funny! Pitiful. But not that exactly, either; sunburned to a crisp, fingers worked to the bone, thin as a paper doll—and her clothes! I nearly cried when I looked at her hat, and her hair that she bobbed herself. But—*valiant!* That's the word for it. Planning on Stanford for her children already. She's the poorest and most cumbered of all the women, but she leads them. 'Married to kind of a twil-dozzle,' one of them told me, 'and there's one of the children that isn't quite right.' She added that she thought it took after its papa who didn't have any more sense than the law allowed. I sent her some books today."

"Snappy work," Rick approved. "We figured there are thirty-five or forty votes up there. Bet Lulie'll get 'em all out for you!"

"She's promised. And Rick, it's incredible the way Hester McGlurk is signing up the Drys for me."

He chuckled. "Lucky she isn't wise to old Ken!"

Kenneth Conway, after a riotous fortnight, had carried out his dramatic intention and set forth with the doctor and novelist who were going to Africa to shoot big game with bow and arrow.

Her face clouded. "I've been miserable about him, Rick."

"Needn't be. Fine trip for him. Make a man of him. I hear a car," Rick listened. "Don, I guess."

There was a strong shaft of moonlight across the porch and Dean clearly saw her youngest brother's expression as he left his car and came toward them."Don! What is it?"

"There's a monkey wrench in the works, allright! Just came from Uncle Joe's, and the Chief was there, and they're wild-eyed. What do you suppose? Old Doc' Howard is back in the race!"

"Don!"

"Yeah. Isn't that a hot one? Dr. William Hanson Howard, who has served his county so efficiently for three terms," said Don, in the tone of one reading from a newspaper, "announces that he is again a candidate for senatorial honors in the twenty-seventh district!"

"Well, the old son-of-a-gun!" Rick exploded.

Dean was astounded. "But, Don, I don't understand it!"

"Yeah. You 'n' me both," he said grimly. "Likewise the Colonel and Uncle Joe."

"How do they figure it, Don?"

"They don't figure it."

"Well, what's his alibi? How does he explain himself?"

"It's a scream. He's giving a statement to both papers for tomorrow, and one of the boys let Uncle Joe in on it. He regrets extremely having to oppose his young friend, Miss Doria D. Yale, but this is a matter of principle with him. He does not honestly believe that a woman can adequately represent this great district of Sacramento."

"Well, I'll be darned!" Rick knocked out his pipe against the porch rail and stood up.

"Don, do Uncle Joe and the Chief think it is very serious?" Dean moved closer to him.

"You're darn right they do! It'll split the vote, you see, three ways."

"But surely, the people who've practically pledged themselves to me—"

"Oh, they'll probably stick, but there'll be a lot who aren't sold on you especially who'll flop, and a great many, Uncle Joe says, who'll figure that the old boy, after his faithful service, ought to have it again if he wants it!"

There was a moment of silence and then Dean said briskly, "Well, anyhow it's going to be a fight, after all! I'm not sure that I don't welcome it! It was almost too easy before, wasn't it?"

"Well, it won't be too easy now, let me tell you." Don was grim about it. "Of course, we're going to make the grade, but, believe me, we've got to ramble!"

His sister went resolutely into the house and they followed.

. . . .

The Colonel and Henry Flint unlimbered their heavy artillery and went into action. Dean was set Herculean tasks in the way of visiting the outlying towns and talking at shops and canneries and factories and clubs. There would be small fine lines about her mouth when she looked into her mirror late at night, and her fingers were lame with the hearty handshaking of the proletariat.

Her managers admitted that it was difficult to tell just how things were going. There were those who expressed themselves with consoling vehemence about the old senator's sudden flop, but there were others, an alarming number of them, who said, "Well, now, I'll tell you! I would 'a' voted for her in a minute. But here's the old Doc' that's given us the best years of his life, you might say, and look at the things you can put your finger on—!"

Dr. William Hanson Howard himself called upon his young opponent at her mother's home and was very regretful and tender about it: the flower of chivalry.

Reporting on the interview to her managers, Dean sighed in exasperation. "The most muddle-headed, mid-Victorian old reactionary in the world today! And the amazing thing is that he's forcing himself to do it! I believe he honestly thinks he's a martyr to the public good! I've thought and thought of it, and I've come to the conclusion that the old doctor's the type that's devoted to the ladies—'the ladies, God Bless 'em!'—but has very little use for women, or belief in them.

"Guess you got his number, all right, Deanie," the Colonel agreed gloomily, but the veteran Ohio politician shook his head.

"No. The doctor didn't arrive at his conclusion alone and unaided. He's been—manipulated. Oh, he's sincere enough about it; no doubt about that! He believes absolutely that he's the lamb of the sacrifice, dragging his tired old carcass up to the capitol again to save the county. He's been very cleverly managed, so cleverly that he doesn't suspect he *has* been managed!"

Dean stared. "But—who, Mr. Flint? I can't imagine—"

"Ah, that I can't tell you yet, my dear young lady. But there's someone—somewhere—who regards you as a disaster to his private plans."

Her face flushed suddenly, hotly, and a tingle of excitement ran over her like a contact with electricity. She was regarded as dangerous, then!

....

The last days of the campaign ran over with meetings and speakings, drives to the outlying limits of her district, interviews, long sessions with the Colonel and Henry Flint, with Hester McGlurk and Belinda Buell, for the publicity woman had come down from San Francisco from sheer inability to keep out of the mess, she stated, and was—in her own graphic diction—"shooting a lot of hot stuff."

The large pink reformer was as disturbed as Dean had ever seen her. Small, malicious rumors were slipping into camp as slyly as little snakes, and as difficult to catch. People on whose support of her candidate she had counted absolutely were avoiding her eye and saying, "Well, but what *I* hear—I guess Dean Yale's not so dry as she might be!" "I don't know how much stock you can take in her being dry. Why, look at the way her folks are, the way she's been raised!" And once, even, "They say she's been keeping company for years with a young feller from up the peninsula somewhere that's just a typical society souse!"

All the Yales foregathered at Yale Acres on the eve of the election, the little Quakeress pale with loyal concern, Hilda, whose hour was hard upon her, chaffing her gallantly, Coburn and Rickford and Donald scrambling eggs and annoying their tearful mother, holding high carnival, with, Dean knew, anxious hearts.

It was more than midnight before she went to her sleeping porch, and Beaver King, chief of the Chesapeake Bays, sat beside her, his chin pressed hard on the edge of her bed, his tail making a soft swishing sound on the floor. As on the night of the Colonel's dinner, she was thankful for his quiet comradeship, and kept a hand on the round dome of his forehead.

She must sleep. Tomorrow would be difficult. And tomorrow night at this time she would be, in effect, state senator for the twenty-seventh district, or she would be that nice Yale girl who was beaten by old Doc' Howard. Well, whichever way. . . . She gave a final good-night pat to Beaver King and resolutely laid herself down.

Election day was the hottest of the year. The first break against them, Uncle Joe admitted. Made it harder to get out the quiet, homekeeping vote, old ladies, cumbered women who "felt the heat," fat men who thought they'd wait till the sun went down and waited too long.

The Yale Acre clan, even to the long-cloaked Hilda, went

"Motion was music; music was motion. It would be the perfect way to go to heaven (if any)—on horseback." Illustration by Harold Von Schmidt. From "Call of the House," *Woman's Home Companion* 53, no. 22 (December 1926), p. 23.

early to the polls, driving along the orchard roads through the sweet and languid air.

For all the times she had driven up to this shabby old ranch house and gone into the dining-room and living-room, thrown together and set with tiny booths, and nodded to the neighbors who sat about the long table calling off names and numbers, there was a thrilling zest of the thing! The other voters, disappearing into their little tents and coming out presently with folded ballots and blank faces—where had they put the little potent cross? She placed her own opposite her name with a firm pressure; it stood out blackly.

DEAN YALE..X

That afternoon with seven or eight dogs streaming after or racing on before, tearing up impossible banks and plunging down vertical canyon walls, she rode Zancudo beyond and above the roads and the houses and the orchards, into the wild country she loved. Well, there would be riding left at any rate—horses and hills and dogs, the scorching sun and the benediction of shade!

There was a telephone call waiting for her when she came back. Everything seemed to be going nicely, her uncle Joe thought. Vote was a little slow . . . too darn hot to hurry 'em. She was to go for old Señora Alvarez and four or five of her kinswomen who had weakened under the thermometer.

A cold shower and the freshness of orange linen, and she was tooling the big family car along the road to San Jose, between the orchards with their little armies of prune pickers on their knees beneath the trees.

It was jolly to pass machines, every few minutes, with big flapping banners which read—

YALE

and whose occupants honked their horns hearteningly or waved to her as they went by.

....

Rickford was waiting for her at Yale Acres. There were one or two more jobs for her. Things were not going too well in San Jose. The word was good from Gilroy, so far, and Morgan Hill, and someone had brought the news that T. Lulie Jessop with her battered car was dragging the mountains for voters. But San Jose was another story. The old Doc' was running awfully strong, and even Dibble was surprising them. And the little snaky rumors were crawling again—she wasn't so *dry* as they made out—and—in the ward where it would do the most harm— "Some say she's awful strong for the Ku Klux. Yeah! Two of her brothers, a feller told me—"

But nothing could dim her high confidence.

"It's all right, Rick! I mean—it's miserable, of course—but it won't beat me! You'll see! Where do I go now? Got a list for me? Oh, only two! That's easy. How's Uncle Joe standing it?"

She threw her hat aside and smoothed her dark bob, and sat hungrily down at the table. "I'm famished, Miss Ella. I hope you didn't count on my being too excited to eat? Oh, by the way, Rick, I met Beverley Blair this morning—he was waiting for a stage right by the Alvarez house." (The dear old thing's face contracted swiftly, his eyes narrowing, his color mounting. Quick! To make him comfortable—) "He looks very seedy, poor old chap; been ill a lot, he said. Digestion all shot to pieces. I told him he must come to dinner soon and bring Cyril. Cyril's seventeen! Imagine it! Well, Beverley must look more like his grandfather than his father. Must be hideous to be sick, mustn't it? Miss Ella darling, I want twice as much as you're giving me! Aren't perfect lady politicians supposed to crave nourishment on election day?"

They all drove into San Jose after supper. Miss Ella, Miss Ada, and Hilda stayed in the car, parked so they could watch the bulletin board, and Dean with her brothers and Mrs. Coburn went on foot among the crowds.

She rather enjoyed being recognized. A nudge, a mumbled word, someone turning round to look at her. "She . . . right in back of you. . . with the white felt hat . . . that's *her!*"

She always smiled and nodded when she could catch their eyes and sometimes they looked a little sheepish, and she was sure they had voted against her, but often they were pleased and friendly and had something encouraging to say.

They went up to the newspaper office and received other returns from a sympathetic young gentleman with a green shade over his eyes. He was not very sanguine, it was clear, but when they came down to the street again there was a heartening report on the bulletin board. Los Gatos, which was the nearest town to Yale Acres, had gone over loyally, royally, for its neighbor. Never in its history had it polled such a vote. That alone, Dean told herself, was an enormous satisfaction. That would take the sting out of a possible defeat. By eleven o'clock she was admitting the possibility of a defeat. The high mood of the morning was wearing a little thin. The remembrance of her freedom from the old silly, cloying romance of her girlhood recurred very often, but the exaltation wasn't quite proof against the determined cheer of her brothers, and the frankly anxious faces of Uncle Joe Dobie and the Chief.

"Oh, blast the old Doc'!" the Colonel cursed feelingly, reading an especially disastrous bulletin.

Someone was honking a horn sharply and insistently—a thin, hoarse horn, and Dean stood still and inspected the machines parked closely along the curb. "Oh, Mrs. Jessop!" she cried gladly, hurrying over to a dust-coated, dented car. "I had no idea—"

"Excuse me for honking at you that way," said T. Lulie, getting nimbly out of her conveyance, "but I was so scared you'd get away in the crowd before I could catch you! Well, I want to tell you that The Women's Improvement Club of Eucalyptus Point went for you, solid! Old Lady Meeks, she was sick-a-bed with the pleurisy, but we just bundled her up in her blankets and put her in my car, and took her! Did her good." The mountain woman was hollow-eyed and haggard with weariness, and her sharply modeled face was grimed where sweat had cut crooked waterways through the dust. "Well, you tell that Mr. Flint—oh, there he is! I didn't see him. Mr. Flint, you said there would be thirty-seven votes up there, and I'm here to tell you I got thirty-six of 'em down to the polls!"

"Great work!" said the Chief, his wooden lips slipping into a smile. "If we'd had a few more like you, madam—"

"I should like to ask," Donald inquired respectfully, "how the other one got away?"

"Died yesterday," said T. Lulie shortly. She raked the bulletin board with bright, feverish eyes. "They haven't put our returns on yet."

Dean looked from the woman to her car. All day long, a broiling day, she had propelled her battered car, her battered self, up and down the difficult mountain roads, dragging indifferent citizens down to vote for her friend. It made her eyes sting.

"Look here," Dean leaned closer to her, "have you had your dinner?"

"Well, not exactly what you'd call dinner, I suppose, but" —she jerked her head toward the corner— "I got me a sack of that awfully good popcorn to take home to the children and I ate some of it."

"And lunch? Did you eat at noon?"

"Oh my *yes!* I had a snack in the car. I put myself up a good big lot of sandwiches, knowing I'd have a big day, and that fool houn' pup of ours, he jumped in, without my seeing him—but there was one that he hadn't touched, really—" She broke off, embarrassed at what she saw in the other woman's face.

"I was just going to have a hot oyster stew," said the candidate, chattily. "We are a family of very sincere eaters, the Yales. I expect we're all going to have something, aren't we, people?"

The Colonel and the Chief elected to stay on the street, and Coburn and his bride stayed with them, but the rest turned into a bright little restaurant and ordered lavishly.

T. Lulie looked round the garish, tawdry little place with wide, impressed eyes. "Of course, I know that too much of it is demoralizing," she said sedately, "but this night life certainly does stimulate a person!"

The Colonel came puffing in, looking like a big abused child. "They won't flash any more on the bulletin board. Come on over to the courthouse!"

They tried to say good night to the mountain woman, reminding her of all the miles, both level and almost perpendicular, which lay between her and home, but she shook her head. The food had revived her, and she was giddily set upon making a night of it. Her bright eyes rested very frankly upon Mr. Rick. "And I guess if this young lady can stick it out—"

She followed them closely in her jangling little old car, parked it briskly, and went up into the great room where the counting was going on—calm, dispassionate counting . . . when it mattered so!"

....

The Chief was of the cautious opinion that they could hardly be sure until morning. There were two or three precincts which would not be in until then. To be sure, they were precincts pretty apt to go their way, but nevertheless— He followed the Colonel, list in hand.

"Well, look what spring has brought us!" chortled Don.

Belinda Buell was charging breathlessly across the wide room. "Just this minute got here—midnight stage. Rotten lunch—planned to be here all day. I adore murders, but they always come when I'm so busy! If we could have a few more dependable murderers, working on schedule—Hello, lambie!" She gave Dean a hug. "How come? Say, listen, I've been getting your news by phone, but wait till you get *mine!*"

"What is it?"

"*Listen!* I'm on the trail of the fox that pepped the old Doc' up to run again!"

"The deuce you are!"

Don and Coburn gave her instant attention, and Henry Flint and the Colonel were listening.

"It was a very slick piece of work, all right. This guy didn't appear himself at all, but for two weeks he had it all doped out so that every day a different person came to the old boy and gave him a spiel, and of course the poor old boob fell for it, like a thousand of brick!"

"I suspected as much," Henry Flint conceded. "It's a San Francisco job, then."

"Yeah," said the Colonel. "The gang didn't want to risk her. Those women in the Assembly have got 'em scared on moral issues and—"

The Chief nodded sapiently. "I had already arrived at the

conclusion myself, Miss Buell, that the thing was a professional manipulation. The Big Boss. Sheriff Rooney—"

"Big Boss Sheriff Rooney your eye!" said the publicity woman rudely. "He was for it, naturally, but he wasn't the main squeeze!"

"Well, who was it then, Belinda?" Uncle Joe leaned nearer.

"Say, listen! I didn't say I had him, did I? I said I was on his trail, and I am, but I can't give you his name and address tonight! He's—there's something funny about him. Lotta fellers talk about him, but nobody claims to *know* him. Lives up north, somewhere, and owns about half of this end of California, they say. Keeps out of sight, and pulls the strings, and—believe *me*—they dance!"

Dean Yale felt again the tingle of excitement running over her, head to heel, like electricity. It made her feel important and potent and dangerous—this knowledge that someone, somewhere, considered her a menace.

"Oh, you aren't listening!" cried little Mrs. Coburn. "The last report—the one those people just brought—it was four for Dibble and seven for Howard and forty-eight for you, Dean!"

And Dr. William Hanson Howard himself was coming toward her, walking a little unsteadily, his eyes bloodshot, his face gray with fatigue. He held out his hand. "My dear young lady, I think you have beaten me."

She took his chilly fingers in a warm and hearty young clasp. "Well, Doctor, I hope I have, but you've given me a terrific battle! And I think it's too soon to be certain."

He shook his head. "No. You've beaten me. Well, I'm a sick man, and I'm tired. It was only because I was over-persuaded. . . . I hope you believe that, my dear." Again he looked bewildered, hurt.

"I do believe it!" She took a step after him. "And if I have—I'll be coming to you often, for help and advice!"

She turned back to the others with very bright eyes. "Heavens, that's pitiful! It was a cruel thing to make him—" she broke off and looked round the circle. "Where's Rick? Where's Hilda?"

"Hospital," Don grinned. "Half an hour ago. Didn't want

you to know. We'll stop by on our way home and see if there's any news. Hil said you weren't to worry, that this was exactly the way she planned it! Old Rick was kind of up in the air."

The returns were all in for the night. Dean Yale, candidate for state senator from the twenty-seventh district, had a lead of a little over a hundred votes and there were three friendly precincts yet to hear from. They said good night to the faithful few who had lingered, and took cordial farewells of Mrs. T. Lulie Jessop, who refused an invitation to stay the night— what was left of it—at Yale Acres, and drove Belinda Buell to her hotel before they went to the hospital.

Rickford, pale and furious, came down to see them. "Of all the blooming smart aleck tricks!" he raged. "Says only one thing would have pleased her better, and that would be to have it born right under the bulletin board to annoy Miss Ella and Miss Ada!"

"But, Rick" —Dean put a comforting hand on his arm—" how is she?"

"Oh, they say she's perfectly all right! Couldn't be better!" he grudged it, plainly feeling that she wasn't getting her deserts.

"And says if it's a girl she's going to name it T. Lulie!"

Dean was determined to stay. Hilda had stood by her and she was going to stand by Hilda. The brothers thought she ought to go home, after her hectic day, but she said they were only thinking of scrambling eggs, which could be done quite nicely without her. Even Rick sided against her, and they sat down to talk it over, and while they were arguing a smiling nurse came down to say that Mrs. Yale sent her compliments and said they might all go home. She didn't need their company, for she had her daughter, Miss Doria Dean Yale II.

AMY BROOKS

Mary Synon

UNDER the smoke pall of the lower West Side lie those streets of eternal twilight which Amy Brooks used to tramp while she studied and worked, fought, lied, and cajoled her way through that small and slightly discredited college where she won the right to put M.D. after her name.

Dun and dreary thoroughfares they are now, shadowed by the imperceptible, impenetrable veil of discouraged souls no less than by the fog of wintry weather. Even on the days when prairie sunshine pours down in molten splendor upon Chicago, the neighborhood just beyond the river catches only enough of the Danäite shower to thicken its grayness of aspect. The gold filters into pale patina on wide-spread ramparts of great hospitals and medical colleges, of Presbyterian and Cook County, of Rush, of Physicians and Surgeons, on dozens of smaller institutions clustered around them, on thousands of shabby houses marked by signs of "Furnished Rooms," and leave so little of its glow that, even in the sunset which thrills the city to flame, the district gives back but feeble flickerings of radiance.

Strangely, though, it stays a land of youth, a *Quartier Latin*

From *Good Housekeeping* 84, no. 3 (March 1927).

of a western world, its gloomy streets ever worn by the restless feet of those who seek the city's guerdons of fame and fortune, its run-down houses shelter for boys and girls ready and willing to battle for their dreams. Perhaps to those crusaders of a later generation's freedom the neighborhood is as brave an Agincourt as it used to be to Amy Brooks and myself when we sought the meanings of life, and love, and death and eternity under the grim palisades of the County Hospital, although it seems duller and more dismal now than it did when we dwelt within it in the poignant days of our own twenties. Places change less than do people, after all.

Amy Brooks was in her last year at the Lister Medical College when I chanced to meet her in the way I met so many of the city's figures of drama, high and low, in the course of a news story upon which I had been sent by the newspaper where I did almost every odd job but society and scrubbing. She herself was not the story's chief actor, but she was its stage director, for she was handling publicity for the college in payment of her tuition, and it is likely that I would have passed out of her ken without much further thought of her had it not been for her extraordinary gift of human sympathy. I was miserably unhappy then, for my mother had just died, and I was wretchedly in love with a man whom I couldn't marry, but I certainly had no intention of confession when I went into the forbidding office of the Lister. Before I came out, however, I had not only swallowed, hook, line, and sinker, the tale she had faked to get mention of the college upon the front page, but I had also told her something of my own, and counted Amy Brooks as my friend.

I saw her often, not only because she fed stories, true, half-true, or not true at all, to the grist-mill of a saffron-hued daily, but also because I lived in the neighborhood of the college, and she fell into the habit of picking me up when she needed companionship—or more probably, when she thought I needed it.

Outside the hours of my own work I went with her through the postgraduate of a liberal education, to clinics at Rush, to court hearings at the Psychopathic, to lectures at P. and S., to open forums at the Mary Thompson, to operations under the vast skylight of the County. I glimpsed the vision of what this group of scientists, some of them famous, some of them obscure, were trying to do for the city and the world. I saw, too, the struggle of the women within the profession, fighting to win and to hold every inch of recognition. They were, with the exception of Amy, continuously earnest, pathetically imbued with the sense of their own responsibility. Amy, however, free-lanced into wider fields than did they. I followed her into Maxwell Street burrows and into back rooms of wine shops in Little Italy. I dined with her in German restaurants on Milwaukee Avenue and in Greek *kapheneia* on Blue Island, breakfasted with her in Syrian coffee shops on Sherman Street, and supped at any night-owl stand which happened to be open when she had ended her apparently leisurely but always definitely motivated pilgrimages. I have seen her bargain with Jew, or Italian, or Armenian for an hour over a matter of ten cents, chuckling with joy at any petty triumph she could secure by haggling, then stay up all night to tend a sick woman or give her last dollar to a hungry child.

The bond between us was our love of the city, but I realized even then that hers was a broader, bigger emotion than was mine. In those days I loved Chicago for its spreading panorama, for the thrill of its power, the vision of its future, the drama of its stories. Amy Brooks loved Chicago for its poor. Her profession was to her, I believe, merely a means to the end of giving service to those who needed it most. That was why, with all her temperamental laziness, all her disinclination to be associated with causes, she counted the cost of struggle not at all when the reward of it came with the ability to help others.

"I'll never make any money with my pill peddling," she told me one night, "but I'll get a whale of a lot of fun out of it."

She was amazingly equipped for her work, with a physical endurance which never failed her, and a shrewdness which saw around corners in everything but her own sentimental affairs. Even by the stretch of kindly recollection she could not be accounted beautiful but she had two assets of lasting charm, the quality of understanding, and a speaking voice with the timbre of Bernhardt's, the sadness of Duse's, and the lilt of Marlowe's. Women liked her without effort on her part, but I never saw either a man who sought her if she failed to notice him or a man who resisted her if she chose to attract him. That was why I did not believe her when she told me that Mark Preston had come to love her against his will and her own.

"You worked for him," I accused her.

"I didn't, truly," she protested. "He was the lawyer for that awful Camiardi, trying to get the children away from that poor woman, and I hated him so that I'd have scratched him if he'd won that case."

"You saw that he didn't."

"Yes, and then he called me at the college and said that he had to see me. I thought it was something about the children, and I let him come. Now I can't lose him."

"Amy!"

"It's true, and the joke of it is that he doesn't really want to love me any more than I want him to."

It was certainly true, as far as outward appearance went, that Preston was the victim of an unreciprocated passion for Amy. He was a young lawyer, struggling, ambitious, taking his ambulance chasing with deadly seriousness, haunting court rooms with biographies of Marshall, or Lincoln, or some other American legal statesman under his arm, apparently to give an impression that his study of them somehow lifted him into their class. He scorned nothing, however, which promised him advancement, and it was as sure as any such prophecy can be that he was going to be a successful attorney, if not a great one. The only surprise about him was his infatuation for Amy, and it is likely that it surprised him more than it did anyone else.

Through the few months which remained of her course at Lister he was literally under her feet, for he waited for her in the gloomy corridors of the college with dog-like tenacity, even after he came to know that she sometimes evaded him by back-door departure. He used for trailing Amy on the devious paths of her working day and sauntering night, the time he had formerly spent in study. He annoyed her at first, then amused her, and gradually she admitted him into comradeship. Together they traversed the highways and byways of her town. There wasn't a restaurant, a dance hall, a theater around the city with which they did not strike acquaintanceship.

"A lawyer's got to know the city even better than a doctor," she told him.

There was not a doubt of her ability to guide him, but he must have rebelled sometimes against her directions as well as her methods. I was with them one night when she literally yanked a girl off a dance floor and took her home to a little cottage on Sedgwick Street, miles out of our way.

"It wasn't your business," Mark told her.

"Well, I couldn't leave her with that drunken beast, could I?" she demanded.

He muttered something about calling the police, but she laughed him back into good humor.

"Mark'll be a great lawyer," she told me afterward, "if he'll ever get to see people as human beings instead of law cases."

She seemed to think that it was a definite part of her relationship with him to lead him to this knowledge, and with her ambition for him grew her desire to give him the wealth of that store of wisdom which was her own. It was the beginning, I think, of her love for him.

That love, nourished by the thousand and one springs of her easily aroused emotionalism, flourished like a green bay tree. If she was no niggard in friendship, she was a profligate in love. The devotion, the self-abnegation, the sympathy which she poured out upon Preston would have sufficed a dozen ordinary women through a dozen lifetimes. In the exaltation of her passion she forgot all those maxims of shrewdness which she had preached to me. So tremendous was the tide of her love that it periled Preston's desire for her, and had it not been for her determination to finish the work she had set out to do for herself, it is likely that she would have lost him through the very violence of her newly awakened wish to hold him.

She had made up her mind, however, to go through an internship in one of the women's hospitals before she married, and nothing Preston could say moved her from that determination.

"I'd be cheating myself and all the other women who try to

be doctors," she declared. "It's too hard to make the grade to let any one slip back before she comes to the top of the hill."

Against Preston's arguments and pleas, against even the opposition of many of the women physicians who did not like her violations of the manners of the profession, she held out for that year of intensive experience, and by sheer force of ability finally won an appointment to work in the Clara Clayton Foundation, which Doctor Anna Lebcovic's surgical skill was already making world-famous.

On the night she took her degree, Preston gave Amy hundreds of roses and an ultimatum that she must marry him the next day. He was going to Texas on a land case which might keep him away for several months, and he wanted her to go with him.

"I can't," she protested, standing among the roses in her cap and gown. "I start at the hospital next Monday."

"Don't you think I'm more important than the hospital?"

"Not more important," she countered, "than my faith in myself. I've set out to do this job, and I'd be losing something vital if I quit now."

"But what are you going to do with it all?" he protested. "You won't want a profession when you marry me."

"I don't know when I might need it."

"Don't you think I can take care of you?"

"Of course, I do," she laughed. "I wouldn't marry you at all if I didn't, but I've seen too many of the accidents of life to let any woman, even myself, go without a means of livelihood when it's within her grasp. Besides, it's something deeper than just that. I'd feel that I'd failed if I give this up, and I don't want to give you a failure for a wife."

"You're quibbling," he declared. "You want this sort of life more than you want me."

"I don't want anything in the world more than I want you," she said, "but I love you so much that I want you to have the best of me. If I went with you now, I wouldn't be giving you that. The hospital people chose me because they think that I have some quality in my work which is bigger than my faults. They turned down three other women, women much more their own sort, to pick me up. Those women have found other jobs. If I back out, it'll mean that the Foundation can't get the choice of interns it could have had a month ago. The colleges are closed, the graduates scattered. It'll mean, too, that they won't let down the bars again for a woman outside their own group. It wouldn't be honest, Mark, to quit now."

"All right," he said surlily, "but I think you're going to be as sorry as I am."

"If I am," she laughed, "I'll run after you all the way to Texas."

For all her work she missed him so much that it is possible that she might have fulfilled her promise had it not been for Dora Lytle. Amy found her, a wistful stray, in one of the wards of the Foundation and took her up in much the same way she would have cared for a sick kitten. The girl was ill and lonely and destitute. She told Amy that she had alienated her family in a little Iowa town by running away with a cheap theatrical company, and that her pride forbade her to appeal to them. Amy anathematized the absent Lytles as hard and cruel, and took upon herself the burden of Dora's care.

The girl seemed to repay her sheltering kindliness by votive gratitude, but there was in her a certain furtiveness which would never have escaped Amy had she been on guard. She was too occupied with her hospital duties and her loneliness for Preston to notice much more about the Lytle girl than her pathetic need of friendship. When Dora grew well enough to leave the institution, Amy found her a job at Lister and a room in the house where she herself had boarded before she went into Clayton. The girl was definitely established as Amy's satellite when Preston returned from Texas.

He came back exultant of his success in his task, and determined to marry Amy at once. He telephoned her as soon as he arrived in town, insisting that she dine with him that night.

It was difficult for her to leave the hospital, but she maneuvered leave for herself and met him in one of the neighborhood restaurants. She was so genuinely rejoiced over his return that he took the occasion to demand that she go with him the next day up to Waukegan, where they could be married with greater legal expedition than was possible in Cook

County. He was so eagerly boyish that she wavered from her resolve.

"If we weren't so short at the hospital, I'd do it," she said.

"Do it anyhow," he urged.

"Oh, it's such a rotten thing to leave them like this," she protested. "I couldn't take my own happiness unless I'd earned it straight."

"You have to take happiness when and where you find it," he threatened.

"I know," she said, "but do you suppose I could be really happy if I knew that I might have saved Mrs. Kozminski by staying on the job and lost her life by going with you?"

"Great heavens, you aren't physician to the universe!"

"No, but I am intern to Ward Three at the Clayton."

"Then you won't?"

"I can't."

"Then we're through."

"Don't be childish, Mark," she pleaded. "You know perfectly well that I'll marry you the last week of next June, and you know you've waited much longer than that for other things you've wanted."

"I've never wanted anything else half so much."

She leaned over the table to touch his hand, and her eyes lighted with flames of devotion. "I'll make up to you every day I make you wait," she told him.

He shrugged petulantly and lighted a cigarette, but he could not resist her voice and her smile. "You win, Amy dear," he said, but she had a curious feeling that she had lost.

Even his good-by, said at the door of the Clayton, seemed to hold a forecast of something beyond temporary farewell.

"I wish I'd told him I'd go tomorrow," she thought as she donned her uniform, but in the pressure of the night's labors she did not revert to regret, and by the next time she saw Preston both of them had apparently slipped back to their attitude of calm acceptance of the situation.

An influenza epidemic, filling rooms and wards of the hospital, kept Amy Brooks on duty sixteen hours out of every twenty-four through the next fortnight. Twice she had to break engagements with Preston. Once, when she could not reach him by telephone, she sent Dora Lytle to his office with a note of explanation. Dora, coming to Clayton the next night, waited with me more than an hour for Amy, eulogizing her so persistently that I was moved to tell her that I had known Amy even longer than had she. Then she swung into queries about Preston. She was talking of him when Amy entered the room.

"I think it's terrible that you treat poor Mr. Preston the way you do," she told her as Amy, exhausted, flung herself across the bed. "Why don't you marry him?"

"I'm going to," Amy yawned, "as soon as I finish my job here."

"In June?"

"In June, but don't expect to hold any bridesmaid bouquet at my wedding. Can you think of anything funnier than a hen medic in a floating veil, with the smell of iodoform drowning the scent of orange blossoms?"

"Are you really in love with him, Amy?"

"You bet I am!"

"I can't understand how you can love him and keep him waiting."

"If you'd seen how my mother had to slave after my father died because she had no training to earn a decent living, you'd understand why her daughter wants an ace in the hole."

"But love—"

"Love's mostly what a woman brings to it. I've known women who thought it was a meal ticket and women who thought it was a shot of strychnine. I've seen them make it a stairs to God, and I've seen them take it as a slide to the devil."

"What is it for you?" I asked her.

"It's Mark," she said. Then, as if she thought the thrill in her voice had betrayed her, she ordered us out. "I've got to sleep," she said.

"Is Mr. Preston a good lawyer?" Dora asked me as we walked to the street car.

"He's a better one since he knew Amy."

"I mean, is he making much money?"

"I guess he's started on the high grade. Why?"

"Oh, I just wondered."

There was a quality of personal speculativeness in her voice which stirred me to suspicion, and I had a thought of warning Amy against the girl, but dismissed it as absurd. Amy and Preston cared for each other with a devotion beyond the reach of such trivial wiles as Dora Lytle's. I knew that Amy was not working quite so hard as she had during the epidemic, and I felt that she was eminently well able to manage her own affairs without advice from any one.

I did not see Dora again for months. Then I met her at the theater with Preston. She tried to avoid me, but Preston greeted me casually, and I had no qualm in passing on the information to Amy as lightly as I could in view of my resentment against the other girl.

"Oh, Mark's nice to Dora," she said evenly, but I caught the surprise in her eyes.

She veered to talk of the hospital, of Doctor Anna Lebcovic's amazing surgical skill, and of her own ambition to serve under that remarkable woman. "I'll call it a day when I can do an operation with her outfit," she declared.

"Wouldn't you fear the responsibility at first?"

"Not if she believed I was ready. I'd do as she does, pray the chances into God's hands, and hold the knife steady in my own."

"When do you think she'll let you take an operation?"

"Heaven knows, but I'd hate to leave Clayton without having had the chance."

The chance did not come to her, however, until long after her world was turned upside down by the news which I had to break to her one April evening when the West Side seemed almost luminously lovely under a smoky, golden afterglow. I found her in the children's ward, reading a fairy-tale to three forlorn children of the city, charity patients of the Foundation. Their faces, lifted to hers, were not more radiant than her own as she made vivid the old story of Snow White. She nodded to me, but did not put down the book till she had ended.

"What's the good news?" she asked me cheerfully as she came across the ward.

"It isn't good, Amy."

"What's happened?" She put her arm cross my shoulder. "What can I do for you?"

"It's not about me. It's—you."

"I? What is it? Is it Mark? Is he hurt?"

"No."

"Then what."

"He's married."

"Married?" Her hand covered her mouth as if to hold down a cry, and her eyes narrowed as if she had been struck.

"He married Dora Lytle today."

"Dora Lytle." She said the name slowly. "The girl I saved from killing herself." She began to laugh sobbingly. "I sent her to him. Now he's married her. Oh, isn't life funny?"

Her laughter lifted to hysteria, and I pulled her through the corridor to her room. There, for a moment, she stood before the photograph of Preston which was the only personal touch in the bare cell.

"I loved you," she said as if she spoke to the man and not to his picture. "I loved you, and I've lost you."

She picked it up from the stand and hurled it against the wall, then threw herself down on the floor beside her narrow bed and burst into a passion of tears.

For hours, as evening dimmed into night and the myriad lights of the city began to twinkle below us, I sat with Amy Brooks as she sobbed out the sorrows of her soul.

"It was my fault," was her refrain. "I had my chance, and I didn't take it. Aren't we fools? We think we can eat our cake and have it. I might have known what would happen. I could have seen it for some one else. Why can't we see around the corner when it's for ourselves?"

Then she would drift to reproach of Preston. "Why couldn't he have waited? It's such a little while to June. June! The hospitals'll be full of roses that people bring in. June! We were going to his old home down in Missouri. Do you think he'll take her there?"

"She wouldn't want to go there."

"That's it. She isn't marrying Mark for what she can do for him. All she wants is a man to give her a home and pay her bills. She's told me that a dozen times. She's said she'd marry

any man who'd earn a good living for her. She doesn't love
Mark. She couldn't love any one. Oh, it'll be disaster for him!
They can't be happy. I know what he'll want. She won't, she
can't, give it to him. What is his life going to be?"

"That's his affair now," I said sharply. "Your only concern is
with what your life is going to be."

"Mine?" she asked dully. "Oh, it doesn't matter now."

"This is just when it does matter."

"Nothing matters." She turned her face toward the wall. "I
had love, and I sold it for a mess of pottage. Now all I can do
is eat the pottage. You can go home now," she bade me, "and
write a story about a fool woman who loved a man, and who
didn't have sense enough to grab him when he wanted her."

"What are you going to do?"

"There's nothing for me to do except—"

The door opened just then, and Doctor Lebcovic came in,
barring my departure by her bulky presence. She was a short,
squat woman with a head of splendid pride and eyes of strange
insight. "I have missed you, Doctor Brooks," she said to Amy
in her deep, strongly-accented, foreign voice. "What troubles
you?" she went on, seeing the other woman's evident distress.
She went to her, and lifted her hand.

"Is it sickness," she asked, "or sorrow?"

"It's nothing," Amy lied.

"It's sorrow," I told her.

"A man?"

"Yes," Amy said.

"You have loved him?"

"I was going to marry him—in June."

"And he goes away?"

"Yes."

"Always," she said sadly, "we are the daughters of Leah, we
women who would blaze trails. Is it ended?" she asked me.

"He married another girl today."

"To be sure," she said. "He was a pigeon who takes a pigeon for a mate, and lets the eagle fly to the sun. Some day,"
she told Amy, "you will go on your knees to thank God that
He saved you from the fate of marrying a coward."

"I love him," Amy moaned.

"You will always love him," Doctor Anna told her, "but none the less you will be glad you lost him. Now you must work." Her voice hardened with authority. "It is your only medicine. You will help me. I will make you ready so that when June comes you will have another kind of glory. If you do what I tell you, you shall be my assistant."

"But—"

"Listen to me," she said solemnly. "Always, while the world endures, there will be love, which we may win or lose, and grief, which we may cherish or abandon, and happiness, which we may hold or throw away; but always there will be sickness, which we must care for, and work, which we must do. With them there is no choice. Doctor Brooks, I need you tonight. Will you come with me?" Her voice was the clarion call of duty, of opportunity, of a future leading to the stars.

"I'll go," Amy said, and followed her from the room.

There began for her that night a course of action which would have taken a more self-conscious woman than Amy out of thought of herself. She worked like a galley slave in wards and operating rooms, and studied like a medieval scholar under Doctor Anna's direction. She was treading the high plateaus of that mountain range of the profession which had lured her into its difficulties and dangers, and she went about her daily tasks with the exaltation of the chosen. She did not even mention Preston to me for weeks. Then one night she flung at me.

"I saw Mark today."

"Where?" I demanded, annoyed less by the fact than by the softness in her voice.

"He telephoned me and said he had to talk to me. I couldn't bring him here, and so I told him I'd meet him at the China-man's place down the street. I lunched with him there."

"You didn't!"

"Well, what was the harm?"

"Why did he want to see you?"

"Why did I want to see him? Because he'd had time to find out that he's made a mess of everything."

"What's he going to do about it?"

"He can't do much for a while, but he plans to have her divorce him."

"She won't."

"That's what I told him."

"Why did he marry her?"

"Why do men marry women they don't really love? Infatuation, passion, anger against another woman. Oh, there are fifty reasons, none of them good, and all of them true! Mark married Dora because I'd hurt him and neglected him, and she was there to soothe his vanity. He knows now what a mistake he has made, and he's going to do his best to make it straight."

"But you can't marry him, Amy, even if he does induce her to divorce him."

"Why not? He loves me, and I love him. Dora's an episode."

"But he's proved to you that he's not trustworthy."

"I can't condemn any one for one such human mistake."

"Then you're going to?"

"Some day."

By her avoidance of me in the days that followed, I knew that she was holding to her decision. I saw her sometimes with Preston, and I wondered what Dora would do when she came to know the situation. I found out before long, for Dora came to me in the newspaper office.

"I've a story for you," she told me, her eyes blazing with fury. "I'm going to sue Mark for separate maintenance and name Amy Brooks."

"You haven't reason for that," I told her.

"Haven't I? He told me this morning that he wanted me to get a divorce so that he could marry her. I'm going to fool them, though. I won't sue for divorce and let them marry each other. I'll hold him by law and ruin her reputation."

"Don't you think you've done enough," I asked her, "by taking Mark from her, without hurting her more?"

"He's my husband now," she said, "and if she doesn't let him alone, she'll have to pay for it my way."

"Why don't you talk to her?" I countered, and from the fear which gleamed in her eyes I knew that she wouldn't.

She had nine points of the law, but she lacked the tenth

point of her husband's love, and she wasn't willing to go into the arena with the woman who had it. She had stolen Preston from Amy, but she couldn't take his devotion, and the consciousness of his revived association as well as of her own treachery would hold her off.

"I'll do more than that," she blustered, but I knew that she had come to me, not because she planned immediate action, but because she thought her coming would be a threat over Amy. "I'll block her game," she said savagely.

She did nothing, however, and Amy went her way of work in the hospital and of leisure with Preston. Doctor Lebcovic must have noticed the change in her attitude, but since Amy was doing all she demanded of her, she was too wise a woman to offer unasked advice in the private affairs of a subordinate. Amy was striving mightily toward the goal of individual responsibility in her work and with the radiance of reassurance was coming nearer to it every day. Doctor Anna's "Soon" shifted to "Very soon," and Amy waited for the command to take into her first operation with the tense eagerness of a runner at the tape. Her months at the Foundation had endowed her with perspective, and her association with Anna Lebcovic had given her spiritual surety in skill as well as an actual consciousness of the demands which the traditions of the profession make upon its votaries. Doctor Brooks of Clayton would have scorned to turn the tricks which Amy Brooks of Lister had played. Even the women of the directorate who had accepted her with misgivings acclaimed her with pride. Except for the shadow of Preston in the background her present was hopeful, her future assured.

May ran into June, and the neighborhood came to pale summering, its only flowers those brought by visitors to the hospitals or sold by dark-skinned vendors on street corners. The fraternity houses along the boulevards began to clear as the colleges closed, but the current of the city's life flowed unceasingly. Great waves of heat rose on the southwestward prairies and rolled over the city, pressing down upon the poor as they sweltered in crowded tenements and hovels. Old men, old women, little children died through the torrid days and breathless nights of misery. Ambulances clanged up Harrison

Street hour after hour, speeding some unfortunate victim to a chance of recovery in one of the big institutions where doctors and nurses fought valiantly to save whom they could. The County was already filled when in the course of a news feature story of the suffering on the lower West Side I found an old woman stricken in a Mather Street warren, and I telephoned to Amy Brooks at the Clayton as a last hope.

"Bring her," she told me. "She can have my room."

I commandeered a patrol wagon and rode with the sick woman to the Foundation.

Amy, pale from heat and overwork, met us at the receiving door. "I'm all in," she said, running her hand through her already disheveled hair. "Morrow was called to St. Louis tonight. They think his daughter's dying there. And Doctor Anna's passed out. She's never stopped for three days and nights until she fainted in the operating room. We're all half-dead."

She swung into work upon the patient, though, as soon as we had put her into Amy's bed, and it was nearly an hour afterward when she came out into the corridor with a sigh of relief.

"She'll pull through," she said.

She sank down into a chair in the sun parlor, yawning prodigiously. "I'd call it a day if there were any one to relieve me," she said, "but I suppose I'll have to stand guard till Temple comes on at six. We certainly need another intern here."

"Had any sleep?"

"Not for fifty-six hours. I'm dog-tired." She stretched wearily. "Why do you suppose people in their senses choose the work we do? Or do you suppose we aren't sane?"

The telephone whirred at the floor desk, and a nurse from the ward came to answer it. "I'll call her," I heard her say, then saw her come toward Amy. "For you, Doctor Brooks," she said.

"Say you can't get me," Amy implored.

"It's Mr. Preston," she said, and Amy hurried to the desk.

"What?" I heard her voice rise in alarm. "How long? Are you sure? Yes, I know Morrow's away. Have you tried any one else? But you can't bring her here! Yes, Doctor Lebcovic is here, but I don't know that she can take a case tonight. It's almost out of the question. Oh, Mark, there are a hundred hospitals in Chicago. I'm sure you can get her in some one of them. Yes, I know it's a question of minutes. All right, bring her!" She came back, waxen white. "Dora's sick," she said. "Appendicitis. She's been Morrow's patient, and he told her that if she had another attack, she'd have to be on the table within an hour. Mark thinks she'll die if it isn't done tonight. I tried to stave off her coming here, but he's set on it. But what'll we do? Morrow's away, and Doctor Anna's sick, and every surgeon on call is rushed to death."

"Miss Johnston," she summoned the nurse, "will you call Doctor Maxwell? And Doctor Blane? And Fishkin? Tell any one of them you can get, it's an emergency appendicitis."

She began to pace the sun parlor. "I don't know what we can do if we can't get them," she fumed. "Doctor Anna's out. There's no one else here. Oh, Lord!"

Up and down the room she strode, restless as a tiger, her weariness dispelled by the driving power of her problem. "I don't see why Mark had to call me," she muttered, resentful of the responsibility of the burdening. "The Presbyterian would have taken her in if he'd fought for it, even if she has been Morrow's case. I should have called there, not let him come here. Don't you see what he's putting up to me? If she went to another hospital, I wouldn't have to think twice about her. If—" She paused, caught by sudden thought of another contingency. "Oh, she won't die," she said bitterly.

The nurse returned from the desk. "They're all working at other hospitals," she told Amy. "Mrs. Blane says the doctor may be able to get here within three hours. That's the best anywhere."

"Too late."

She went back to the instrument as it buzzed again. "Mr. Preston's downstairs," she said.

"Send him up."

Amy went forward to the elevator to stand beside it with martial attention as Mark Preston came out with Dora on the rollered cot which two attendants were pushing.

"You've got some one?" he asked Amy.

"Not yet."

"You won't let me die?" Dora gasped between her groans. "You won't let me die?"

"No," Amy said. "Take her down to the operating room," she ordered the attendants. "Stay with her, Miss Johnston. You'll have to be the scrub for any one who takes it."

She turned to Mark as they bore Dora down to the corridor. "Do you want Doctor Lebcovic to operate?"

"Any one you trust."

"I'll see if she can."

She ran down the stairs, leaving him standing in troubled distress. What was he thinking, I wondered, as he waited her return? Was his desire to save Dora merely common honor, or was it strengthened by some force of that infatuation which had led him to her from Amy? Would he be glad ultimately to be free to marry Amy, or would he choose Dora, with her trivialities, her pettiness, her dependence upon him? He had been a coward when he had married Dora. Would he be coward enough now to see nothing in her death but release? Whatever his thought, he awaited Amy in troubled silence.

She came slowly up the stairs, holding the rail as if for support as she faced him.

"Doctor Lebcovic can't operate," she said. "She broke down tonight, and she daren't try now."

"But she must know some one," he declared.

"Yes," she said, her voice trembling with excitement. "She knows a doctor who has never yet performed an operation but whom she'd been training for months."

"She's here?"

"Yes."

"We'll take her."

"I don't know if she dare," she said slowly. "She'll need all her nerve for it, and this is the one case where she hasn't it."

"Why not?"

"It's myself. Doctor Anna has left it to me. She said that if I feel ready, I can take it. Do you think I dare?"

"But if—"

"Amy came slowly up the stairs. 'Dr. Anna can't operate,' she said. 'She says that if I feel ready I can take it. Do you think I dare?' Preston watched her with pleading eyes. 'I can't tell you what to do, Amy.'" Illustration by Leslie L. Benson. From "Amy Brooks," *Good Housekeeping* 84, no. 3 (March 1927), p. 85.

"If she lives," she said, "she stands between us now. If she dies under my knife, she stands between us forever."

"I can't tell you what to do, Amy." He watched her with pleading eyes.

"No," she said, "You can't. No one can tell me what to do." She stood a moment, staring down the corridor toward the operating room, then lifted her shoulders. "All right," she said. Chin up, she repeated Doctor Anna's creed of crisis, "The chances in God's hands, and the knife steady in my own."

From the operating room came the sound of Dora's groans. "Coming, Johnston," Amy Brooks called. "Get little Sawyer for the anesthetic. I'll be there in five minutes."

Five minutes later, swathed in the enveloping white apron and tight, white cap of the surgeon, she came back through the hall from her room, her arms bared in readiness for the nurse's scrubbing. Not one look did she give to Preston as she passed. Miserably he moved after her as the door of the operating room closed. Wretchedly he strode the corridor as she came out, pallid as her raiment.

"Safe," was all she told him.

A nurse came breathlessly up the stairs. "Oh, Doctor Brooks," she cried, "a child's just been brought in with a broken pelvis. It's another emergency operation. Do you think you can take it?"

"Yes," she said.

She stood aside as the nurses wheeled Dora into the hall. "Take her to forty-one," she bade them.

She did not even give Preston a glance as he followed Dora's bed down the corridor, but she spoke to me before she went back to the table.

"Tell one of the nurses to take your old woman's temperature every hour," she counseled.

"Yes, Doctor Brooks," I said, for I knew even then that the last of the old Amy Brooks, who had played, and strolled, and laughed through gay days and gray with me, had died in the operating room instead of Dora Preston.

EVE GOES ON

Sophie Kerr

Sophie Kerr, a prominent writer of the period, published this serial in the
Ladies' Home Journal *from March to June 1928. When we meet Eve Archer
she is nineteen and the very unhappy daughter of a mother who favors Eve's
older sister, Bernice. With dreams of achievement outside marriage, Eve is a
misfit in her home town of Cadeville, a place that bores her and pains her
with its provincial values. When Bernice steals the heart of a young man
named Randall Clement whom Eve has attracted, she runs away from home
to New York City, where she is aided by a police matron, Mrs. Rich and her
daughter Irma, until she can afford a place of her own. Eventually, Eve secures
a job making salads in a cafeteria, where she becomes friends with a number
of women, including Amy Blake, a college graduate and an outspoken feminist. In this episode, a crisis develops at the cafeteria when the female partners
who own it sell to the Woodser chain, which imposes petty rules on the staff
and lowers the food quality. The new manager is patronizingly authoritarian
to the women and immigrant men as well as lewdly suggestive to the younger
employees. After Eve resists his advances and the staff walks out in solidarity,
she and Amy establish their own cafeteria with the old employees and become
successful businesswomen. In the last installment, Eve visits Cadeville after a
five-year absence and finds that Bernice has grown fat and bitter in her marriage to Eve's former sweetheart. Moreover, Eve has outgrown Randall, an
unhappy businessman of conventional views. The past now resolved for Eve,
she returns to New York, her stimulating life at the cafeteria, and a budding
romance with Amy's brother, Frank.*

From *Ladies' Home Journal* 45, no. 5 (May 1928).

"THAT funny old fellow who fusses about everything was here again today. I don't know why he comes; nothing ever suits him. And he won't hurry; he holds up everybody." Jennie, one of the counter girls, was speaking at the kitchen luncheon table.

"He is one who likes a grievance," said Helga. "I worked for a lady like that when I first come to this country. All I did wass wrong. I cried myself to sleep every night."

"She probably put it on to keep from paying you fair wages. Lots of people do that with greenhorns," said Marta, the pastry cook. "Try the apple pie, Helga—I had luck today."

"You always have luck, Marta," said Helga.

Carlo, one of the Italian bus boys from outside, came in and sat at the foot of the table. "I went to the opera last night—it was *Aida*. Oh, that big first aria for the tenor—*splendido, magnifico!*" He bunched his fingers and threw an ecstatic kiss to the world that afforded him such delight.

Eve said nothing. She liked to sit and listen to them. Gradually she had come to know them and her first despising had changed to respect, to which presently liking had been added, with two exceptions. Linda—she had never been able to endure Linda, and her feeling was heartily returned.

And Miss Woodall! Miss Woodall was undoubtedly capable, efficient, the sort of person who comes grandly to the fore in an emergency, who never admits defeat. And a worker! "She iss quick like the egg beater," Helga said of her. But she was petty, eager to get even for any disrespect, real or fancied. There was democracy in that kitchen and it extended to the counter girls and the bus boys outside, even to Mrs. Cleeve and Miss Fraley; but it never reached Miss Woodall. She never let anyone forget that she was a superior, a ruling power. An appeal to Mrs. Cleeve she regarded as a personal affront, and she could not rest until she had scored off the offender. She would not eat with the others, but filled a tray and sat outside, like a patron. The kitchen was glad of her absence, but resented the gesture. Miss Woodall suspected everyone of the worst. No one ever gained her trust; she praised nothing.

Eve knew them all now. How different they were from her first estimate! The two bus boys went regularly to the opera;

it cost them nothing because they belonged to the claque. They knew more about music than Eve had ever suspected, and they were always greedy for it, never sated.

Then there was Amy Blake, counter girl beside Jennie. Amy was a college graduate who was learning cafeteria management with a view to owning her own. She had, it seemed, always wanted to run a restaurant of some kind or other, and having worked in tea rooms and wayside inns had decided that the cafeteria offered the best return for the investment of time and money. An odd, diffident girl, Amy, hard to know; but when Eve told her that in common with Cadeville, she had believed all rightful interests of college women to be high in the brow, they laughed themselves into friendship. Helga, too, was a friend, and a friend worth having. That serene, self-contained and forceful creature dominated the kitchen by the right of personality far more than Miss Woodall by vested authority. Helga was always kind, and whatever she said was sound. She was a supreme cook, possessing the art of divining flavor, and she willingly passed on to her assistants all of her knowledge that they could absorb. Miss Woodall, it was observed, walked a bit light about Helga, didn't chip at her so sharply as she did the others.

Marta was another story—Marta, the pastry cook. Nervous, temperamental, soaring one minute, groveling the next, Eve had seen her weep frenziedly when a batch of muffins scorched, and sing for joy over a superfine lot of cakes. She was wrinkled and worn, and though she was an excellent cook she worried unceasingly about possible failures. Sometimes she was inclined to be absent-minded and silent, and it was whispered about the kitchen that her boy was on another spree. She adored that boy, her only child; he was definitely no good, but she loved him the more to make up for his shortcomings. Eve had won her gratitude on one of those bad days when she was sick with anxiety by making her own Cadeville gingerbread to supplement the desserts Marta could not finish. It made a success with patrons and Marta begged the recipe and used it thereafter, calling it "Eve's Ginderbread." Mrs. Cleeve had been pleased about it.

Marta was a reader, with a passion for the Russians. She

loaned Eve worn volumes of Dostoyevsky, Chekhov, Tolstoy, Turgenieff; and, once Eve had read them, discussed them with her passionately. It turned Eve's ideas upside down to find in this cafeteria kitchen animated informed talk of books and music and general aesthetics, much of which was over her head, when on her first day she had classed her coworkers as ignorant, stupid, debased. They told her of the free lectures and concerts and exhibitions open at night, the museums available on Sundays, the entertainment and instruction which the city lavishly offers to those who care for it. Eve rushed about madly trying to taste it all, sometimes with Amy, sometimes with Irma. But Irma had acquired a heavy suitor and was much engaged in the evenings. His name was Robert Anderson, and he worked with a firm of certified accountants and aspired to be a partner. His object was clearly matrimony. And as he was a solid young man, with a good salary and not much family, Mrs. Rich approved of him, while he had enough lighter traits to make him a possibility also in Irma's opinion.

It was for Eve an exciting, evolutionary winter. She had become quickly skilled in her work, and had lost her first disgust for it. There was a quickest and best way to make every salad, she thought, and she worked out each one, thoroughly. Once a satisfactory routine was established it was all easier, and gave her a sense of mastery. But she had gone farther than routine and after some experiment had suggested several new salads which Mrs. Cleeve approved, and tried out on the patrons. Two proved instantly popular and were put on the menu frequently as specials, and two others failed to please the public taste and were dropped. Mrs. Cleeve told Eve to go on and try other combinations—a novelty on the menu was always welcome. Miss Woodall, however, discouraged these attempts, and as she had charge of giving out supplies Eve found herself constantly checked and blocked for want of ingredients. Miss Woodall was a strong conservative; in her own words she didn't believe in letting a salad girl imagine herself a French chef! But Eve did not bother much about Miss Woodall. She had too many other things to think of.

There was, to begin with, the constant adventure of living on her wages. Fifteen a week is sixty dollars a month, save for those blessed four months when there is an extra pay day. Rent for the room shared with Yriane was twenty-two fifty. Out of the remainder Eve must manage everything else. Even on the seventy-five-dollar months there was a small enough balance, and on the other four-pay-day months she had only a trifle over a dollar a day for all expenses beyond the rent. To make it fixed, she took a dollar for each day of the week, put it in her purse, and set the rest aside.

Food for supper she reduced to the plainest and least expensive things. A fifteen-cent loaf of whole-wheat bread made toast four nights, and this, with a glass of milk, and a bit of fruit, was sufficient. Or hot cornmeal mush, with butter or milk, made a supper equally good and more filling. A string of dry figs bought at the nearest Italian grocery or a box of raisins provided sweets. An occasional bag of peanuts was a treat.

It was Spartan, but it brought her food within a dollar a day, and she had more to spend on the things she craved—theaters and music chiefly. And since she had been obliged to pay her first share of the rent out of her saved money, she wanted to fill up that hole, and add a tiny bit now and then to her fund.

Clothes were the hardest of all to get within her budget. She bought cotton crepe and made underwear that could be washed and dried in an hour, and needed no ironing. But shoes and stockings she could not make, and since she was on her feet so much the shoes must be of the right sort, strong and well-fitting. Jennie told her of the people who sell coats and dresses on the installment plan, and she bought some much-needed garments in this way.

. . . .

She looked about her constantly for some way to escape from Yriane, but there seemed none. She couldn't live by herself on the money she was making, and be as comfortable as she was here. She had not found anything else to do, and she really didn't want to find anything else. She liked the cafeteria, its order, its organization, its capable, efficient system. Mrs. Cleeve was a wizard at arrangement, and always looked out for improvement. She and Miss Fraley, Eve had learned, lived together and had pooled their resources in this venture. Each had served a sound apprenticeship in other establishments before starting this, and they were both hard workers. If any one of the staff was absent, or on days when there was an overwhelming rush of customers, Mrs. Cleeve would step in and help, steady everyone, keep things going smoothly; and no matter what the task was she did it so well that her assistants were forced to admire. Miss Fraley could not be so omnipresent—the cashier's desk chained her so long as there was a patron in the place—but early in the morning, and after lunch was over, she was as active as her partner. Eve and Amy watched them and discussed them.

"They make the whole thing dovetail so neatly," said Amy. "Fraley keeps the accounts, attends to the banking, runs the desk, but manages to be about behind the scenes a lot too. And if there's anything gets by Mrs. Cleeve, I don't know it. I tell you, this is the sort of place to have—in a good business district—serve lunch only, no dinner."

Eve had been impressed, each morning and each evening, by the great army of women workers which she joined, and she felt a certain loyalty to them. There were her comrades, the poor old broken scrub woman, the stenographer, the clerk, the cook, the waitress, the seamstresses and millinery workers, the factory girls—and, finally, Helga, Marta, and the rest, even Linda and Miss Woodall. They were all fighting for their lives, some of them for the lives of others as well. They weren't all good soldiers—no army is composed of virtue only—but they must all fight, and if some of them don't fight fair, why, even so, Eve did not want it on her conscience that she had tried to shove them out, to take away their weapons. Miss Woodall was cranky and arbitrary; Linda was mean and willfully inefficient; but they might need their jobs.

Still, it was hard to bear Miss Woodall's constant nagging. She nagged at Eve more than at anyone else in the kitchen. If there was a spot on a lettuce leaf, if the cheese balls were not exactly the same size, if a scrap of peel stuck to a tomato she could see it three yards away and denounced it loudly at the same distance. Her enmity grew fiercer after the day when Mrs. Cleeve asked for less noise in the kitchen just as she was scolding Eve for leaving an orange pip in a fruit salad, and was augmented by the evident pleasure of Helga and Marta when they heard her thus rebuked. She didn't dare nag Helga and Marta.

"She hass it in for you—you should watch your step," counseled Helga, later, "I haff seen her take distaste to people before; she always gets them out."

But one day Miss Woodall and Linda went too far in nagging Eve, and Mrs. Cleeve got to the bottom of the trouble.

"Do you suppose you could do part of Miss Woodall's work?" she asked Eve. "In the storeroom, and checking the supplies that come in, I mean? And at the same time keep on making the salads if we got you a helper? I've thought for quite a while that this was too small a concern to have a regular kitchen supervisor as they do in the larger places, especially since I'm in and out all the time, Well, what about it?"

"I'd like to try it."

"That's the way to talk—never refuse responsibility. That's another business axiom. Well, I'll let Woodall and Linda go tonight—lucky this is Saturday and you can begin on Monday. We'll raise you to twenty. That all right?" she smiled at Eve.

It was more than all right to Eve. As she went back to the kitchen she heard Mrs. Cleeve say to Miss Fraley: "Oh, they both had to go; spite and lying I will not stand from anyone."

....

Eve's second summer at the cafeteria had begun with a fortnight of sticky, soppy heat. The kitchen, in spite of fans and ventilators working at top speed, was a Turkish bath. Everyone was peevish, and inclined to give the sharp answer that increases wrath rather than the soft one that turns it away. Work went on to an obligato of recrimination. Even Helga the serene was heard to raise her voice in impatience and unreason.

When the nerves were fretted and tried, the mind is less guarded, reserve is broken down, and a great deal is said that is far too frankly true.

Hidden tragedies came to light. One of the assistant cooks had a husband who beat her and took away her wages. Ben, the man who did all the heaviest work in the kitchen, had a child who was dying with tuberculosis of the bones. Ben spent his Sundays beside his little son's hospital bed. The woman who had taken Linda's place as vegetable washer was married.

Her husband had been hurt in a factory accident and the insurance company had found some flaw in the case whereby they could refuse to pay his rightful compensation under the law. All the discord was not in the kitchen. It was whispered about that Miss Fraley and Mrs. Cleeve were at odds—that Mrs. Cleeve wanted to get married again, and Miss Fraley fought it, seeing it as the end of their partnership and their friendship. The employees watched them. They were often red-eyed, formally polite where they had always been easily familiar.

Helga was moved to philosophize. "It iss always from hearts that the worst troubles come to us. If we love people, there iss nothing steady, nothing sure. Why should Mrs. Cleeve, here with a good business and making money every day and all running so smoothly, and living so nice with her good friend—why should she wish to take another man and make things out of joint? Oh, she iss a fool!"

Helga had said another truth to be remembered when she called out at lunch, when everyone had been bemoaning his or her own particular distress: "I am sick to death of such gloomingness. Thiss world iss not so bad, but if you keep talking that it iss, you make it so. Get another girl, Carlo, and you, Marta, let your son go to jail. Then your aching teeth will be drawn."

They had all stared and then laughed, somewhat shame-faced, but when the great heat abated a day later the depression was over. Eve was glad of it and glad that she had told them nothing of herself.

She had never told anyone but Mrs. Rich and Irma and they never reminded her of it. Her intimacy with Irma was waning, for Irma had at last set a wedding date—early fall—and was absorbed in preparation. Amy was taking Irma's place with Eve.

Amy had a home of her own with a father and older brother, otherwise she and Eve might have taken an apartment together, but Eve had found no other girl with whom she could have lived any more satisfactorily than with Yriane.

Eddie Craig hung on. Eve had discovered that it was possible to like a man very well and find him a frightful bore at the same time.

There was another young man who showed the same symp-
toms as Eddie Craig—one Harvey Harrison, salesman for a
firm of wholesale grocers, who specialized in cafeteria staples.
Now and then, when Mrs. Cleeve was busy, it fell to Eve to
see young Harrison and order supplies, and after the first time
he made a point of coming into the kitchen for a few minutes
whenever he called. He was jolly and slangy and irrepressible,
asking Eve endless personal questions and begging that she go
out to dinner and a show with him. Eve evaded him and put
him off. She thought him common. All the same, she was
pleased.

But she really preferred to go about with Amy, the two girls
together—second-balcony seats for the theater, standees in
the top gallery at the opera, or long Sunday hikes in the country. Amy's brother, Frank Blake, sometimes joined them on
these. Now and then he treated them to things they could not
afford, for Amy, except in the matter of paying no rent, lived
on her earnings as Eve did. It annoyed her family, but she
insisted.

Eve enjoyed the occasional evenings she spent in Amy's
home, an apartment up the Drive, where the park and the river
could be seen at their most dramatic. Old Mr. Blake liked to
have the two girls at the dinner table. He was a semi-invalid,
and a little deaf and withdrawn, but kind. He could not understand Amy's restlessness, her choice of occupation, and he
did not like it, but as he was magnificently tolerant of all other
human beings, he did not bar her way. The Blakes lived well,
with a formality and ease that were precious to Eve in contrast
to her own necessarily meager ways. She speedily grew fond
of Mr. Blake, but the brother, Frank, she did not at first like at
all. He was sufficiently older than Amy to treat her—and her
friends—as children. He teased unmercifully, and laughed at
them more, Eve thought, than was pleasant. After a little she
saw that whenever Frank teased or laughed there was justice
in it, and though he frequently infuriated both girls, also he
frequently kept them from being swept into wild enthusiasms
and partisanships. Jollying was his mode of control, Eve observed—and it was better than scolding—of tendencies and
traits in Amy which needed check or redirection. He was spe-

cially hard on her strongest obsession—a loud dislike of men. Amy was an advanced and rabid feminist and the verbal stabs she dealt the other sex never failed to amaze Eve, and her first real liking of Frank Blake came when she saw how much this abnormal complex in his sister irked him, and their first personal conversation was started by it.

"Can't you help her get away from it?" he asked. "It's bad for her. Heaven knows she's had her own way ever since she was a baby—father and I give in to her and spoil her in every possible way—and yet she's always suspecting us of trying to put something over on her because we're men, and when I bring any of my friends home she's as sour as a quince. You're the first girl she's liked who wasn't the same stripe; I've felt that might be a hopeful sign. What do you think?"

"I'm not so crazy about men, but I don't hate them and I'm not afraid of them as Amy is. I don't understand why she's that way. Sometimes I think it's uncertainty—uncertainty of herself, I mean."

"Amy says you're the most extraordinary person, full of ability and decision and—" Amy came in and stopped the conversation. Eve was glad and sorry.

Thereafter she knew that her status with Frank Blake had changed. He was less high-handed with her, and though he didn't stop teasing, the sharpness of it was gone. And now and then he said a word or two that showed he considered her an ally in the reformation of Amy's attitude toward men.

Inevitably this changed Eve's own attitude toward Amy. Hitherto she had deferred to her knowledge, her taste, her wishes, feeling her comparative ignorance. Now she rose to equal ground, but their friendship did not weaken. The two girls complemented each other. Where Amy wavered, Eve went steadily ahead. Yet, except for a superabundance of caution, Amy had qualities that Eve could not match, and she knew it. Amy was a born organizer, she was by far the most efficient of the counter girls in the cafeteria. There was something in her manner that helped the hungry customer, hesitating between pot roast and fricasseed chicken, to make up his mind at once and not delay the line. She served portions with exactness but with a beneficent flourish that seemed generous.

And she had an eye for side issues. She would warn the kitchen when the cream pies or apricot puddings were going to be popular, she could tell by instinct when there would be a run on muffins, and she overlooked Eve's new salads and predicted accurately which would be liked and which would be passed by.

"How do you do it?" Eve demanded. "You can't make a salad to save your life, and you don't even like to eat them."

"It's my restaurant instinct. Wait till I get one of my own; I'll make this place look amateurish."

"But I thought Mrs. Cleeve and Miss Fraley were doing awfully well."

"They are—but it's because of the location and quality of the food. Of course those are the two great essentials. But there are lots of details they neglect. And I tell you," declaimed Amy, warming to her subject, "when I start my cafeteria it's got to be successful. I'd consider it a disgrace to my sex if I failed! But I want my place to be an outstanding success, an inspiration and a help to other women who go into business. And it will certainly be a satisfaction to me to be able to hire and fire men and boss them around! I think I'll have a man chef, just to be able to give him orders."

Eve remembered Frank's admonition and answered accordingly:

"If you have a man chef, you'd have to have men assistant cooks for him, I suppose, because surely you wouldn't let him have authority over women, would you? Maybe you'd like a whole kitchen staff of men."

"I haven't made up my mind."

"Well, don't let your prejudices run away with your sense."

"Oh, you're hopeless; you actually like men!"

"Of course I like men," said Eve. "And I expect to keep on liking them. They're not so bad."

"I believe you're in love with this Craig person you go out with."

"Eddie'd be flattered at your expression. You look as though you wanted to order him the rack and the bowstring, possibly the bowl of hemlock. No, I'm not in love with Eddie, though he has his points."

Their conversations usually dwindled off in this manner. But in spite of their differences of opinion Eve liked Amy more than any other girl she had ever known. And now and then, when Amy came to their apartment, Eve was secretly gratified by the way she dealt with Yriane, putting that bumptious young woman very much in her place.

Yriane's last year in art school was over, but her affair with her young playwright, Otto Garrish, was not. And though she kept telling Eve that she was going to Woodstock for the summer to join an outdoor sketching class, she lingered on through June and July. Secretly Eve wished with all her heart that Yriane would go to Woodstock, though she didn't see how she could manage the rent by herself.

She reduced it to plain terms. To be able to live by herself she must earn more money. She wasn't likely to get more money at Mrs. Cleeve's. Therefore she must look for another job. With the experience she'd gained she thought she could find something where the work would be no harder, but where she could draw at least five dollars more wages a week. On the floor above herself and Yriane there was another one-room apartment, smaller and with lower ceilings but costing only forty-five a month. It was unfurnished, but Eve believed that her mother would, if sufficiently urged, send her the shabby things she had had in her room at home, and these would suffice.

Amy objected. "It is economically unsound to pay so large a per cent of your cash income for rent," she expounded. "One-third is the highest that is safe."

"See here, Amy, why don't you hunt another job too? Maybe we could get one together."

"No. I'm helping Miss Fraley with the accounts occasionally now, and I want to find out a lot more about it. I don't think they carry enough general liability and workmen's compensation insurance. I'm working out the proper ratio for the help and the number of customers."

"My heavens!" cried Eve. "The restaurant business is certainly complicated. I don't even know what general liability and workmen's compensation mean!"

"Go on and dump your little art friend and get your apartment," said Amy. "You are positively naive when it comes to the A B C of business. And listen to me: Before you go out and snatch another job, speak to Mrs. Cleeve about it. She might well prefer to raise your salary rather than break in a new girl. She made a highly economical move, you see, when she got rid of Woodall, who was paid a high salary, and gave you a small raise, and added a cheap helper for you. She must have saved forty to fifty dollars a month right there. She might rather share that with you than let you go. And she's so disturbed about the row Miss Fraley's raising over her getting married again that she won't be so keen on getting someone new in your place. When the business is prosperous and your boss is somewhat distracted by outside matters is a fine time to ask for a raise."

In this Amy was perfectly right. Mrs. Cleeve, when approached by Eve, added five dollars a week to her pay without a murmur. It was so easy that Eve was indignant with her own stupidity for not asking sooner. And that very night she rented the apartment upstairs, wrote to her mother and broke the news to Yriane, who was most unpleasant about it.

"I should think, in gratitude to me for taking you in here, you'd stay on," she said. "You've used my things, you've met my friends, I've done everything I could for you, just as if— just as if—"

"Just as if I didn't work in a kitchen," finished Eve tartly. "Well, I've done a good bit for you too. I've kept this place clean and made up your bed; I've pressed your clothes and mended them when they got too awful. That pays for the use of your furniture and linen." Then she felt a pang of remorse. "Oh, Yriane, why do we fuss so? You were awfully good to take me in with you, of course, and you've taught me such a lot about pictures and painting and artists—I do appreciate all that. But I think you ought to have somebody more congenial with you. You don't like me; I can feel it all the time, and it rubs me the wrong way. You're always saying something hateful about the work I do and the people I know. That's why we're better apart."

"But what am I going to do?" wailed Yriane. "You know I can't pay the rent by myself. You don't care what happens to me. You'd be glad if I had to give up my career and go back home. I know you would. You've always resented that I'm an artist and you're only a servant—for that's all you are and all you ever will be."

Eve was not sure whether or not her mother would send her furniture. She might have to buy the absolute necessities on the installment plan—a scheme she didn't relish. But finally a letter of acquiescence came, accompanied by reproaches as usual. ". . . you never let me hear from you. . . . I have no idea what you are doing. . . . people here in town think it very strange that you don't come home and stay with me, now that Bernice is married . . . knowing my state of health . . . but you were always an unnatural daughter. Bernice and Randall are very, very happy, and though his means are not large, she makes the best of everything and has a perfectly lovely apartment in the nicest locality in Baltimore, and has gathered round her a delightful circle of friends. She is more beautiful than ever, and Randall is so proud of her . . . I'm thankful to have one daughter who is a credit to me. I'm sending your furniture, though it leaves the house very bare. But that's all parents can expect these days—their children leave home without permission, and strip the homestead. . . ." Once started on this strain, Mrs. Archer found many things to say. Eve thought of the old ottoman and whatnot. Evidently they had become treasures in her mother's eyes—a change indeed.

And the vision of Bernice and Randall Clement, very happy, in a lovely apartment, in the nicest locality, surrounded by a delightful circle—this she pushed resolutely away from her. But it came back again and again, with that familiar, hateful stab of pain.

"I wish you hadn't got this place," said Eddie Craig morosely. He was helping Eve put her new room in order.

"It looks awfully nice," said Eve, not paying the least attention to his discontent. "You certainly were the best help ever to me."

"I didn't do it willingly."

"No matter, so long as you did it well. How's that for a polite speech?" She ran about the room, pushing the furniture into new positions. "Look, that's the ivy Amy brought me.

And Mrs. Rich went over all her china and glass and gave me the pieces she didn't need. I told her she'd better save them for Irma and Bob, but she said they sniffed at her things. I didn't sniff. I grabbed them. But listen, Eddie, you don't know the funniest. Yriane and her playwriting boy got married day before yesterday at City Hall. Yes—imagine! It seems he had a play accepted and got a five-hundred-dollar cash advance, so they rushed right off and got married and he's moved in, in my place. So now I suppose Yriane will forgive me, even if she won't speak to me."

"Five hundred dollars for anything that goof could write? Whoever paid it ought to see an alienist. All the same I think they were sensible to get married. Eve, why don't you marry me? Oh, you know I've wanted to ask you. You've been choking me off—I suppose you don't care anything about me."

"I like you. I like you so much," she began, "that I would be ashamed to marry you—"

"Now what d'you mean by that? It sounds ridiculous."

"I mean I wouldn't do you the wrong of marrying you without loving you. And I don't love you, Eddie."

"I'd love you enough for both of us."

"You know that wouldn't work."

"But I want to take care of you. It almost kills me to see you slaving your life away in a place like Mrs. Cleeve's, with such people around you."

"I can take care of myself. And the people I work with are as good as I am, and some of them are a lot better, and more clever, and more capable, and more educated too. I thought at first it was quite a comedown for me, but I soon saw that I was in another world where the tests are quite different from Cadeville tests."

"Another world? You talk in such a queer way."

"It's the world where you're measured by the kind of work you can do, and how well you can do it, and how much it's worth. I'm not worth much. Oh, when I think of the wicked injustice of bringing up a girl and teaching her nothing that's any use if she has to earn her own living! No parents in the world would willingly maim or cripple a child physically, I mean—but they think nothing at all of maiming or crippling their children's minds and abilities."

"We seem to be getting away from what I asked you," remarked Eddie.

"But I've answered you, I'm sorry, but that's the only thing I can say."

"You're in love with somebody else. I know it. I can feel it. Every time I've tried to be loving with you, you've slipped away from me. I've been up against a blank wall. You are in love with somebody else, aren't you?"

"I suppose I am."

"And he's not in love with you. He must be a fool. Why do you waste your time on him if it's hopeless?"

"Eddie, are you going to forget me and think about some other girl?"

"You know darned well I'm not. I would if I could, but I can't."

"I would, too, if I could—but I can't." Eve waited a moment, and then went on: "And just because I've told you this, don't think that I want to talk of it again. It's not something to be dragged out and dangled about if you happen to think of it. When everybody in the cafeteria had that burst of telling their hearts' secrets there was the most terrible time afterward—everybody so suspicious and so uneasy. It was the most awful warning about confiding in your friends."

Eddie was offended. He got up and took his hat. "I see what you think of me. It's not flattering, I must say. Well, I'm going. If you have any more odd jobs you want done, let me know. In the meantime, I'll try to be discreet."

"Now I've made you cross. My tongue's always running away. Eddie, I do thank you for all you've done—and please forgive me, for everything."

"I suppose you wouldn't want to go to dinner and a theater with me on Saturday."

"I'd love it, and you know I would, only—only—don't get it into your head—"

"—don't get it into my head that you'll ever want to marry me. There's no law that I shouldn't keep on hoping, is there?"

"There's no law, but—it's no use."

He went at last, and she was glad of it. She didn't want to think of Eddie Craig, but it had to be done. The first man who had asked you to marry him—and quite possibly the last, she owned to herself. She was glad he had asked, it was over, and he wouldn't do it again right away.

"Mother'd say I ought to jump at him," she told herself. "Mother'd say a young doctor with money of his own was quite a catch for me. Indeed, she'd think Harvey Harrison was plenty good enough."

But she would never marry, never, never; and if Eddie Craig was persistent she'd stop seeing him. She wasn't going to be bothered, and she wasn't going to let him run on to false hopes, for that wouldn't be fair. She wished that she could exhibit Eddie to Cadeville, assembled, and let them know that he was in love with her. It might change her status from being merely Bernice's sister. In Cadeville a girl who has a bona-fide suitor was so much more important than one who has not. Eve wondered why this was so, and could find no answer. Maybe it was some deep racial reason; maybe it was merely a more luscious topic of gossip.

．．．

Everyone in the kitchen should have been busy, for it was ten o'clock and lunch should be well under way by that time. Helga should have been mixing the day's dishes in her great caldrons, Marta should have been putting pies in the oven and beating icing for cakes, Eve should have been concocting the more intricate salads, and throughout there should have been a bustle of quick and ordered industry. But no one was doing anything. Instead they were standing stock-still, as if an evil fairy had dropped in and put them under a spell.

Helga had a big spoon in her hand, but it was motionless. Marta had put down the rolling-pin, and Eve's slicing knives were in their rack. The girl who washed vegetables had turned off the faucet and stood beside the sink.

And all the assistants were equally motionless and silent. And for once, poor battered Ben, the odd-job kitchen man, was the center of attention.

"I tell you, it's time," he said in a husky undertone calculated not to reach beyond the kitchen doors. "I heard it straight. Mrs. Cleeve has sold out to the Woodser people, and it is going to be added to their chain. A fella I know who works in the Fifty-eighth Street."

"Maybe he's mistaken," said Marta.

"Maybe he didn't hear right."

Ben took this as a personal affront. "How could he be mistaken? There ain't nothing to be mistaken about. Besides, you seen that chap snooping round here last week and week before we all thought was a sanitary inspector or something? Well, he's the man who always looks over places for Woodsers. I described him to this fella I know, and he says that's the very fella."

"What does your friend do, that he knows so much, Ben?" asked Helga soothingly. "I believe you, you know, but sometimes things get mixed."

"He's the porter in the offices, and he's all over the place. He's real sharp, and gets onto lots of things. He's not got anything mixed. He's nobody's fool."

"Mrs. Cleeve's got a right to tell us if they've sold out," said Marta angrily. "I don't want to work for Woodser—bunch of slave drivers, they are. I know, I was in one of their branches till I couldn't stand it. List of rules as long as your arm, and fine you for everything you do. If you're a minute late, costs you a nickel. End of the week they got a big slice of your pay."

"And they don't pay so well to begin with. They get help cheap, and drive 'em," went on Ben. "They're always changing."

"I don't hold wiss changing," said Helga. "Here we stay pretty much the same and the work goes easily. Change often and work iss harder, for everybody new has to learn."

"If we've been sold out to Woodser I'm going to do some changing myself," snapped Marta. "Right off, I'll look for something new."

"It iss too bad," said Helga. "We all get along fine here. Don't jump too quick, Marta. We do not yet know when the change comes, nor how. And look at that clock. I must hustle."

They all looked at the clock and hustled. Ben lost his importance. Marta flew at the pastry board, and Eve turned toward the waiting salad materials. The various underlings went vigorously at the nearest task. Conversation became strictly limited to the necessary directions and requests. But the threatened change hung over them, bothered them all. When Mrs. Cleeve came in they all looked at her intently, trying to read in her expression some hint of the future. There was nothing new to see. She had been nervous and fidgety for a long time, and not so careful in noticing details of the work, but of late she had seemed somewhat more like her old self. Everyone had been reassured; gossip assumed that she had sent her suitor packing and made it up with Miss Fraley, and it was the consensus of opinion that this was the right thing for her to do. Now came this subterranean bomb—the cafeteria sold, and no one in on the secret. It was unfair and unkind, a slight put on her faithful, loyal helpers.

In the after-luncheon lull, when the general cleaning was in progress, Mrs. Cleeve came out to the kitchen to check up supplies, and Helga rose and addressed her ceremoniously, as one power to another.

"Madame—we hear that you have sold out to Woodser, and we are disturb. Will you say if it iss true or if it iss not true?"

Helga had spoken distinctly so that the whole kitchen could hear, and the whole kitchen heard and turned, silent and expectant, for Mrs. Cleeve's reply.

And this was as plain as Helga's question. "I had intended to tell you as soon as the final arrangements were made; until then I thought it best to say nothing. But since you've heard rumors, I know you want the truth. Yes, Miss Fraley and I have sold out to Woodser, and we have stipulated that those of our present employees who wish to stay on under the new management shall be allowed to do so, at their present wage scale. I hope you will all stay. The Woodser people are reliable and energetic, it's a big concern, and you'll all have more chance with them than with us. I can't begin to tell you what your faithfulness and efficiency have meant in the business; without it we never could have succeeded. And before we go we shall express our appreciation more substantially."

"But when do you go, madame?" asked Helga.

"The first of the month, if they accept our terms," Mrs. Cleeve looked about at her staff. "You've all been splendid and I'm proud to have worked with you, and had you for my friends."

After she had gone out no one spoke for a while. Then Helga said, sighingly: "So, that iss how the world goes. You think you are settled, and everything iss sure and going fine, and along comes a big upset. That iss life."

"D'you suppose the Woodsers will stand by what Mrs. Cleeve said—that we can all keep our places at the same money?" anxiously asked one of Helga's assistants.

"No, certainly not," spoke up Marta. "They promise that, but if they want to get rid of us they'll make it so hot for us we have to get out. Then they put in somebody cheaper. I know; I tell you. I've worked for them. They're a mean lot. They're the kind that starts decent people to praying for the revolution."

"Oh, you and your revolution," said Helga. "Here in America there will be no revolution, not in our time, nor in our children's. There iss no revolution where people are fed and have good shoes and good clothes and go to school, and get plenty jobs at good money. It iss no work, and starving and bad, unjust laws that make revolutions. All the same, I am sorry those Woodsers come. I see a bad time for all of us with them. And I am sorry Mrs. Cleeve and Miss Fraley are to go. They are good women, square to everybody. Eve, you have said nothing at all. Are you not thinking something?"

"I'm thinking; but what good does it do? We'll have to wait and see what happens."

"Now, that iss good. No use to cry out before we are hurt. If these Woodser people treat me right, I'll do as much by them. After all, the day's work iss the day's work, no matter who iss boss."

Marta was not subdued by all this weight of wisdom. "You'll find out quick enough what you're up against. I'm going to leave as soon as I can find something else."

But Marta did not go at once, as she had threatened. She waited and croaked her dismal prophecies day after day, until she had them all on edge. The negotiations were finished at

last, Mrs. Cleeve and Miss Fraley said good-by and gave each
member of the staff a ten-dollar bill as a parting good wish.
And the Woodser manager and his aide came in on a rainy
Monday morning, on a full tide of curiosity and apprehension.
The new manager, Mr. Dewson, was somewhat inclined to
stoutness and had a fat man's ingratiating smile. His aide, Mrs.
Canning, who was to be cashier, was a subdued and neutral
little woman, without color, age or significance. She said nothing, looked at no one, but she was a wizard at computing a
tray and making change. Mr. Dewson came out to the kitchen,
told them all heartily how glad he was they were to stay on
and work with him, promised cooperation and interest, and
ended his words with a genial "Now, boys and girls—let's
go!" then he posted up a list of rules and retired to his little
office outside.

"He sounds all right," said Helga, doubtfully, after he
had gone.

But Eve had taken one of her instant dislikes. "He's got a
cruel mouth, and all that boys and girls stuff isn't sincere. I
don't like him."

They read the rules. There were a great many, even as Marta
had said. Aprons, white coats and uniforms must now be
bought from their employers; Mrs. Cleeve had supplied them.
Employees' lunches were limited to two dishes, with either
coffee or tea, and bread and butter. No one had ever eaten
more than this, but it was hateful to be told they must not.
There were fines for lateness, for leaving before the hour of
five had struck, for absence, and for breakage over a certain
per cent. No pay for absence on account of sickness. One
week's vacation, without pay, allowed employees who had
been there for more than one year.

"Well, I wonder who they think they are?" said Eve. "It
sounds like Simon Legree in an Uncle Tom's Cabin show. All
Mr. Dewson needs is a long whip and a couple of bloodhounds."

"You see I was right," said Marta, triumphant.

More and more they saw that Marta was right. Mr. Dewson
was tireless, and his eyes saw everything. He was particularly
keen on wastage, and would like, Helga declared, to make

soup out of garbage! The counter girls, Amy reported, were instructed to cut down on the portions served, and Eve was hauled over the coals of his wrath for making salads that were too lavish. "What d'ye think this is?" he bawled. "A Park Avenue joint where they begin with a dollar cover charge?"

In the storeroom, too, she had to deal with this unpleasant trait. He checked and double-checked every item she handled. The brands of tea and coffee were changed and quality gave way all along the line for inferior goods, bought in enormous quantities by the whole Woodser chain. Not too inferior—they were smart enough to shade it only slightly—but the aggregate saving was large. Seconds, instead of firsts, in butter and lard and other fats, seconds in canned goods, in sirups, and dry groceries, in fruits. "If you season things right, nobody in the world can tell the difference in taste," said Mr. Dewson at Helga's protest.

Very shortly, on slight pretext, one of the assistant cooks was discharged, and no one was engaged to fill her place. This made more work for Helga and the remaining assistant. Next, one of the two odd-job women disappeared, Mr. Dewson holding that there was not sufficient to do to keep her busy.

He systematically harassed each department, concentrating a few days on this one, until it was properly speeded up, then a few days on the next, then the next, until he had completed his round, when he would begin all over again. He had jollying ways, would put his hand familiarly on the arm of Jennie or Amy as he talked, called them "girlie" and "dearie" and "sweetheart," stood too close to them, looked over their figures with appraising eyes. Amy drew off, flung off his hand, reminded him of her proper name, gave him back a level, contemptuous stare, but Jennie was softer, afraid. She needed her job, and she endured this familiarity shrinkingly. Tacitly the counter girls never left one of their number alone with him, unless it was unavoidable. They watched him and blocked his advance with silent, innocent feminine strategy.

In the kitchen he was less offensive—the women there were for the most part older, mature and not attractive to his type—but presently Eve found that he was calling her into his office to talk to her about the storeroom supplies, and that he

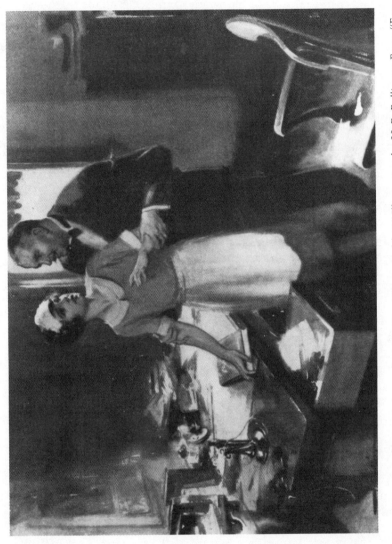

"'Why don't you stop all this upstage stuff and be agreeable?'" Illustration by H. R. Ballinger. From "Eve Goes On," *Ladies' Home Journal* 45, no. 5 (May 1928), p. 40.

would shut the door of the tiny place, tell her to sit down beside him at his desk, and lean his shoulder or press his fat knee against her.

The first time Eve kept her head, reached over and opened the door. "It's too warm in here," she said. "We need some air." But Mr. Dewson was not to be rebuffed. The second time she did it he closed the door again. A salesman, calling opportunely, released her. The third time brought the climax. "I want to talk to you confidentially," said Mr. Dewson. "I don't want the others to hear. Why don't we get along better, girlie? I could do a whole lot for you if you were nice to me. Now, that assistant of yours—you don't really need her. It'd be easy for a smart girl like you to do all that work, but I haven't fired her just because I like you and I want to be kind to you. Why don't you stop all this upstage stuff and be agreeable? I got a lotta influence in this company; I could get you more money, and—" He put his hot fat arm around her shoulders, drew her toward him, and at his touch Eve went into a panic.

She opened her mouth to scream, but he clapped his hand over it. "Shut up, you little fool. Don't you make a yip," he whispered. "If I'd a-thought—weow—" for Eve had bitten his hand with all the strength behind her strangled voice, and blood spurted from it. He let go his grip on her at the sudden fierce pain, and she seized the door and got through it, out into the darkened restaurant, bare of patrons, where Amy and Jennie were giving the final polishing of the coffee and tea boilers. Mrs. Canning was just coming in from the kitchen where she had been giving out the weekly pay envelopes.

"That—that horrible pig tried to take hold of me," cried Eve at the top of her voice as they turned startled faces toward her wild appearance. But Mr. Dewson was close behind her. "You little liar," he said. "Shut up your mouth. I tell you—"

But Amy, comprehending instantly, rushed to the kitchen door and flung it open. "Come in here, quick, all of you," she called, and as they trooped in, with Helga's magnificent height in the lead, she said, "Mr. Dewson tried to get fresh with Eve just as he's been trying to get fresh with the girls out here ever since he came. What are we going to do about it?"

"You're not going to do anything about it," snarled Mr.

Dewson, nursing his injured hand. "Here, Mrs. Canning, get me some iodine, and some cotton. And you all of you get back to your jobs, except you—" He turned viciously to Eve. "You're fired."

Helga advanced, taking off her apron. "If Eve is fired, I also am fired," she said, and snapped her strong fingers under Mr. Dewson's pudgy nose. "As for you, fat booby—you are not worth spitting at. I go."

"And so do I," cried Marta. "Let's all go."

They tore off aprons, jackets, flung them on the floor. "Sure, we'll all go!" they cried exultantly. Pandemonium reigned. Mr. Dewson, seeing the predicament he would be in with his superiors, began to cringe and beg, to run from one to the other, appealing, promising anything, his face twisted into abject fright. "Eve, I didn't mean anything—I didn't do anything to you. Tell 'em—tell 'em God, this is terrible—this'll be the end of me. I'm a married man with three little children—listen—listen—Eve—Helga—Mrs. Canning—talk to 'em for me—"

But Mrs. Canning declined to interfere, and Mr. Dewson begged and pleaded in vain. Very shortly the entire staff of the Woodser—late Cleeve Cafeteria—was standing out on the sidewalk in a compact group in which there was now that first rift of doubt which invariably follows a splendid gesture.

"Served him right, the dirty dog," exulted Marta. "I'd like to hear the string of lies he'll tell the general manager. I'll bet it'll be wonderful."

"It's a good thing it was pay day and we got our money," said Jennie. "I'll have to hunt something else right away."

"I wish you hadn't done it on my account," said Eve. "I feel responsible—I suppose I oughtn't to have made such a fuss."

"No, you did right," was Helga's decision. "It was bound to come, sooner or later, with a bad man like that. We go all together, instead of one by one; that iss the only difference."

"I'm only sorry I didn't give him a good poke in the jaw," growled Carlo. "What say we fellows go back and beat him up?"

"That's fool's talk," said Helga. "It would get us all into bad trouble—police, and courts, and maybe jail. No, Eve has damaged him sufficient."

Amy had been standing by listening, and now she drew them around her. "You know I've been intending to start a restaurant myself," she said. "I've only got a little money, and I've been afraid to try it—it seemed like taking such a chance. But this thing has made up my mind. I can borrow some, and I'll get right at it, and—well, why don't you all come and work with me? We'll get a place right near here, as close as we can, and put up a sign that we're the old Cleeve crowd, and I know everybody who ate here will come to us. We'll have a ready-made clientele, for everybody knows us. Give me all your addresses and I'll go to work like a demon, and you'll hear from me right off whether I can raise enough capital to put it over. I won't try to do it, though, unless you all promise to come with me."

"But we can get temporary jobs—we don't have to stay without work till you're ready, do we?" asked Jennie.

"Of course—go ahead; only promise you'll come with me when I'm ready. That's all I want."

"I'll come," said Helga. "We can make a new place go well, just like the old one did, I know it."

They all wanted to come. They promised, they gave Amy their addresses, and at last they drifted off, leaving Eve alone with Amy, both of them wildly excited and trying to keep cool.

"Have you got any money?" asked Amy.

"About three hundred, saved up, that's all."

"D'you want to put it in, and come along with me as a partner?"

"I'll gladly put it in, but it's not enough to make me a partner, Amy. Don't be benevolent to the poor."

"It's not being benevolent. I can't manage this thing alone. I'm scared to death of it, now the moment's come when I've got to do it. I wouldn't tell another soul, but it's been nothing but that horrible inside cautiousness of mine that's kept me back. Now you've got nerve—"

"Oh, I haven't."

"Yes, you have. Part of it's from ignorance, to be sure, because you don't know what we'll be up against; but all the same you've got it. And I need your nerve, just as you need my practical experience, and my knowledge. We can work together too. That means a lot. And don't you fret, but it'll be a frightful lot of work."

"Amy, I'd work myself to little bits of pieces for a chance like this."

"All right, my dear; you'll probably have to. And now, as our dear Mr. Dewson was so fond of saying, 'Boys and girls, let's go.'"

HALF A MILLION

Zona Gale

IN the late forenoon of an autumn day Mrs. Marian Burleigh walked through the harmonious rooms of her well-ordered house. The maids had finished grooming the floors and the furniture, fires burned lightly in the fireplaces, the vases had been filled with asters from the garden, the house was placid and expectant, waiting for its day to begin. In her dining room the luncheon table was laid for twelve, and Mrs. Burleigh, too, was waiting for her day to begin. Well gowned and well groomed, the fires of middle life burning lightly in her eyes, the flowers of autumn touching her cheeks, she was placid and expectant, like her house.

She stood looking from a great leaded window down onto a lawn of beeches, and she saw her day file past: Her luncheon for twelve; the rush down to the Fortnightly to hear the lecture; tea, in the rooms, for the English lecturer; dinner alone, probably on a tray in her room. Then the concert. Then home once more, to meet the dark house and the long night. Then the day again.

Her home, her maids, her car, her friends, her club were all that they should be. Since Mr. Burleigh had died, two years

From *Ladies' Home Journal* 45, no. 4 (April 1928).

ago, and Camilla had married, six years ago, she had filled her life as best she could. And now the thing that she wanted, more than anything in the world, was to empty her life of everything with which she had filled it and to begin at some beginning.

"I'm only fifty-four," she thought, coming back to the fireplace mirror. "With these brands of cold cream and powder, I could pass for fifty. There are years of work in me yet."

Camilla's lovely photograph was on the mantel—Camilla, in her wedding gown, conscious, expensive, happy. She looked in her mother's eyes, confident of having done all that was required of her. She had married well, she had a little girl five years old, and a charming apartment in Park Avenue. The years stretched before Camilla, filled to the brim until her children, too, should be married. Mrs. Burleigh looked at her daughter's likeness and sighed.

"I shouldn't want it all to do over again," she thought. "I'm free now for something else."

For what else?

When the bell rang and a telegram was handed in, it was as if Camilla had spoken, not as an answer, but in absorbed preoccupation with her own affairs. The message was from Lenox, where they were staying for the moment, and read:

BOB HAS INHERITED HALF A MILLION FROM HIS UNCLE DAN. WE ARE COMING DOWN TONIGHT FOR SUNDAY. LOVE.   CAMILLA

Half a million. For Camilla who loved beauty and had never had enough, even with her modestly brilliant marriage. Nobody could possibly enjoy half a million more than Camilla.

The luncheon guests began to arrive—Mrs. Barnaby Maltby, a widow with two married sons; Mrs. Larry Marks, twice a widow, childless, not yet fifty; Mrs. LeMarr, her husband in business, her children married.

They were all women of position, dignity, respectability, substance, family. Mrs. Burleigh went through the dreary catalogue, looking at these guests of hers, wondering if they were as serene as they looked. How, she wondered, had they solved or dismissed the question that faced her—the spending of a presumable twenty-five years in elegant leisure, a leisure which they called being "rushed to death"? Mrs. Burleigh looked down her table and suddenly asked them: "What does a woman of fifty do with her life? Whatever it is, I'm keen to begin."

They all inevitably said that they were not fifty and they didn't know. They laughed much and speculated lightly:

"She loafs."

"What else should she do with her 'splendid idle forties'?"

"Her share of work is done; now let her play."

"She's earned some rest—before she has to rest."

"The woman of forty-odd with money and married children is the most fortunate woman alive."

"She is—if she is!"

Mrs. LeMarr looked up from her plate and produced an electrical silence when she said: "I'm forty something, my husband is a successful enough business man and my daughters are married. But I'm not the most fortunate woman on earth." They waited, not knowing what was coming. "Because," Mrs. LeMarr proceeded, "if I lift my hand to be useful, outside my home, my husband thinks I'm going to die next day of a nervous breakdown."

Mrs. Burleigh lowered her eyes lest her guests should see the answering fire in her own eyes. Not for any treasure would she have confided to them that her husband had felt exactly the same way.

"I can go to luncheons and dinners and bridge, I can dance all night; but if I want to take one step toward any work for the town or a school or a charity, Joseph thinks I'm overdoing. 'Write them a check,' he says, 'and stay away.'"

Her husband to the line, Mrs. Burleigh thought. It seemed almost disloyal to the dead to recognize him so sharply.

"What would your husband say," she asked Mrs. LeMarr, "if you wanted to take a position for pay, such as I'm looking for?"

"That's what I'd like to do," Mrs. LeMarr cried, "but Joseph would perish—he'd just naturally perish. Joseph Le-Marr," said his wife with spirit, "would like me to sit all day long in the chaise lounge in my room and wear a peacock blue house gown. When he comes home he wants me to be there."

It all came back to Mrs. Burleigh—her own endless arguments. She had almost forgotten them—the evenings when she had wanted to go to a lecture or a meeting, and her husband had said: "Now you'll be nervous if you do that. Let's get a couple in and have some bridge." In vain she had told him that bridge made her nervous. He could never be persuaded. He wanted her there.

For two years she had been to the discreet lectures and meetings which her mourning had allowed her. Now she wanted to know what to do with her time—for pay. What would he have said to that?

"And I'll tell you," Mrs. LeMarr cried, "of a job that I had offered to me only yesterday. I didn't even mention it to Joseph; I knew better. It's to be chaperon in the Madora—the new business woman's home. Two hundred a month, and the chance to know all those girls. Do you want me to speak for you?"

"Rather!" cried Mrs. Burleigh. Her eyes sparkled, she seemed almost young when later, in the drawing-room, she talked about this. "A chance to be useful, a chance to be a part of the world, and for the first time in my life, to feel myself able to earn," she said almost passionately. Mrs. LeMarr arranged to come next day to take her to interview the president of the Madora board.

Camilla's lovely face smiled down on her mother from the mantel. And when the guests praised her daughter, Mrs. Burleigh said gayly: "Next to seeing Camilla happy, the best thing that I can think of on earth is the new job—if I get it!"

There was no question about her getting it. The president of the board, tremendously impressed by the fact that this was *the* Mrs. Marian Burleigh, wife of the late Seymour Burleigh, promised to let her know next morning, but he gave her to understand that there was little question about the board's decision. On Saturday morning he telephoned to her, congratulating himself, he said, on securing her.

Mrs. Burleigh turned from the telephone and walked through the harmonious rooms of her well-ordered house. Floors and furniture were dusted and groomed, fires burned on the hearths, the vases had been filled, and the house lay, placid and expectant, as it had done daily for twenty-five years, waiting for its day to begin.

Well—now her own new day was about to begin.

Abruptly she felt that she hated all the well-groomed quiet of her house. This was no existence for a woman alone in the world—"alone in life," as they said. She stood before the mantel, and Camilla's lovely face smiled out at her. How glad of all this Camilla would be.

"Camilla darling," said Mrs. Burleigh aloud, "for the first time since you stopped needing me—you did stop needing me, you know—and since father went, I may have my place in the world too."

Camilla and Bob and little Margot and the nurse came down from Lenox just before dinner that evening. Mrs. Burleigh's car was at the station, and her erect and modish figure was in the back seat. She gathered Camilla and Margot in her arms, kissed Bob and was so gently exuberant that Camilla said:

"Oh, mummy darling, you are glad to see us! And how adorable it is to run down to see you. Is everything just the same?"

"Not with you," said Mrs. Burleigh.

"Oh, not with us—no! Rather not. Bob's poor Uncle Dan, dying in South Africa at Something-dorp and leaving no will at all—and Bob being his nearest relative, Bob whom he never saw. . . . Isn't it too exciting?"

"I saw him when I was two," Bob corrected her mildly. "I didn't think I made the slightest impression; in fact, I didn't think anything. Poor old boy, I wish I might have done something for him."

"Because he'll be doing something for us and for Margot for years and years."

Margot now took her part in the exchange. "Daddy and mummy have some new money," she explained to her grandmother, "and we're going to have fun. New fun."

At table Mrs. Burleigh asked them their plans. "What's all the new fun?" she wanted to know.

"Europe," said Camilla instantly. "Bob and Margot and nurse and I."

"For a year?" her mother asked.

"For forevermore!" said Camilla firmly. "No more America and no more grind for Bobby and Camilla. Just joy."

Mrs. Burleigh looked at Bob Mallory. Bob was looking in his plate.

"Swiss and French schools for Margot," Camilla was going on, "Paris and music for me. Travel and ruins and libraries and leisure for Bob—yachts and friends and the whole wide world to roam in. Think of it, darling! For our whole lives."

Mrs. Burleigh looked puzzled. "It sounds a quite perfect vacation," she said. "But what shall you do after that?"

"That's just it!" burst out Bob Mallory violently.

"Now, Bob darling!" Camilla coaxed. "Don't be horrid before mother."

"A life of hotels and yachts and traveling—a life of loafing, Mother Burleigh. Isn't that outrageous for a well man?"

Camilla was very lovely in cream lace which her mother thought became her delicacy as a web becomes a rose. "You see, mother," she said, "Bob is American—provincial American. He doesn't know that there is anything except work. He simply cannot imagine leisure. Isn't it too absurd?"

Bob left his salad, lifted his six feet into the upper reaches of the room and began to stalk about the floor. "I am American," he said. "I know that work is the only decent occupation for any man."

"But what does he work for?" Camilla cried. "To support and educate his family; to get a few pleasures for them and for himself. Well, here, Bob dear, is your little family all supported and its education all provided for forever, and all the part you have left is the pleasures. Can't you see that?"

Bob leaned over Camilla's chair. He adored her—that was plain to all, in the way that he touched her shoulders, in the way that his lips brushed her hair. "Don't tell me," he said, "that you don't know that work is more than that, more than a bribe to the universe to get the fat things of life. Work—why, work is work, Camilla."

But you have the chance now to lift yourself and your family into the life we were all meant for."

"Meant for! Meant to be a lot of jolly loafers?"

"Sit down, Bob dear," said Mrs. Burleigh, "so that I can ring for dessert."

Mrs. Burleigh smiled into his eyes, and as if he had caught an ember of understanding in her look he sat down meekly enough, and even smiled; but Mrs. Burleigh noted the strong firm lines of his still boyish face and felt a sudden sympathy for him and an impatience with Camilla.

Camilla said with dignity when the maid had gone: "But the world is full of things to do besides working for a living! We won't loaf. We'll live—at last."

Bob looked at her wistfully. "Haven't you liked it, dear," he said—"my going off to the office and coming home—having things to tell you that went well?"

"Having worries and disagreeable people and stupid journeys and overwork and nervousness. Why don't you paint it as it is?" Camilla cried. "A lawyer is a slave. You've never been anything else."

As they went up to the drawing-room Mrs. Burleigh thought that he looked very unlike a slave—this tall broad brown independent youth who was trying to hold on to the thing he believed worth while.

"What is it that you propose, Camilla dear?" her mother asked.

"I want Bob to leave the firm," she sobbed. "I want us to do Europe for a year or so, and then settle down in France—not too far from Paris—and have the Riviera and the M-Mediterranean—and leisure—and life."

"Gosh!" said Bob. "I've got a life now—and I'm sorry you haven't."

Camilla stood up, with a manner of being brought to bay, before Bob. "We've got to settle it quickly," she said to her mother, "because Bob was just going to make some frightful journey West."

"Oh, come now, Camilla! It's to California, mother. To Sacramento—with some mountain stuff thrown in."

"And if he's going with me somebody else should be sent out there. We really came down here to talk it over with you, mother—and take your advice. I knew you'd agree with me," she ended girlishly.

Her husband's ear had caught only one sentence of this. "If I'm going with you. . . ." he echoed. "Then you—"

"I'm going anyway, Bob, for a year," said Camilla steadily. "I can take my own money that I've been saving for Margot. Oh, Bob!" she cried. "For a year—for a year! Compromise on that—a year with me over there—"

"It's a crucial year in my practice, Camilla," he said; "you know that."

"If you love me better than your practice—Mother! Make him see!"

"This is between you two, dear," Mrs. Burleigh said.

"If Bob loves me—Bob, darling?"

Camilla put her arms about Bob's neck, her cheek against his. And Bob suddenly said, "What a fool a man is. All right, Camilla. I'll go as you say—for a year."

"Mother, isn't it glorious?" Camilla cried.

"I hope so, dear," said Mrs. Burleigh.

"But I'm going to have the trip to Sacramento first," Bob made it clear. "I really must go there. After that the year is yours."

So Camilla brought her maps, and they sat before the fire and planned. Camilla planned, rather, and her husband and her mother listened.

"And now, darling," said Camilla to her mother, "when will you be joining us, and where?"

"I?" said Mrs. Burleigh, startled. "Oh, not at all, Camilla. I haven't told you that I have a plan of my own." She told them—the empty days, the Madora, her own good fortune. "From the first of October," she said, "I shall be on duty every day from nine until five—busy, and almost happy."

She looked up with a kind of pleased complacence. She saw Bob smiling and nodding his approval. Then she saw Camilla leaning toward her, white lipped and stern. "Mother Burleigh," Camilla cried tensely, "are you proposing to take a job?"

"But certainly! And isn't it enormously clever of me to get such a good one?"

"Mother!" said Camilla. "Mother!" And burst into a passion of tears.

"Camilla—what on earth—," her mother tried to say.

Camilla sank into her chair and sobbed without speaking. Mrs. Burleigh and Bob stared at each other, then Bob knelt by Camilla and her mother leaned and caught her hands. And they heard Camilla's sobbing words: "All my life—since I was a little girl—I have seen you in this house—the m-mistress of it—looking like a queen and—and entertaining our friends. And to think of you taking a job—going off like any agent, mother—"

"Camilla!" Her mother spoke sternly. "Don't you see that this is a great chance for usefulness that has come to me?"

"You don't need to be so useful as all that!" Camilla cried. "You are useful, just by being beautiful and gracious and yourself. You have a position—"

"I have a position," Mrs. Burleigh agreed, "at two hundred dollars a month, Camilla."

"Mother, I can't bear it—I just can't bear it!" Camilla sobbed. "It'll spoil every bit of my pleasure in the money, it'll spoil every bit of Europe."

"But you have gone away from me, Camilla. You have your own interests; let me have mine."

"Why, darling," her daughter cried, "you don't know what a big part of my life you are. I've always thought of you here—here, in the home. I don't know what I'd do if I couldn't think of you here." She dropped down beside her mother and buried her face on her mother's knee. "Dearest," she begged, "you've sacrificed a lot for me all your life—I know that. Give me just this one little bit of a thing more, so that I can have all our good fortune—and nothing will be spoiled. Please, dearest, please."

Mrs. Burleigh and Bob looked at each other above Camilla's bowed figure. He shrugged and lifted his brows and turned away. Camilla's mother looked down at her for a moment. Then she stroked her bright hair.

"I've always lived in your happiness, Camilla," she said. "Very well—I'll do as you like. But," she added firmly as Camilla struggled up, dabbing at her eyes, "but if you want to think of me here, it's here that I'll be. I'll not sail a foot toward Europe!"

At this Bob laughed, and Mrs. Burleigh laughed with him, a good deal ruefully. And Camilla cried:

"Mother! Bob! What adorable angels you both are to me. Only I'm sure you'll see in time that it's the sensible thing to do."

Toward ten o'clock that evening Mrs. Burleigh sat with a novel before a bright fire. When the telephone beside her rang, the voice was a woman's voice, apologetic but determined.

"Mrs. Burleigh, this is Mrs. Harden, at the Madora. I oughtn't to call you, but there is something that only you can handle."

Mrs. Burleigh said that she was extremely sorry, that her plans had changed, she would not be coming to the Madora, and she would not therefore be of any use. But the hurried and determined voice persisted:

"Yes—forgive me. This has nothing to do with your coming here. This is about someone who mentioned your name."

Then Mrs. Burleigh listened.

"Iris Valentine." Mrs. Harden continued, "from Sacramento—who has come to New York to see your son-in-law."

"But he is on the point of going to Sacramento."

"To see her, she says. We read in the paper tonight that they had come back to town and were with you. She hadn't been able to reach him at his office. And she wondered if she could possibly see him."

"Let her write to him and make an appointment."

"Mrs. Burleigh," said Mrs. Harden slowly, "this is something very, very important, or I should not ask it. His office says that he is away for the month. The paper says that he is here for the weekend. If she could reach him before he leaves—"

Mrs. Burleigh agreed to let Mr. Mallory know, and then sat staring at the fire. When Camilla and Bob came in from their concert and sat before the hearth over the little supper that she had herself prepared, she listened to Camilla, in her high spirits, and looked at Bob, who smoked in silence, and wondered how she was to see him alone. She had an uneasy sense that this was a matter which it would be better not to share with Camilla at the moment.

This point Bob seemed to settle for her. When Camilla rose he opened the door for her and said: "I think I'll have another cigarette before I come up, dear." Camilla was, Mrs. Burleigh thought, still almost indecently affable about having her own way.

As soon as they were alone Bob said: "Mother, if I ever reneged I'd renege on my promise to Camilla to knock off work for a year."

"If I ever reneged, so would I!" said Mrs. Burleigh. But at that Bob stared a bit. "Oh, but come now," he said. "For you that's not half bad. You have your home and your fortune and your leisure—"

"So have you!" she cried, and smiled.

But Bob said, and frowned: "It's not the same for a woman." And she said no more. "Anyway, I've got one last fling," he said, "on my Sacramento case. And it's likely to be a nasty one, and may keep me out there for some time, thank the Lord."

Now Mrs. Burleigh said: "I suspect that you needn't go out there at all, Bob. Iris Valentine is here in town."

Bob cried "Here!" in a manner of stupefaction, discounted her words, then demanded: "But how did you know her name?"

While Mrs. Burleigh explained she was watching him closely. For this man had Camilla's happiness in her keeping. But when she had finished he merely said: "Thunder! Now I won't get even my one last fling at work—and the mountains."

Mrs. Burleigh felt a quick relief, told him that he would have certain mountains in Europe, and waited for him to impart something or other.

"Look here," he said instead, "do you think that you and I could slip down there tonight? It isn't only that I've absolutely got to get up to Boston early tomorrow. But Camilla—you understand, I don't want her worried."

"Quite so," said Mrs. Burleigh, feeling less relief than she had thought, and telephoned to Mrs. Harden.

The matron's voice came back briskly: "We're still sitting over the fire," she said. "I've been hearing the whole story. Come by all means."

"So she's been hearing the whole story, has she?" said Bob grimly.

Aston, Mrs. Burleigh's reserved chauffeur, in the long tenure of his job had never yet been called out by his lady at that hour of night. But he said: "Yes, madam. As quickly as I can dress," without a shadow of surprise—a restraint which Mrs. Burleigh felt herself to have equaled as she drove at Bob's side without a question.

Bob told it all at once. "Iris Valentine," he said, "claims to be my Uncle Dan's legitimate daughter. Rather, her mother claims to have been his wife. The mother has just died, I believe—I heard from her lawyer just before I had the word from Africa. That was why, of course, I've held out on the Sacramento trip—but I've said nothing to Camilla. I don't think there can be anything in it. Only, how did they know so soon? That worries me. If she can establish herself, since he died without a will—"

"Oh, poor Camilla!" Mrs. Burleigh said.

"Exactly," said Bob only.

The Madora office was dark and forlorn at this hour. But Mrs. Harden's room was warm and bright. The figure that rose from the hearth side was that of a uniquely beautiful and distinguished girl in her early twenties.

When they were seated, "Will you give me your facts, Miss Valentine?" Bob said only.

This girl, gentle, controlled, with the clear skin and delicate features of a good inheritance, began to speak simply and reasonably. She said that she had been born in California twenty-three years before; that her father was Daniel Valentine, and her mother Gwendolyn Fear. That her father and mother had lived together but three years, and that in California. That since that time he had sent a monthly sum to her mother. That they had never been divorced; that her mother had died but a fortnight before; and that it was just before her death that a friend in Johannesburg, who knew all the circumstances, had cabled the news of his death. It was her mother's lawyer who had written at once to Bob, of whose relationship to her husband she had always known, and it was her wish to retain him to push their claims. Also it was her mother who had exacted a promise that she would come to New York at once. All this she related in a trained and resonant voice, with an enunciation definite and delightful. At the close of the concise and ordered study she took from her bag her father's and mother's marriage certificate, her own birth certificate, and a dozen letters bearing the signature which Bob knew to be that of his uncle.

"Your thought is, of course, Miss Valentine," Bob said without expression, "that you are your father's heir, since he died intestate."

"That was mother's thought," said Miss Valentine.

"What do you propose?" Bob asked.

Mrs. Harden intervened. This woman was small, with a large square head which she energized as she talked. "I always look out for the welfare of my girls," she said sharply. "I have been advising her to see what you would propose under the circumstances."

Bob turned to Mrs. Burleigh. "I expect," he said, "those papers and letters being what they are, we should better explain this to Camilla. If we can make an early appointment at your house, I'll wait over for an hour in the morning."

They appointed an hour which found Camilla still in a blue silk gown and on a blue velvet chaise lounge, with a cup of chocolate.

"We'll have her up here, if you don't mind," Bob said. "My train doesn't seem to run by your schedule. But I'd better tell you first what it's about, darling."

He sat on the foot of the chaise lounge, looked at his mother-in-law for support, and said rapidly, with his bluntest attorney-at-law manner: "Camilla, dearest, Uncle Dan seems to have had a daughter, who may prove to be his real heir."

"Instead of us?" Camilla stared at him. And at his almost guilty confirmation she cried: "I'll not believe it!"

"Not yet, at any rate," he said cheerfully. "We'll wait till she gets here."

"Mother!" Camilla appealed. "But why on earth should I see such a person?"

Mrs. Burleigh said somewhat stiffly: "Nonsense, Camilla. She is a lady—"

"I suppose even people who are not ladies might legally inherit money," said Bob crossly. "Wasn't that the bell?"

Camilla set down her cup, drew a gold satin quilt across her knees and waited, like an indignant queen, for the cat to enter.

Iris Valentine came in, wearing gray, well and recently cut. Almost upon Miss Valentine's gray heels moved Mrs. Harden, taking personal charge of her. And to Camilla, Miss Valentine repeated her story, produced her papers, showed her father's signature, and waited.

"And upon these things," Camilla said excitedly, "you hope to establish that you are Uncle Dan's sole heir?"

"In case no will is found," Bob interposed.

Miss Valentine said nothing, because Camilla's high voice went on: "How is it that we have never heard of this wife and daughter of Uncle Dan?"

"But really, no one heard much of him himself, I fancy," said Miss Valentine. "And he said almost nothing about himself when he came to see us, about ten years ago."

"Was he in America ten years ago?" Bob demanded in amazement.

"You see!" said Miss Valentine quietly. "We didn't know it, either, until he came to the door. He never told anyone anything, apparently."

Camilla sat up in her blue and gold surroundings. And to Mrs. Burleigh, watching a Camilla strange and new to her, it occurred that a contest for money will change the actual features of folk. Only Iris Valentine—her features seemed not to have changed.

Camilla's voice came cutting its way again: "Evidently," she said, "there must have been a divorce and a settlement and you are keeping it from us!"

Miss Valentine flushed and looked faintly astonished. She said nothing.

Camilla dropped her voice. "Bob," she said audibly, "her claim is perfectly absurd. Of course Uncle Dan's lawyer would have known if he had a wife."

Mrs. Burleigh was seeking to remember whether Camilla herself had ever seen the man whom she was calling "Uncle Dan." As if Miss Valentine had caught that thought from the air, she said to Camilla: "Pardon, did you ever, then, see him— my father?"

"I never saw Uncle Dan," Camilla said majestically, "but I know something of the law." This inconclusive statement hung upon the air and died of its own weight. "It's your idea," Camilla now said, "that your father's entire fortune should be yours?"

"Of course that's her idea," declared Mrs. Harden forcibly.

Miss Valentine was silent. She was looking at Camilla speculatively, collectedly, and with some amazement.

"You are alone in the world. What would you do with half a million dollars?" Camilla pursued. Again her mother looked at her. Was this Camilla at all?

Bob interposed hurriedly: "Most of us could find uses for another million, I fancy."

"What is your work, may we ask?" Camilla now asked Iris Valentine.

Miss Valentine regarded her steadily. "I have no work now," she said, "but I am interested in the stage."

"An actress!" Camilla cried. "Then even a million wouldn't last you long."

Suddenly Mrs. Burleigh rose and crossed the room to Iris Valentine. "My dear Miss Valentine," she said, "I'm sure we all want to do the right thing. Bob, perhaps Miss Valentine will give us her idea of what that will be?"

Miss Valentine was silent, looking from one to another.

"Her idea!" cried Camilla. "Her idea is, of course, to have her father's fortune and to shut us out. Naturally."

Miss Valentine turned to Camilla. "Shut you out?" she repeated. "I did not know that this concerned you at all."

Bob Mallory looked at her, but her face was smooth and without a shadow. For the first time it occurred to him that she did not know that he himself had been notified that he was next of kin, and heir of his uncle. Miss Valentine had come to him solely to protect her rights, because he was—he gathered—her cousin. "My dear Miss Valentine," he cried, "my wife of course has supposed that you know that I have been declared my uncle's next of kin, and his heir."

Now as they looked at this girl they saw relief and relaxation take her features. She smiled a little. "Oh," she said, "so that's it!"

"That being the case, would you be willing to come to a settlement?" Bob asked hurriedly.

Mrs. Burleigh leaned forward and looked in Miss Valentine's face. "You understand," she said, "my daughter—this has been a great shock to her, when she had been thinking of herself—"

"Oh, naturally!" cried Miss Valentine quickly. "Oh, now I understand quite, quite!" Her face was almost joyous.

"Miss Valentine," said Bob, "will you tell us exactly what you think ought to be done?"

Miss Valentine sat, her poise that of the woman who knows quite how to take care of herself, in spite of all the Camillas and all the Mrs. Hardens. When she spoke she addressed Mrs. Burleigh and Bob.

"I thought," she said—"and you understand, Mr. Mallory, that I was consulting you merely as the lawyer naturally most interested—I thought that I should like to have enough to keep myself until I get established in New York—say four or five thousand. And I should like to send two young people through college—neighbors of ours in Sacramento. That's all."

There was silence until Mrs. Harden burst out: "Well, of all the crazy—," and Bob put in gravely, "You mean four or five thousand a year, I take it?"

"Oh, no!" Miss Valentine said composedly. "I shall find my work in a year or two; I feel certain of that. Really, ten thousand all together would be quite all that I had thought of."

"But you know," said Bob earnestly, "that your father's fortune was very large?"

"I suppose it must have been," said Miss Valentine: "poor father made such a slave of himself getting it together."

Bob looked at Camilla. And it was at Camilla that Mrs. Burleigh looked, and with a manner of gentle triumph.

And Camilla incredibly cried: "Bob! Mother! Now we know she's an impostor, or she wouldn't be asking for such a ridiculous sum as that!"

At that Iris Valentine got to her feet. She spoke with a power and a fire no one would have guessed to be in that clear and transparent vessel of hers, with her gentle speech and manner.

"People like you," she said, and now she spoke to Camilla—"people like you haven't the smallest idea of what life means to people like me. It doesn't mean idleness and amusement and it doesn't mean having things put in one's lap. It doesn't even mean money. It means just one thing—work at something one loves, and getting somewhere oneself through work that one has done. I don't want father's half million dollars, or whatever he had, and neither did mother. All my life she taught me that there is no happiness except in work that you love. Well, I love the stage. I've worked at it on the Coast. Now I have a chance in New York. I didn't come East primarily to see you, but because this chance had opened. But mother made me promise that I would see you, and she and I thought out together what might be arranged. When your office said you were leaving for the West, and when Mrs. Harden mentioned Mrs. Burleigh and said that you were here for the weekend, she was good enough to arrange—I'd gone to the Madora because I haven't much to get along on, but I have enough. Don't think that I want to upset your plans or take your fortune. I want one thing—success on the stage—and I'm willing to work till I die to get that. I know you won't understand. People like you could never understand. But there are people who do."

"I'll say there are!" cried Bob, and sprang away from Camilla and walked the floor. "It's what I understand better than any other one thing. I'd rather be a big attorney than a little millionaire. I know what you mean, Miss Valentine."

Mrs. Burleigh's rich voice took up his period. "With all my heart I understand, my dear," she said. "If you don't find your happiness in your work you don't find it—that's all."

Camilla threw aside her gold coverlet and stood up. She was looking at Iris Valentine. "Do you mean," she said, "that you would give up a fortune for the stage?"

"Haven't you known," said Iris Valentine steadily, "of women who have given up fortunes for love of a man, and never regretted it? Well, my love happens to be the stage. Oh, I'm not stage-struck. I know what I can do—I've begun to prove it, ever so little. And a fortune is nothing beside it. But whether I win or lose success, the work is what I want."

"But couldn't you have a fortune and succeed on the stage too?" Camilla demanded.

"I wouldn't work hard enough then," said Miss Valentine. "I'd get soft and self-indulgent. I'd have a divided mind.

No—some people might do that. But if I had half a million dollars now, no matter how much I loved my work, all the softness and ease would poison it. I expect you won't understand that either."

Camilla said strangely: "No, I don't understand that. But I respect you no end—and I have to ask your pardon. I've never met anyone like you." Then she looked at Bob and at her mother, and was silent.

Bob was arranging for Iris to come to the office when he returned to New York, and as she put out her hand Camilla quite suddenly kissed her. Mrs. Burleigh thought grimly: "Camilla is certainly a lady when she has her own way."

"I think Miss Valentine's pretty silly, if you ask me!" said Mrs. Harden gratuitously as the door closed.

Bob turned to Camilla. "So then you're still a half millionairess, anyway darling," he said absently.

Camilla hardly heard him. "Oh, Bob," she said, "you must settle thousands on her without her knowing a thing about it. Some day—"

"Some day she may be willing to give in and sell out," said Bob bitterly.

Abruptly Camilla cried: "Bob! Mother! Do you really feel about work as she does? The stuffy law, and that awful place at the Madora—do you?"

"Yes. Only worse," said Bob.

"Mother?"

"Absolutely, darling. But that's all put behind us, isn't it?"

"No!" said Camilla. "Oh, no. That girl—oh, I expect it was her wanting her work more than the money—oh, Bob! Give me the summer, and then if you want to come back and go to work I'll come too."

"Brick of the world!" said Bob.

Mrs. Burleigh said nothing. She sat looking at Camilla in Bob's arms. Then Camilla cried to her: "Mother darling, what a pig! I believe you've wanted all your life to have a job—even when father was living. Didn't you?"

"Ever since I can remember."

"And all I could think of was just that I wanted you at home—there—"

"That's what they always want of women—want them to be there," Mrs. Burleigh said.

Camilla drew Bob along and came and kissed her. "Go on down to your messy old home," she cried. "And just you try to forgive me."

Margot was brushing at the door, and she pushed in, looking adorable. "Daddy," she said, "can I have some of our new money to get me a honestly doll wiv really hair and a truly squeak?"

"Our new money can do lots of things, darling," said Bob. "Maybe even that."

He turned to Mrs. Burleigh and said: "But really, mother, why don't you just enjoy your well-earned leisure now? It is different with a woman."

Marian Burleigh laughed. She said only: "I'm going to do something for Iris Valentine, too—whether she likes it or not. I owe her something myself."

MEN ARE LIKE THAT

Eudora Ramsay Richardson

EMMA Morrison swung herself through the revolving door conscious that the elasticity had gone from her. In the rest room she hung her hat and coat on the usual hook and studied her reflection in the mirror. Yes, she looked her twenty-four years and perhaps one or two more. There were shadows beneath her dark eyes. Listlessly she started toward the rear of the bank.

There he stood—the new trust officer. Emma saw him talking to the president; saw him, and hated his earnest good looks. From the beginning he would be her enemy. She was sick to death of seeing men climb past her. At his new desk across the aisle sat Herbert Harris, yesterday promoted from will soliciting to manager of new business. There was no reason why she should not have been given his former work—anything to take her from the hopeless rut. But no, she was needed in her important service position. Dearly she had paid for having made herself indispensable.

The president smiled and with a stubby forefinger beckoned to Emma. Rotund old gentleman with flabby cheeks and squinting little eyes that looked out from enveloping flesh folds with the obtuse kindliness of a tame elephant, so pleased

From *Ladies' Home Journal* 45, no. 5 (May 1928).

with the economic scheme! How could he understand unrest of any kind?

"Miss Morrison," the great man patronized, "the new head of the trust department, Mr. Wainwright. You'll find this girl superb, Wainwright. We couldn't do trust business without her."

Emma tried to smile. Thank heaven these men couldn't read the cynical thoughts she had learned so well to suppress, couldn't know that after five years of work praise was not enough.

"I'm afraid I'll have to depend on you at first," John Wainwright replied.

There was nothing surprising in that. Emma was entirely used to being depended upon by officers of the bank.

She murmured something—it couldn't matter what, for no one would be listening—and lifted her great ledger from the drawer.

A new trust officer, and Emma Morrison his bookkeeper and untitled assistant—the same old story reënacted! There was no use fighting against the system. Obviously, not having studied law, she could not hope to become trust officer; and there seemed no chance of being transferred to another department in which promotion would be logical.

That afternoon Emma was about to open the filing cabinet when John Wainwright came to her side and stood a moment waiting. Not until she turned did he speak. At the Mercantile Bank men were all business in their methods. Could it be that this man was combining with his work social amenities he had learned elsewhere?

"When you have time, Miss Morrison will you go over the real-estate files with me?" he said, and added with a half apologetic smile, "You see I'm going to be a burden to you."

"I can stop what I'm doing now," Emma replied. "Perhaps it would be as well to work here where we can be near the files."

"All right," John Wainwright agreed and immediately drew a chair to Emma's desk.

Emma knew the trust department's entire story. She had kept its books, guarded its records, watched its growth for the five years of its fiduciary existence. It was easy enough to tell

"These men couldn't know that praise was not enough." Illustration by
Dudley Glayne Summers. From "Men Are Like That," *Ladies' Home Journal*
45, no. 5 (May 1928), p. 29.

it all—to explain the loans and produce the mortgages, the insurance policies. When she had finished, John Wainwright, with elbow on the desk and chin in the palm of his hand, leveled his eyes with hers and was silent for a moment. Then abruptly he rose.

"Thank you," he said. "I'd no idea the work of years could be made clear in an hour."

"Let me know when you're ready to go over the bonds and wills," Emma continued. She tried to speak as impersonally as one might dictate into the gaping mouth of a dictaphone.

"Tomorrow," John Wainwright replied. "I'm due now at the executive meeting."

Emma watched him go. There would be no difference. Like his predecessor, this man would depend on her, and she would remain as stationary as the filing cabinet. The president marched pompously toward the carpeted elegance of the board room. The vice presidents sauntered after with scarcely less grandeur. The cashier followed, and now came the three assistant cashiers. Last of all, like a bantam rooster in the Plymouth Rock's seraglio, strutted Herbert Harris, calling attention to his recent elevation by a throat clearing which seemed to Emma to resemble a faint crow. How utterly absurd ever to have hoped one day to be a part of this procession!

Emma glanced across the elegant tops of many desks behind which revolving chairs evidenced recent desertion. It was the flippancy of others for which she paid. One little stenographer with hair as short as the brains it covered had left her typewriter to talk to the veritable reflection of herself who operated the switchboard. A file clerk coquetted with a youth who kept books. Not a girl was at her place now that the officers' surveillance was lifted. These—these silly children who in their thinking were as far removed from Emma Morrison as the president was from the office boy—helped men to form their estimates of women, chained the ambitious ones to typewriters and adding machines. Emma swallowed hard and returned to her work.

Almost at once she was startled by the metallic notes of a voice which came to her like a scale run in high trebles. "Will you get Mr. Wainwright for me?" a woman was asking precisely as she might have spoken to her chauffeur.

Emma looked appraisingly from the high-heeled slippers upward along the coat that dripped with fur, to the gloved hand that held an ornate bag, and to the other whose too many rings lay exposed upon the mahogany rail. From head to foot this woman proclaimed that she was neither created nor dressed for toil.

"He's in conference now," Emma replied with deliberation. "Won't you sit down and wait?"

The woman smiled a bored little smile and shrugged her bored little shoulders.

"No, no," she said with the air of one enduring a wrong. "If you're his—er—clerk, stenographer—whatever it is—tell him that Mrs. Wainwright will not wait to go home with him this evening."

Then she was gone, and Emma's corner was filled with the aroma of gardenia perfume as sweet as death flowers. So this was John Wainwright's wife!

Emma was closing her desk for the afternoon when John Wainwright returned from the executive conference. Before going out, she stopped at the swinging gate to deliver the message.

"Your wife asked me to tell you," she said in her best business tone, "that she will not remain to go home with you."

"That's rather good," the new trust officer smiled. "I'll have to be late, and waiting isn't one of the things she does particularly well."

Emma could have guessed as much. Perhaps in John Wainwright's mind there was tolerance for all his wife's foibles. Perhaps he enjoyed humoring her whims. Men are like that.

At the door Emma almost ran into the former solicitor of wills who waited watchfully. Though the youth bored her a trifle, she was glad today that he joined her. From fashion plates and the local ad club he had selected all the best selling points with a result 100 per cent American and not unpleasant.

"I feel like celebratin' my new job," he began. "How 'bout dinner downtown and a show?" Emma nodded. It was amazing that this boy liked her—this flapping trousered, pomaded youngster whom she had always helped with whatever inside work his will soliciting involved.

Over dinner Emma inquired politely concerning the new position. "You like the desk with your name on it," she said disconcertingly, "but I'm afraid having to stay in the bank part of the time will bore you terribly."

"You're dead right," the boy replied. "There's a lot about the files I don't understand . . ."

Emma toyed with her salad. The new-business department had been run for a long time in a slipshod fashion. It would be fun to establish a system that would function like the one in the trust department. She would not offer! Long enough she had been cutting the path to success—for others.

Herbert Harris passed his hand across the sleek surface of his head and then fumbled the silver beside his plate. This youth, whose gift for dealing with people of all kinds had won for him his recent promotion, was obviously embarrassed. Emma was sorry for him, foolishly sorry. After all, the boy was a good sort.

"Oh, say, Emma," he began at last, "can't you come over and sort of straighten things out for me? Organize the department? I—I can't get anywhere the way things are."

"You see, Herbert," Emma parried, "I'm very busy just now."

"Yes, I know, but you do your work so easily. Oh, please, Emma!"

"All right. Meet me an hour earlier tomorrow morning."

Several hours later Emma talked things over with her mother. "I'm just discouraged, mother," she choked. "Do you suppose I'll ever accomplish anything?"

"You've done well, honey," Mrs. Morrison consoled. "So young and making a hundred and fifty a month."

"Oh, bother the salary! I want a chance. Ten years from now I'll still be an untitled clerk. Men can see just two types of women—their wives and the stenographers who work just long enough to get some pretty clothes and a husband." At nine o'clock the next morning, however, she was having an excellent time among Herbert's disordered files. John Wainwright had probably been watching her some time when she became aware of his presence just beyond the boundary of the new-business department. There was, of course, no reason for her to be self-conscious, but she was.

"I'm just helping Mr. Harris," she explained evenly, but she patted her hair in that nervous little way she detested. "He claims that getting things systematized isn't his line."

"Decidedly it seems to be yours," John Wainwright added.

"You should have said unfortunately," Emma corrected.

"And why?"

"Because men think what I am doing indispensable but of less importance than the work they like," she replied with a little edge to her voice.

"Their error," was the laconic comment.

The day began monotonously—and ended with Emma crossing again with Herbert to the new-business department and working entirely heedless of the passing minutes. The street lights were sending their reflections through the windows when she closed the cabinet satisfied that she had reduced a section of Herbert's chaos to order. In its depopulated state the bank—despite the flowers here and there that tried to mock the solitude—looked to Emma like a vast, ornate prison. For a moment she thought that only she and Herbert remained. Then she heard the click of keys across the marble aisle and saw that John Wainwright was closing his desk. A sigh from a teller's cage two windows away revealed a youth who mopped his brow in anguish.

"What's the matter, Bob?" Emma asked. "Settled out again?"

"Oh," came the despairing groan. "Gets worse every time I go over it. Ten dollars out. Please see if you can't find it, Emma."

As Emma began her tedious checking of the teller's day, she saw that John Wainwright sat in his revolving chair with the afternoon paper open before him. In thirty minutes she found the mistake and turned accusingly to tell her beneficiary.

"If you don't tell the president how many times I've done this for you," she said with an irritation that sent the smile from the young man's face, "I'll never help you again."

"Oh, Emma," the teller quavered, "do you want me to be fired?"

But Emma did not reply. She was hating herself for the resentment she felt and for letting John Wainwright hear her. But when Wainwright joined her at the door there was nothing in his manner to indicate that he had taken note of the unpleasant remark. "I've worked late, too," he said. "Let me drive you home. Where do you live?"

The next morning she experienced a mild return of her old cheerfulness. Something would turn up—something must; and in the meantime she was young and healthy and pretty enough and doing work that interested her. Since there was nothing more to explain to John Wainwright, her old routine was undisturbed. Emma was again intent upon doing only that which was expected of her.

The morning held John Wainwright in conference in the outer office. Whenever Emma lifted her eyes, she could see him looking earnestly into the face of the person to whom he talked. His brown hair waved back from a smooth, high forehead; his lean, well-chiseled face was more that of scholar than banker. Impelled by a motive she did not analyze, Emma looked at herself in the mirror of her hand bag. Serious, wide-set eyes, a nose with a bridge too Grecian for the mode American, a chin that balanced the nose, a forehead there was no way to conceal. The lips were not very firm, and they had a provoking way of betraying her by a quiver. But her straight hair was like sun upon ebony.

Then suddenly from the outer office words bored into Emma's consciousness. John Wainwright was considering a request for an increased loan on Alta Vista real estate—a rather remote suburban section which Emma knew to have undergone a reaction following a period of inflated values.

"At the time I requested the loan," a man was arguing, "I needed only about a quarter the house's appraised value. You lend up to fifty per cent, don't you?"

John Wainwright nodded. "In other words, you want us to increase the loan on another first mortgage substituted for the old?"

"Yes," the man replied, "and I'm in need of the money right away."

"Miss Morrison," John Wainwright directed, "will you bring me the data relating to the Craig loan in Alta Vista?"

Emma found the papers, handed them to John Wainwright and returned to her desk. She knew it was all as the man had indicated. The appraisal of the property showed a valuation of $20,000. Only $5000 was lent, but she knew that elsewhere in the files was the record of changed conditions which would certainly make a new appraisal as low as $10,000 and the present loan on the property the maximum the bank was permitted to make.

"Drive out with me and look over the place," Craig urged, and John Wainwright accompanied him immediately.

Emma sat going over the situation in her mind. The trip to Alta Vista would not reveal what she knew to be true—that two proposed factories were ruining the section for residence. John Wainwright had been in the city so short a time that he could not know what Emma had learned through the years. The executive committee of the bank had long ago formed the habit of accepting the recommendation of the trust officer. Wainwright's predecessor had made no mistakes, and only Emma knew of several she had been able to avert. Little good her vigilance had done her. It was absurd to continue— certainly if her opinion were not asked. Let Wainwright take the consequences that would be justly his. She tried to finish her work but failed. There was within her no spirit for anything at all. Perhaps the way to be happy was to lay aside ambition and turn to other things. There was Herbert Harris who liked her, while to him she had always been indifferent.

Emma walked across the bank to Herbert's alcove. She had intended to ask him to take her somewhere to dance that night. Instead, she stood waiting while Herbert read a letter so engrossing that he did not even see Emma's approach. Finally he looked up and smiled in an embarrassed way that changed him from self-confident young salesman to just boy.

"Sit down, Emma," he invited. "I've—I've got something to tell you."

"No more work for me, I hope," Emma smiled.

"Not on your life—not now at least," Herbert replied without committing himself to a future policy. "You see I've been waitin' to make more money. Got a girl, you know. Back home. Now we can get married. Want to see her picture?"

From a bill case Herbert extracted a photograph and handed it to Emma. He was the very incarnation of Jack Horner on one memorable Christmas morning. The girl that looked out from her sepia background had a face baby-round and dimpled. The hair curled above a forehead that stood for beauty rather than for brains, and the shallow eyes were placed quite close together. "Send her my love, Herbert," Emma said.

The boy wrung Emma's hand gratefully. "You're the best pal a fellow ever had. Betty'll love you," he prophesied.

A few minutes later Emma returned to her work. Tomorrow perhaps she would smile upon the young teller whom she had helped out of many difficulties, but now she was in no mood to extricate her mind from the slough into which it had descended. She pressed the cool tips of her fingers to her eyes and held them there for a long moment, envisioning her future, steeling herself for the struggle.

A step in the outer office; voices—Craig's and Wainwright's. Wainwright was agreeing to recommend the loan. An hour of silence on Emma's part, and it would be all over. For once it should be simple to attend to only that which was strictly her business.

In a moment John Wainwright was alone at his desk. Emma could see the scholarly stoop of his shoulders as he bent over the papers before him. His first important step in the bank would be an error. He did not deserve that beginning. Suddenly Emma ceased futile arguing with herself. Automatically she took some papers from the drawer and carried them to the outer office.

"Don't recommend that loan," Emma jerked out the words nervously. "Look at this material and you'll see why."

She handed him all she had gathered together concerning Alta Vista. Five minutes later she heard a long whistle.

"Miss Morrison," John Wainwright said with conviction, "you ought to be trust officer of this bank."

"I haven't an LL.B.," Emma smiled.

Then the smile was lost in the old misgivings. Like all the others, John Wainwright would probably exploit her judgment. There was no use combatting it. Men are like that. And she would go on being exploited. That was her way. Women also are sometimes like that. But Emma was not unhappy. A new exaltation lifted her spirit and sent it soaring.

It was toward noon the next day that John Wainwright sought her for the first time since the epochal interview. Looking up from a monthly statement she was tabulating, Emma saw that he stood by her desk. "The president wants to see you," he said.

John Wainwright's eyes were darker and more deep-set than they had seemed before. His eyebrows came together more closely, and new lines had carved themselves into his face. It was a simple thing he said—"The president wants to see you"—and yet John Wainwright was deeply moved.

Emma left him standing there and crossed to the soft-carpeted sanctum of the bank's chief executive. The portly old gentleman adjusted his pince-nez, consulted his watch, lifted and deposited again the paper weight that lay upon his pile of open letters—all very deliberately—before he asked Emma to be seated.

"To be quite frank," he began at last, "I've had my eyes opened by someone who—er—sees from the perspective of being new to the scene. Never thought of your wanting to be pushed along. Now the boys—you know how they are. If we don't change them once in a while, they leave, but raises generally satisfy the girls. They're all thinking more about getting married than getting famous."

"But some do want to get ahead—want terribly," Emma argued.

The president cleared his throat and continued. "Yesterday Wainwright told the executive committee how you saved him from a bad mistake, mentioned that you straightened things out for the boys whenever they got in tight places, added that you were unhappy about your prospects here."

"He told you that?" Emma gasped, but the president seemed not to hear.

"So I nosed about. Several of the tellers added to the story. The upshot of it is, if you want the chance the men get, it's up to us to give it to you."

"Oh, I do want it!"

"Well, here's the idea. Your genius seems to be for organizing. There're several departments that need going over now. Start in as a kind of efficiency expert, and in a month we'll talk things over. Of course there'll be a bit more salary."

As she passed from the president's office between the pillars that made the aisles of the bank, she saw that doors had been closed to customers and that employees were leaving for luncheon. John Wainwright still sat at his desk while all about him the bank was deserted. He rose to open the little swinging gate, and Emma passed into the enclosure that belonged to the trust department.

"I want to thank you," she said, holding tight to the desk light. "In a few days you have seen what in five years no other man has guessed."

"You should have told them that you were not content to be stranded in the trust department. Men have to be told things like that."

It seemed to Emma that John Wainwright's eyes looked from depths remote yet very near, and she wondered why they filled her with a longing as sharp as pain.

"I did not tell *you,*" she said.

"I knew."

Looking into John Wainwright's eyes, steadily now, Emma understood what his stumbling, inadequate, man-made words could never convey.

"I had known only two types of women till I met you," he continued. "I thought there must be another. One type here—our wives the other—you the third!"

"And I," Emma faltered, "I had only known men without discernment."

For a moment John Wainwright's face was darkly shadowed by the things he could not say. Then a smile broke through, and Emma was at ease again.

"Life is full of little ironies," he said.

"And compensations," Emma added.

"Yes," John Wainwright answered soberly as he went out to meet his wife for luncheon.

BIRD GIRL

Vivien R. Bretherton

PERHAPS, if Brian Scott had first met Vandy Cameron at one of those infrequent moments when she was more débutante than bird girl, he might have looked at her with eyes that saw the fascinating cap of her dark curls and the scarlet mouth that matched in charm her *farouche* little face. In that case, anything might have happened—Brian Scott being who he was, as adventurous as the career he followed. But the first time he set eyes upon her, she was stunting above the Cameron flying field in a wicked-looking, little Waco single-seater, and doing it with such beautiful ease that she made recklessness seem casual.

Brian, who knew just how far from casual her exhibition was, squinted his gray eyes in her direction gave a low, admiring whistle, and asked the man beside him, "Who's the chap above?"

The man, who happened to be Vandy's father in addition to being the head of Cameron Aeroplane Corporation, grinned and said, "That's Vandy Cameron—not so bad, eh?"

"Bad! I'd like to meet that bird! Belong around here?"

Martin Cameron eyed the stunting ship above. "Only runs the place," he remarked dryly, "me included."

From *Good Housekeeping,* 88, no. 3 (March 1929).

Even at that Brian Scott didn't understand, for everybody knew that Martin Cameron, who would have given half his fortune for a son, had none. Not even when Vandy, making a perfect three-point landing, swung her slim lithesomeness over the cockpit and sprang to the ground, a straight, boyish figure in trim flying garb and concealing helmet, did Brian imagine he'd watched a girl flirt with death in the clouds above. It was only when Martin Cameron said, "Vandy—my only and most exciting daughter," that Brian realized who and what she was. The surprise left him speechless.

It wasn't often that Brian Scott, looking as he did and being who he was, found himself tongue-tied before a girl. But this time, evidently, the girl wasn't expecting much from him. She merely pulled off her helmet, making her black elfin locks stick out all over her head in quirky curls, and remarked coolly and not at all as if she were impressed by being introduced to a national hero:

"Hullo—I've heard a lot about you."

Brian recovered his tongue and his breath at the same time. "And I've seen enough, in the last five minutes, to tell me a lot about you. By George, that was pretty stuff!"

Vandy eyed him silently for a moment. Like the rest of America she had read much of this sensational young flyer, most of which had exasperated her because of its maudlin sentimentality. Because she envied him above all men she'd been afraid to meet him—afraid lest the extravagant worship of a nation had spoiled him. But suddenly, meeting the steady gaze of his gray eyes, she knew that all the finest things she'd heard of him were true. She flashed him a rueful smile and said:

"Gaudy—but safe. If I'd known you were watching, I wouldn't have been showing off."

"Why me?" He said it simply.

Vandy sighed contentedly. "I might have known you'd be like that. Come along—Dad's taking us to lunch. I want to ask you—oh, millions of things! And has Dad persuaded you to take charge of all this?" She waved a careless hand towards the Cameron air field with its surrounding hangars and factory buildings. "If so, he won't need to fly for a week. He'll be walking with his head in the clouds."

Brian Scott grinned—and went to lunch with her. It was a new experience for him to find a girl who looked like a vivid little creature of eighteen and knew almost as much about flying as he did. And the two of them sat and talked until the afternoon was nearly gone—Brian Scott, who flew because it was the thing he'd been born for, and Vandy Cameron, who flew because she couldn't help it.

Vandy Cameron. She had tumbled out of her crib at three months, preferred a tricycle to her own pram at three years, sent her mother into hysterics over her proficiency on skates at the age of six, and from that time on had scooted, raced, and swooped through life on a series of speed-provoking conveyances that began with a woolly lamb on wheels and ended, when Vandy was eighteen, with an aeroplane. In the interim Vandy's mother, having found the pace too much for her, had died with the firm conviction that she'd soon see Vandy on the other side of the River Styx, leaving Vandy to race unchecked along her swift, reckless way.

If Vandy had been a boy she would have been, by the time Brian Scott encountered her, one of the bird men of her generation. As it was, she knew as much about aeroplanes as her father, who made them. More, in fact, for Vandy's was the training of an army pilot. She could check her ship, from prop to rudder, in thirty-five minutes. She could read a meteorology map as expertly as she could follow the newest dance step. She could tell the minute she lifted into a fog if it was the low-hanging type she had to fly above or the ceiling-high kind she had to fly blind, and every pilot in her father's employ knew that Vandy Cameron had the "feel"; that hers was the gift of "flying before her engine," which meant, in other words, that no matter what happened to her motor, in that split second when her engine went dead and before her plane could take that first plunge that sends a ship into its fatal nose dive, she had touched her controls, nosed her plane down for flying speed, and sent it in a safe glide to earth.

If Vandy Cameron had been asked to write her own biography after the manner of modern biographies, she would have said that she hated inertia, ruffled dresses, teas, cowardice, and men; that she liked the wind in her face, the roar of a motor in her ears, cold showers, and men. Which sounds contradictory, as far as the men are concerned, but wasn't at all. She liked men when she could admire them and when she could envy them for the things that, being men, they could do. And she hated them when they turned from adventurous creatures into figures of earth who became sentimental, and were sure that she was going to kill herself, and finally proposed, offering themselves as a substitute for the passion of flying. And propose some of them did for various reasons; because she was Martin Cameron's daughter, for one, and because she combined a scarlet mouth, a whimsical face, and black curls like an elf's cap, for another; none of them very good reasons, to Vandy's way of thinking, for she had no time for love. Not, that is, until Brian came over her horizon.

Not that Vandy bracketed Brian and love together that first day she saw him—or the next—or the next. It was just that somehow, at the first sound of his voice, her heart had turned over and then swooped suddenly up, like a plane lifting into the bright blueness that is the highway of the winged ones. For a moment, until she was sure what the world and its adulation had done to him, her heart had hung in mid-air. Then, her last doubt forgotten, it had soared off in a rush of wings—a flight that was unbroken in the days that followed.

Why tell of those days, save that they were heavenly blue and of the fabric that only youth can weave? Why tell of the things these two talked about, save that the hours sped by as swift as the ships they flew, and at the end of them it was as if they'd known each other since the world began? Suffice it to say that, before a week had gone its way, Vandy Cameron had fallen in love—cracked up—crashed down to earth, as it were. Though Vandy, so naturally had the whole thing happened, hadn't the slightest idea of that. It took Narcissa Elliot to teach Vandy the pattern of her heart.

Vandy heard of the meeting of Brian and Narcissa from Narcissa herself; Narcissa, who had just come back from three years in Paris and looked it; Narcissa who was like her name, white and lovely and exquisite looking, with a beauty that was so authentic that it was like day and night—something you just couldn't deny.

"And to think," rippled Narcissa when she sought out Vandy, for Narcissa was ever one to look to her own fences, "that you've had him almost a month, Vandy, and never shared him!"

It wasn't exactly true that Vandy hated Narcissa from that moment, though perhaps that was the first time she was afraid of Narcissa's beauty. Vandy and Narcissa had gone to school together, and even then, at sixteen, Narcissa had been one of those lovely, virginal-looking girls whose sly, silky, little ways had never been the ways of Vandy. Now, looking at her, Vandy remembered all the things she knew about Narcissa—remembered, and felt her heart stop like a motor suddenly gone dead.

She said evenly: "He's in business with Dad, you know, Narcissa, and if he hasn't gone about and met people it's been because he was busy, I suppose. As for sharing him—I'm not his jailer."

Narcissa's eyes were a heavenly blue. They met Vandy's with a gaze that would have seemed childlike to anybody who didn't know Narcissa.

"Oh, don't be angry with me, Vandy, dear. I didn't mean anything! Of course, you aren't his jailer—I don't think he's ever had one. A girl can tell, you know. And he's just too adorable! He—well, he just sits and looks at me, you know!"

Vandy, too, looked at Narcissa and told herself that any man with eyes in his head would do just that!

"She's entirely too beautiful!" thought Vandy desperately, and all her own vivid, boyish charm seemed smudged into oblivion by comparison. "You wouldn't expect any man to see anything but her beauty! It—it wouldn't be natural! But oh—she's not good enough for Brian! She's not!"

"And so insistent, Vandy! He's giving me the most fearful rush. I suppose you think I'm silly, for you never care about the different ways a man can look at a girl. But Brian—well, of course, he's awfully famous—and I can't help being flattered."

Narcissa rose, having said the thing she'd come to say, and the sunlight on her hair turned it to a flame of gold about her head. Even Narcissa's hair, Vandy told herself miserably, was made to make a man forget all else. But she managed to smile and say politely, all the while wondering what would happen if she throttled Narcissa:

"Yes—he's very nice—and yes—he's quite famous. It was nice of you to come, Narcissa, when I hadn't called on you. But I didn't even know you were back."

"You're always so busy, Vandy, flying about in those terrible planes. You never did have time for parties and foolish, romantic things. Though I don't see why Brian didn't tell you we had met. And do you know, Brian says you're not a girl—you're just a bird creature. I'll tell him he's right, when I see him this afternoon. He's driving me out into the country, you know."

"Brian? This afternoon?"

Vandy caught herself. She wouldn't—she simply wouldn't—let Narcissa know how that cut her. She said jerkily, answering Narcissa's blue questioning eyes:

"Oh—it wasn't anything. I just thought—there's a new ship ready this afternoon—but Brian can take it up tomorrow, you know."

Vandy thought, when she was alone again, that that was what hurt most of all. "To think that Brian is content to drive out in the country—with the new plane ready! Why—she's already made him forget the thing he lived for, before she came!"

But that night, when she lay in bed and stared with hot eyes into the dark, she faced things as they were.

"I love him—I didn't know it but there's no use pretending it isn't so. I love him—terribly—world without end. I've cracked up—crashed down in a nose dive—and Brian doesn't care. I'm just Vandy—somebody to fly with—while Narcissa is the girl of his heart."

And then, because it was Vandy's nature to be logical, though it nearly killed her to be so: "Of course he's in love with her. What man would look at me with Narcissa—so beautiful—so everlastingly beautiful—about? And she'll be helpless—and afraid of things—I know her ways—and Brian will fall for it—men always do—and want to protect her! If it were any one else, I think I could stand it! But Narcissa! Men are her meat! . . . She's out to marry Brian—because he's famous and has money. And Brian should be loved for what he is!"

And so on and on, until Vandy, her throat as tight as a drum, cried herself to sleep.

Because she was young, and each morning offers a new lease on life to the heart of youth, Vandy woke to sunlight and a saner viewpoint—even a faint hope.

"I'm probably making up most of it in my own mind," she told herself, refusing to remember how lovely Narcissa was to the eye. "Perhaps he isn't in love with her—perhaps Narcissa is making up most of it—perhaps I'm not even in love with him myself!"

But that was pure braggadocio, as she herself knew. She was so completely in love with Brian Scott, now that she was awake to it, that everything he said took on a sharper meaning. That was why she knew, five minutes after she met him on the flying field that morning, that all the things she'd feared were true.

Brian, already inspecting the new plane, met her with a rueful smile.

"This was ready yesterday—and I forgot it!"

She made his excuse for him.

"Perhaps I didn't tell you the finishing date."

"Not you. I was the one who forgot—and we talked about it, too. I'm awfully sorry, Vandy."

"It doesn't make a bit of difference, Brian. We can try it out today."

Brian ran a lean hand through his hair. "That's just it—I'm tied up today. But you go ahead—take it up and test it."

Hope, that had flamed up in Vandy with the morning, trembled and died. A month ago—a week ago—nothing short of death would have kept Brian out of that cockpit.

"He's got a date with Narcissa," Vandy told herself miserably. "But if he just doesn't tell me so—"

Brian did, grasping the opportunity. It was plain that he wanted to talk about Narcissa.

"It's like this," he said, trying to seem casual and not making much of a success of it. "I met a girl—don't know if I told you—Narcissa Elliot. She's a dear friend of yours, which rated her pretty high with me. And today—"

"It doesn't make a bit of difference," broke in Vandy, tugging on her tight little helmet and hiding from sight all her black elfin locks. "You can try it out tomorrow."

"Narcissa—you've known her a long time, haven't you, Vandy?"

"We were little girls together, Brian." But to herself she cried out, "Oh—why will he make me talk about her!"

"Isn't she—isn't she beautiful!" he burst out. "Enough to take your breath away?"

"Awfully beautiful, Brian." Vandy swallowed the lump in her throat and thought, "It's true—he loves her!"

"You know, Vandy, first time I met her, I thought she wasn't real. Oh, gorgeous to look at! I simply sat and stared at her. But—funny thing, how you get the wrong impression of people—I thought she was, well—cold. The perfect coquette, I'd have called her. But d'you know what she said?"

Vandy shook her head. "That she wanted to fly with you!"

"That's just it! She didn't I—you know, I guess I'm a fool to feel that way, but I've met so many girls that wanted that—just to fly with me—until I feel like a performing monkey on a stick every time one says so. But Narcissa—she said, 'I want to know you, Brian Scott, but I don't want to fly with you.'"

"Oh—how clever of her!" thought Vandy fiercely. "Of course she would say—just that!"

"And then she said," went on Brian eagerly, "that she was afraid to fly. She's a funny little thing—afraid of so many things. She told me afterward she hated to confess it because she thought I'd be so disgusted I'd never look at her again. But she just had to say it—it was the only way not to sail under false colors. Can you imagine that?"

Vandy couldn't—not of Narcissa—but she didn't say so. It was curious, the feeling that kept Vandy's lips closed. It wasn't that she wanted to be loyal to Narcissa, but she just couldn't betray her. It wasn't "cricket"—and being "cricket" was a thing you didn't reason out. It was something you just were.

"Narcissa always was afraid of things," said Vandy gently. "I guess—she was born that way."

"And you were born loving danger."

A new expression came into Brian's eyes. The dreaming look was gone—that was for Narcissa—but a glow lit his face. "Vandy—you're the only real pal I've ever had. D'you know that? With most girls—why, I'm as dumb as an oyster with Narcissa. She makes me tongue-tied. But I rattle like a bell-clapper when I'm with you. Lord, I'd be lost without you!"

"Lost? With Narcissa here?" The words came in spite of Vandy.

"But that's entirely different." Brian's look had no reticence in it. "Narcissa—she is the girl you dream of having. But you—you are something I have, Vandy. Always here—that I can count on. Dependable, like the motor of a plane."

"A motor!" cried Vandy's heart. "And Narcissa is the dream in his heart!" But she only said ruefully: "You'll probably be the one to go away, Brian. I—belong here."

But Brian didn't go away from Vandy, either in spirit or in body. Gone were the long evenings they once had shared together; gone the jolly dinners when they had bumped their heads over head winds and tri-motor planes and wing improvements. The evenings were Narcissa's now, and the dinners Brian attended were a process of triumphant social occasions. But the mornings and the bright, clear afternoons—the camaraderie of the flying field and the highways across the heavens—these were still Vandy's. To give them up was something Brian had never thought of doing. Nor to give up Vandy and what her comradeship meant to him.

It was Narcissa who sensed this first, and she made up her mind to eliminate Vandy. It maddened her that, as the weeks slipped by, Brian did not propose to her. The Galahad in man had never been enough for Narcissa, and that Brian was still dreaming over her she did not know. Because she couldn't understand a man's friendship for a girl, she reasoned that somehow—in some way—Vandy stood between her and the thing she wanted. She set herself to discount Vandy as a result; not openly, Narcissa was too clever for that, but in her own way.

She took to including Vandy in plans for herself and Brian,

making such a point of her acceptance that Vandy had but two choices open to her—to decline and show herself up as a sullen girl refusing Narcissa's generous impulses, or to accept, though Vandy knew, as well as Narcissa, that no girl could register when Narcissa was near by; that Brian wouldn't even see her with Narcissa's beauty to fill his eyes. She knew it more than ever on the night of Narcissa's dancing party when Brian, with the evening half over, hadn't come near her for a single dance.

And then, suddenly, there he was before her, saying so naïvely and never thinking he was showing up Narcissa's hand:

"Vandy—you've got a list a mile long—wallflowers and what-nots—for me to whirl. She said you were so popular you didn't need me, but I got fed up at last. How about this one? May I have it?"

He could—and Vandy, in his arms, thanked the little Gods of Chance that, whether her hair was golden or not, she *could* dance. They hadn't circled half the floor before she knew that Brian knew it, too, and she wouldn't have been human if the knowledge hadn't warmed her blood like a draught of wine. And then the dance was over, and into her dreaming crashed Brian's voice.

"Why, Vandy, you're a marvelous dancer!"

The surprise in his tone! Oh—did Brian think Narcissa was the only girl who knew how to dance? Something flamed up in Vandy Cameron, something that made her tremble with rage as she said fiercely:

"What if I am? Did you think I wasn't like other girls? Did you think I was just a machine that sat in a cockpit and flew a ship?"

She whirled about and rushed out onto the dark terrace, where she could cry if she wanted to without any one to see. But she couldn't, it seemed. For Brian, bewilderment written all over his face—what on earth had come over Vandy?—was at her side the moment she sank down on a garden bench.

"Good Lord, Vandy, what did I say? I didn't mean to make you angry!"

She couldn't harden herself against him; it wasn't in her to do that. She said wearily:

"Never mind, Brian. It wasn't anything. I'm just tired, I guess, and cranky."

The dress she wore was like a warm, glowing marigold, and the quirky, black curls on her head were more like an elf's cap than usual. In the shadows her scarlet mouth was sweet and arresting, and Brian, suddenly aware of her as a person apart from airplanes and disguising helmets, felt as if he were seeing her for the first time.

He said curiously, "Vandy—how strange you look—tonight!"

She wished he'd go away, and she wondered how she'd stand it if he did.

But she only said, fiercely flippant, "Me and matches—we show off better in the dark."

He put a hand out, following an impulse he couldn't define, and traced a finger across her soft, flushed cheek. At his touch the flippancy flowed out of Vandy like water from an upturned goblet. She looked at Brian because she could not help it, looked as the first woman might have looked at the first man. And Brian, curiously stirred by that deepening, shadowy glance, whispered huskily,

"Vandy—your eyes—"

It was Narcissa's swift laughter—laughter that held a touch of panic, for Narcissa knew that she had made a mistake ever to have given Brian the chance to see this new, breathless Vandy—that broke in upon them. It was Narcissa who was beside Vandy with a little rush, tilting her flittering head against Vandy's dark curls, who cried out:

"Isn't Vandy the dearest girl, Brian? Say she is for me! Tell her she's pretty—and that she ought to give less time to flying and more to dancing."

And all the time Vandy, standing there so quietly, feeling Narcissa's beauty as keenly as if it had been a hurt, thinking hotly, "Oh—she's clever—she knows men never look at the girls they're told to look at!" watched Brian's eyes turn to Narcissa's flower face and rest there like a pledge.

Brian, being only a man, slept like a baby that night; and if any thought at all crossed his mind, it was of Narcissa's last words:

"Tomorrow, Brian, we'll run away—into the lively sunshine. I want to play gipsy, Brian. We'll take a picnic dinner into the hills."

And Vandy, being the girl who loved Brian, sank into the depths of despair, saying fiercely:

"There's nothing for me to do but cut and run. How beautiful she is! Her beauty isn't the least bit like her, but Brian will never find that out. How can he? She'll never let him get a peek of the real her—she'll only show him the outside. And that—" cried Vandy despairingly—"is like a song, or a symphony—"

But Narcissa, lying on her own white bed, narrowed her blue eyes and said to herself: "I shan't do that again! Vandy is too clever! As for Brian—I could choke him for being so slow! But if he's going to be such a saint, I'll make him ask me—tomorrow—"

And so the morrow came, almost too dazzlingly blue to be endured, and Brian and Narcissa drove off into its enchantment in Narcissa's canary-colored car that matched her bright head in color, while Vandy, trying to wear herself out, spent the long hours of the afternoon doing mechanic's work on a double-seated Waco that had been giving trouble of late.

It was late when she finished, the long shadows already tracing their pattern across the field, when Vandy decided to take the Waco up to test her work. She slid into the harness of her parachute, because Vandy was too good a pilot not to take the necessary precautions, noted casually that the extra parachute lay on the second seat, climbed into the cockpit, and started her engine. The motor roared, the plane hurtled unsteadily forward, gained speed, and in another moment lifted from the ground.

Once well up, Vandy took her hands from the control sticks, stretching into an easier position. But though she seemed to sit there oblivious to the plane, her eyes kept sweeping back to the indicators, and now and then her hand went back to correct her course.

The plane drove blindly ahead, now steadily, now lurching at an air pocket, and Vandy, her thoughts on Brian and Narcissa, scanned the countryside below her, though she herself was unconscious of seeking them. The world below, etched in the faint shadows of late afternoon, held the delicacy of a watercolor, but Vandy was blind to its beauty. She flew on and on, as if escaping from her own thoughts, and the open country beneath her gave place to the fir-covered slopes of the forest altitude.

She was flying low—not over two thousand feet—idly watching the flashes of water as she sped over a string of mountain lakes—when suddenly her eyes were caught by it, a flash of yellow. It was tiny; eyes less keen than Vandy's would never have seen it. Or perhaps it was that Vandy's eyes had been, all unknowing, seeking that same small dot of color. The thought flashed to her, "Narcissa's car," but with it came denial. Narcissa's car would never be parked in that lonely spot. This was some fifty miles from town. Narcissa and Brian, wherever they were, would be speeding back by this time.

And yet—

Unconvinced, Vandy circled back, and as she dipped lower and lower toward the earth, the roar of her motor reached the two tiny figures beside the yellow car. One of them—a midget speck—ran out into an open space beyond, waving his arms.

Again Vandy circled, dipping nearer to the earth, and as she did so something, she didn't know what, told her that her first instinctive thought was right. That was Narcissa's car down below her, and those tiny figures—surely they were Brian and Narcissa. She could only guess what might have happened— engine trouble that had stranded them in this lonely place. For a moment she thought of flying back to the field; of sending help out to them. But with that thought came others. It would be midnight before a car from town could reach them. Midnight—and perhaps later. And Brian, the idealist—what would his reaction be?

Something primitive flamed up in Vandy again. "Narcissa— she's managed this somehow. If she knows Brian—and Narcissa knows men—she knows he'll ask her to marry him tomorrow, after this sort of mess. Brian would."

She knew instantly what she would do. Land, no matter how mad the experiment. She circled again, scanning that open spot. Not so mad, after all, she decided. It was like a small plateau down there, narrow, not any too long, but long

enough, she calculated swiftly, for her to make a forced landing. As for taking off again—well, she could do that, too.
Vandy knew her own ability.
She circled once more, heading into the wind. Then, shutting off her motor, she throttled it down to a glide. Like a
swallow the heavy two-seater swept earthward, and when
Vandy was within some sixty feet of it she kicked her rudder,
side-slipped her plane, and fan-tailed into a landing. The earth
loomed up beneath her. She felt the wheels strike, bounce off
and strike again, then race over the uneven ground until, with
the farthest line of trees not fifty yards away from her, her
pace slacked, and with a few last lurches the plane stood still.

Before Vandy was out of her chute harness, Brian was beside the plane, Narcissa at his heels.

"By all that's miraculous!" cried Brian gratefully. "A rescuer
from the skies! Vandy, you were a little idiot to land—but
Lord, how glad we are to see you!"

Vandy, catching a glimpse of Narcissa's face, doubted if she
was as glad, but she heard that clear, flute-like treble lifted.
Narcissa, evidently, was adjusting herself to this sudden change
in events, no matter what her private thought of them.

"Oh, Vandy!" wailed Narcissa, clinging to her with a pretty
show of gratitude and plainly determined to do all the talking.
"It was all my fault! You know I always was a rattle-brain!
They told me at Daddy's garage that my gas tank needed looking at, but I was so eager to go gipsying today—I just forgot!
And while we sat here—having such fun—eating our silly
little picnic supper—the gas just leaked out! If you hadn't
come, I don't know what would have happened!"

Beyond that frantic gabbling Vandy felt Narcissa's nervousness. As if any girl would swallow that story, even though a
man blinded by Narcissa's beauty might!

"She's afraid I'll say something to make Brian doubt her,"
thought Vandy.

But Narcissa's hands, soft and warm, were cuddling into her
own, and Narcissa's voice, pleadingly caressing, was caroling
in her ear.

"And it was so wonderful to see you coming down to us,
Vandy! I was frantic—thinking we would have to stay out

here all night! Thinking of what people would say! And did you look down from your clouds, Vandy, darling, and see my gaudy little car and say to yourself, 'Stranded again the little idiot, I've a good mind to leave her there and teach her a lesson.' But of course you wouldn't. You never deserted anybody in your whole life. And to desert me—why—" the blue eyes sought Brian's face— "Vandy and I have been the dearest friends since we were tiny girls!"

Vandy stood there, slim and straight and gallant-looking, though she didn't know that. And she, too, looked at Brian, and weariness fell upon her heart. For Brian's eyes were all for Narcissa—his quiet, steady glance. Vandy, watching, thought quietly:

"Well, she wins. You believe every word she says. You always will."

With a curious tightness on her scarlet mouth, she smiled at Narcissa.

"It's all right, Narcissa. I didn't do anything wonderful. It was a lark for me—always did want to try my luck at this sort of landing. The question is—what good do I do now that I'm here?"

They talked it over, Narcissa rattling on in relief, now that she was sure Vandy believed her, and Brian, though it seemed to Vandy that he was quieter than usual, summed up their problem.

"If you think we can take off again, Vandy, we'll all fly back. Simplest thing. Send back tomorrow for the car."

"Fly? Oh, I couldn't! I'd be afraid," whimpered Narcissa.

Did a shade of irritation cross Brian's face? Vandy couldn't tell, but his voice, when he turned to Narcissa, was considerate.

"I guess it's a question of necessity, Narcissa, unless you want all three of us to spend the night out here."

"But—you will pilot, won't you. I know Vandy is marvelous, but I'd feel safer with you, Brian! I know you'd take care of me."

Vandy flicked an expressive hand. "Of course, Brian will fly us. Why not?"

Why not anything? Vandy didn't care, now. Nothing was left worth caring for, in the world.

Narcissa turned to Brian.

"And I can sit beside you, can't I? I couldn't stand to be alone in that teeny back seat!"

Brian smiled at her, but his eyes sought Vandy's.

"And I wouldn't put you there, Narcissa. I don't want to worry about the passenger behind me."

"You think I'm silly," Narcissa pouted, "but you can't expect me to be like Vandy—not afraid of anything."

"I don't expect any girl to be like Vandy," returned Brian quietly, "but there's nothing to be afraid of. Now—slip into this and let's get going—" and he held out to her the harness of the second parachute.

"That?" Narcissa drew back. "What is it?"

"Parachute," explained Brian patiently.

"But I'm not going to jump in one!"

"Of course not. But if anything should go wrong—"

"How can it, Brian, with you flying? Oh, I'd much rather trust myself to you, Brian, than to that ugly thing."

Brian, all airman now, shot a helpless look at Vandy—the look of a man embarrassed by too much flattery. And Vandy, shrugging her shoulders, turned to Narcissa.

"The better the flyer, Narcissa, the more he insists upon precautions. That's all a parachute is. Brian is giving you his—put it on and let's hurry."

At the thought of Brian giving up something for her, Narcissa yielded. Allegiance, even in the form of anything so unromantic as a parachute, was food and drink to her.

"And I'll be very brave," she promised Brian, her small hand on his arm. "I'll make you proud of me, Brian."

Vandy, busy with her own harness, smiled grimly to herself. Narcissa was spreading it on pretty thick. That stuff about being brave! Bravery, to people like Brian and Vandy, meant something so much bigger than putting on a parachute and riding in a plane. And that transparent twaddle about a leaky gas tank! As if the man who cared for the Elliot cars would have told Narcissa about it! He'd have fixed it—or sent her out in another car. But perhaps Narcissa knew that any man who looked at her would believe anything she told him.

Vandy's thoughts were interrupted by the roar of the motor.

BIRD

By VIVIEN R. BRETHERTON

"I'll be very brave," Narcissa promised Brian, her small hand on his arm. "I'll make you proud of me, Brian." Vandy smiled grimly. Narcissa was spreading it on pretty thick

PERHAPS, if Brian Scott had first met Vandy Cameron at one of those infrequent moments when she was more débutante than bird girl, he might have looked at her with eyes that saw the fascinating cap of her dark curls and the scarlet mouth that matched in charm her *farouche* little face. In that case, anything might have happened—Brian Scott being who he was, as adventurous as the career he followed. But the first time he set eyes upon her, she was stunting above the Cameron flying field in a wicked-looking, little Waco single-seater, and doing it with such beautiful ease that she made recklessness seem casual.

Brian, who knew just how far from casual her exhibition was, squinted his gray eyes in her direction, gave a low, admiring whistle, and asked the man beside him, "Who's the chap above?"

The man, who happened to be Vandy's father in addition to being the head of the Cameron Aeroplane Corporation, grinned and said, "That's Vandy Cameron—not so bad, eh?"

"Bad! I'd like to meet that bird! Belong around here?"

Martin Cameron eyed the stunting ship above. "Only runs the place," he remarked dryly, "me included."

Even at that Brian Scott didn't understand, for everybody knew that Martin Cameron, who would have given half his fortune for a son, had none. Not even when Vandy, making a perfect three-point landing, swung her slim lithesomeness over the cockpit and sprang to the ground, a straight, boyish figure in trim flying garb and concealing helmet, did Brian imagine he'd watched a girl flirt with death in the clouds above. It was only when Martin Cameron said, "Vandy—my only and most exciting daughter," that Brian realized who and what she was. The surprise left him speechless.

It wasn't often that Brian Scott, looking as he did and being who he was, found himself tongue-tied before a girl. But this time, evidently, the girl wasn't expecting much from him. She merely pulled off her helmet, making her black elfin locks stick out all over her head in quirky curls, and remarked coolly and not at all as if she were impressed by being introduced to a national hero:

"Hullo—I've heard a lot about you."

Brian recovered his tongue and his breath at the same time. "And I've seen enough, in the last five minutes, to tell me a lot about you. By George, that was pretty stuff!"

Vandy eyed him silently for a moment. Like the rest of America she had read much of this sensational young flyer, most of which had exasperated her because of its

18

From "Bird Girl," *Good Housekeeping* 88, no. 3 (March 1929), pp. 18–19.

GIRL

She Flew Full
Tilt Into Danger and
Came Out
With Colors Flying

Illustrated
By Haddon Sundblom

maudlin sentimentality. Because she envied him above
all men she'd been afraid to meet him—afraid lest the
extravagant worship of a nation had spoiled him. But
suddenly, meeting the steady gaze of his gray eyes, she
knew that all the finest things she'd heard of him were
true. She flashed him a rueful smile and said:

"Gaudy—but safe. If I'd known you were watching,
I wouldn't have been showing off."

"Why me?" He said it simply.

Vandy sighed contentedly. "I might have known
you'd be like that. Come along—Dad's taking us to
lunch. I want to ask you—oh, millions of things! And
has Dad persuaded you to take charge of all this?" She
waved a careless hand towards the Cameron air field
with its surrounding hangars and factory buildings. "If
so, he won't need to fly for a week. He'll be walking with
his head in the clouds."

Brian Scott grinned—and went to lunch with her. It
was a new experience to him to find a girl who looked like
a vivid little creature of eighteen and knew almost as
much about flying as he did. And the two of them sat
and talked until the afternoon was nearly gone—Brian
Scott, who flew because it was the thing he'd been born
for, and Vandy Cameron, who flew because she couldn't
help it.

Vandy Cameron. She had tumbled out of her crib at
three months, preferred a tricycle to her own pram at
three years, sent her mother into hysterics over her proficiency on skates at the age of six, and from that time
on had scooted, raced, and swooped through life on a
series of speed-provoking conveyances that began with a
woolly lamb on wheels and ended, when Vandy was
eighteen, with an aeroplane. In the interim Vandy's
mother, having found the pace too much for her, had
died with the firm conviction that she'd soon see Vandy
on the other side of the River Styx, leaving Vandy to race
unchecked along her swift, reckless way.

If Vandy had been a boy she would have been, by the
time Brian Scott encountered her, one of the bird men of
her generation. As it was, she knew as much about
aeroplanes as her father, who made them. More, in fact,
for Vandy's was the training of an army pilot. She could
check her ship, from prop to rudder, in thirty-five
minutes. She could read a meteorology map as expertly
as she could follow the newest dance step. She could
tell the minute she lifted into a fog if it was the low-
hanging type she had to fly above or the ceiling-high
kind she had to fly blind, and every pilot in her father's
employ knew that Vandy Cameron had the "feel"; that
hers was the gift of "flying before her engine," which

19

Illustration by Haddon Sundblom.

The next instant, as she started to climb into the rear cockpit, she felt Brian's touch on her arm. He looked down at her, straight into her clear, lovely eyes, and he smiled. Vandy, who didn't know he'd had his world knocked out from under him during the last few hours, wondered at that smile. Then he lifted her over the rim, looked at her again, and said quietly.

"Thanks, Vandy."

With that he was gone.

Vandy looked, wondering, at the lean figure swinging up over the fore cockpit. What was Brian thanking her for? Surely not that matter of a forced landing. That was the sort of thing each would have done unquestioningly for the other. She found no answer to her own question.

Brian's take-off was a thing of joy, but Vandy hardly noticed it. The plane took the air, fought for a moment, then lifted triumphantly, but there was no soaring in Vandy's heart. She had saved Brian from Narcissa's trick of the moment, but his eyes were still blind to everything except her beauty; would always be, thought Vandy hopelessly. And that, she told herself, was that.

So sunk in her own despair was Vandy that she was only mechanically aware of that first sputtering of the engine that came before the plane had been in the air for fifteen minutes. It was Brian, in the cockpit ahead, who whipped into instant action. He saw, in a flash, that the needle of the indicator was dropping. As swiftly he turned to the hand pump. Not until then did Vandy, her brain as well as her eyes snapping out of their lethargy, realize what had happened. Her eyes, too, flew to the indicator; saw the needle pause for an instant, then go dropping down again. In the same instant she felt the plane swerve as Brian turned it about and knew that he was trying to get back to the clearing they had just left.

She knew what had happened—their gas line had broken—and she knew, as truly, that they'd never make the landing. As she watched, the linen around the fuselage began to burn, and she realized, as she knew Brian must, that with fire around the motor it would be a question of minutes before the plane burst into flames.

She thought swiftly: "We'll have to jump for it! It's not bad country—but Brian!"

Brian had no parachute. Her mind caught instantly at a substitute.

She saw that Brian was bending over Narcissa's now genuinely terrified face. He was shouting to her—probably giving her the formula:

"Count one—two—three—four then pull the string! No danger—keep your head—don't straddle anything when you land!"

Lifting her own voice, she screamed, "Brian! Brian!"

He turned—read the pantomime of her hands—knew that she was telling him to drop with her. It could be done. Both of them knew that. If Brian crooked his arm through the harness of her parachute, it could take them both down. They were high enough—a little over two thousand feet—to make the attempt reasonably sure.

She caught Brian's eye—saw him nod his head. Then he was lifting Narcissa over the edge, shouting,

"One—two—three—four—pull!"

Narcissa, now that her life depended on it, had thrown away all pretense of helplessness. She held the release ring desperately, and something in her face told both Brian and Vandy that she would keep her head and do as she was told. The next moment she had dropped into nothingness.

The two who watched her waited tensely as they counted. Then they saw Narcissa's hand flash out, saw the parachute burst into blossom, and almost instantly the sprawling figure was floating down toward earth, hidden from their eyes by the wide, silk umbrella top.

They forgot her immediately. The fire was nearer the gas tank now—and if the tank exploded—

Vandy stood, clinging to the edge. Her eyes were strained as she watched Brian climb back to her. Then he was beside her, steadying her, shouting encouragingly in her ear, thrusting his arm through her harness. Somehow, Vandy never knew how, they climbed to the rim of the cockpit. Minutes were like seconds racing by.

Vandy caught the flash of a mountain lake far below— shouted, "Ready?" heard Brian's "O.K.," and the two of them were over the edge, falling into space in a welter of arms and legs. The plane, above them, lurched heavily on its way. Vandy shut her eyes, counted slowly to four, and pulled the release ring. The jerk with which the chute opened, bearing that double weight, seemed as if it would tear her out of the harness. Her feet dropped beneath her, the parachute careened wildly, and she looked up and saw what had happened; the extra weight on the ropes had torn loose several of the points, and the chute, taking the air unevenly, was swaying like a drunken thing.

Almost simultaneously she felt Brian's body sag, saw his face, so close to hers, turn suddenly gray.

Even as she clutched the arm caught in her harness, crying out, "Brian! I'll hold you!" she knew what had happened. His arm, in that unexpected jerk, had been pulled from its socket. Brian, helpless and in agony, hung half unconscious at her side.

They fell—all too swiftly. Vandy's mind was a tumult of confusion. Death, so unexpected and suddenly so near, stamped her own face with a pallor but still she tried to cry to Brian, reassuring him.

"I'll hold—Brian—you're—all right!"

He opened his eyes; his gray lips moved. "Vandy! Too— late—"

She clutched him to her convulsively, trying to think, trying to forget the earth below, rising so incredibly and so swiftly to meet them. She couldn't control the chute—it fell crazily, swaying drunkenly from its broken points. Trees—to crash into! That meant death. And the earth—they were falling so fast—that meant death, too!

"Vandy!" Brian, fighting back his agony, was trying to beat death and tell her something.

But Vandy wasn't listening. Her eyes were strained upon a flash of water below—that little mountain lake hemmed in by trees. If they hit the water—together—they would surely drown. Brian, helpless, and she strapped into her heavy harness, would be smothered and trapped beneath the folds of the collapsed chute. In another minute—

But Vandy needed no other moment. Her mind worked like lightning. Of the three of them, two had a chance to live. Narcissa and—Brian. She could save Brian if she acted instantly. The lake was less than fifty feet below. Brian—if he hit the water clear of her—would get himself out. The shock of the cold water and the instinct of self-preservation would save him, in spite of his helpless arm. And she? Vandy gave one wild sob. Who was she—the third corner of that triangle—to want to live!

Brian's free hand was clutching the ropes above his head. She knocked it suddenly loose. She tore at his useless arm, thrusting it back through the harness, letting the weight of his body pull it through.

Brian, rousing from his half-stupor, realized too late what she was doing. Even as he cried frantically, "No—together, Vandy!" she had him free—felt his body sliding clear of hers— saw him fall like a plummet to the lake below. Then she shut her eyes and waited.

Brian, stunned for a moment by the impact of the water, was snapped back to consciousness by its icy touch. He fought to the surface, struggling madly. He had faced death with the ripping of those parachute points, but he'd faced worse than death when Vandy had cut him loose—saving his life even as she went to her own death. He looked wildly about—saw the wilted flower of her chute floating on the water some twenty feet beyond him, and knew that Vandy— the only person in the world who mattered—was beneath it!

How he reached her, he never knew. A strength not his own—the strength that comes to men when the women they love are in danger—kept him going. But reach her he did. And somehow, incredibly, he tore away the silken folds and freed her from her harness. As he reached the water's edge and felt firm ground under his feet, he sprawled forward into blackness that reached up for him. But he didn't care now. Vandy was safe. That was his last conscious thought before the blackness engulfed him.

He woke to a sharp stab of agony as Vandy, white-faced and desperate, braced her knee against his shoulder and jerked his dislocated arm back into place. For a moment pain swept through his body like a wave, then slowly it receded. He looked up into the face of the girl who held him in her arms.

"Vandy!" he whispered. "Oh, Vandy!"

Her eyes were wet. She said shakily, "Did I hurt you—very much, Brian?"

He thought he had never seen anything so beautiful as Vandy with the tears upon her lashes.

"I thought," he said simply, "I had lost you. I thought—I'd never have the chance—to tell you—I love you."

A little cry broke her lips. "Oh—don't say it, Brian—just because I—"

"Because you saved my life?" He turned his head, kissed her arm where it lay against his cheek. "When death was—just around the corner, Vandy, I knew it was you—only you. Is that enough—to make you believe me?"

She met his eyes steadily. "And—Narcissa?"

He said, once and for all time: "She was just a dream—but never a real one. I knew that, today. You see, there was never anything wrong with her gas tank. I looked. I suppose she drained it when I wasn't looking—the ground beneath it was soaked. I—I had two hours, Vandy, before you came—to face the fact that, because of her, I might lose you. I knew then—"

And Vandy? Vandy, the Bird Girl? She looked into his eyes and read the truth there, and into her heart rushed the flight of wings. Night was coming on—Brian's arm was useless—Narcissa, wailing and terrified, was somewhere to be found—they were lost, and Death had had its finger-tips upon them! But what did it matter! What did anything matter now, save Brian's lips on hers!

HENRY'S DIVORCE

Edith Barnard Delano

WHEN Henry Bronson passed through the room where the filing clerks were, on his way to the elevator, little Miss Carson, whose hair was red, looked after him.

"Gee," said she, "what that man needs is to get caught in a raid on a night club or some'n'. I bet he never had a thrill in his life, the poor fish. He'd never ast a girl to go out to lunch with him or anything—not him!"

But Miss Carson wronged Henry; that was just what he had done. Moreover, he was no fish; and though thrills may vary, the all but invisible jauntiness of his step was indicative of the odd little thrill that had been running through him ever since he had talked with Mrs. Moffitt over the telephone that morning.

Of course he had not placed the voice at first. Ordinarily nothing infuriated him more than to be asked to guess who was at the other end of the telephone; but when at last she announced herself as Mrs. Moffitt—the Adele Martin of his younger days—his ire vanished. And presently he had asked where she was lunching.

It was not until he drew within sight of the liveried giant at

From *Ladies' Homes Journal* 46, no. 16 (June 1929).

the curb that he realized he had named a place he had often heard Cookie mention. It was not so far from the great department store where she worked; remembering that, a quiver of distaste ran through him. Not that Cookie herself was anything but proud of her job; she flaunted it before all their world. When she had been promoted to be the head of the fashion department, whatever that was, hadn't she even given a party to her associates, to celebrate? That had been all very well for Cookie and the people she worked with; but what had he felt like—with everybody there calling her Cook or Miss Lee too?

Addie rose as he entered the vestibule; of course she was a good deal plumper than she had been in the old days, but youth flooded back upon them as they walked side by side toward the dining room. An assistant head waiter gave them a table rather too near the door, but neither of them got the significance of that.

"Why were you frowning so when you came in?" Addie asked when they were seated. "I don't believe you're a bit glad to see me! I hope you don't think it was terrible of me to come to lunch with you alone."

Henry's frown was no longer there, and he answered—as he hoped—appropriately. Addie's eyes widened when he discarded the menu and ordered an excellent luncheon; then he leaned toward her across the table. They both laughed a trifle nervously.

"Will you smoke?" he asked, producing a cigarette case.

Mrs. Moffitt's head turned slightly aside, but her look met his coquettishly. "Now, now!" said she. "So that's what you think of me!"

"I think you are very charming," Henry informed her. "Life has certainly dealt well with you. Tell me about it."

"Ah," she said, and her eyes looked dewy. "I've had my troubles, Henry, but I hope I have known how to bear them. Every woman wants to be—well—cherished, you know. Mr. Moffitt—Oh, well, it is all over now."

"I—er—I didn't know," said Henry, thinking how gentle and womanly she was.

Addie shook her head. "It doesn't do to talk about our sor-

rows," said she, "but you'll agree, I am sure, that we ought
not to lose sight of old friends the way we do. Why, just to
think, Henry, I didn't even know you were married until your
mother told me."

"Oh," said Henry. "Then you have seen my mother?"

"Indeed, yes! She's invited me to make her a little visit before I go back to Ohio. She says your wife is quite an artist."

Yes, that was of course what his mother would have said,
Henry himself had often heard her say it, for the elder Mrs.
Bronson resolutely closed her mind to all the unpleasant facts
of life, as she tried to do to all its improprieties. Her grandmother had been a Peabody, and her father a judge. An earlier
ancestor, to be sure, had engaged in the mercantile trade of
the Salem of old days; but that sort of thing had long since
become associated in people's minds with romance and India
shawls and old Lowestoft—and possibly spices. To work,
however blithely and lucratively, in a department store—oh,
no! To Mrs. Bronson, senior, dear Beatrice was quite an artist.

"She says your wife is very modern, too," Mrs. Moffitt
added. "But I can see that she takes good care of you, Henry."

They talked over their sole Marguery; it was wonderful
how much they both remembered of the old days. People of
whom they were oblivious passed and repassed their table; the
only warning that Henry had of someone's pausing beside
them was when he caught the startled widening of Addie's
eyes. He looked up quickly. A hand tapped his shoulder.

"Hello, lamb," said the slim, girlish person who had
touched him. She nodded brightly to his companion, and
passed on, followed by her companion. Henry had got hastily
to his feet and was staring rather blankly after them. Then he
sat down.

Mrs. Moffitt's lips were parted, her cheeks were a deeper
rose. "Why, Henry!" said she. "That—er—that was my wife,"
said Henry. "And Mr. Furness, her—ah—assistant."

"Your wife!" Mrs. Moffitt turned and looked.

The couple had gone directly across the broad room to a
table beside a window; apparently it had been reserved, and
the girl—she did look like a mere girl—nodded to the head
waiter as he drew out her chair. Mrs. Moffitt could not fail to

observe the smartness of the small close hat, the luxuriousness of the fur that dropped carelessly backward, the gesture of the man as he flicked a cigarette lighter and held it across the table toward the lady.

"Why, Henry—," she said again, and added, "My goodness!"

"I—er—want you to meet her," said Henry lamely.

He was slightly constrained during the rest of the meal; when he put his guest into a taxi he thought he detected a shade of pity in her eyes. Damn it, he thought, there it was! Pity. Every sweet womanly woman like Addie Moffitt would pity him; he knew his mother pitied him. Doubtless every man of his acquaintance who didn't pity him held him in secret scorn for being willing that his wife should work. What they would think of him if they knew the ways in which Cookie otherwise conducted her life, he was not willing to think of. Even that ridiculous insistence of hers on the use of her maiden name, B. Cook Lee—oh, in business, to be sure, and by people who knew her in business—put shame upon him. There was no sense whatever in Cookie's persisting in working at all. There never had been; but he had wanted Cookie, been willing enough to take her on her own terms. Now, however, after five secure years of marriage—

But something that thought suggested brought him up short; he even carried a faint uneasiness with him during the rest of the afternoon, and when at last he started uptown the disquieting thought persisted. Just how much security did he really have? He knew well enough where Cookie stood in his life, but just where did he stand in hers? It had been all very well to say, before they were married, that of course she must go on working, go on fulfilling herself—that was one of her phrases; but did not the whole experience of the world indicate that a woman could only fulfill herself, really, in the role of wife and mother? He had to admit that Cookie ran the house excellently, and all that; but he had put up with—well, damn it, with other things—long enough. The time had come for him to assert himself.

Yet, after all, he had had his five years with Cookie; passing a florist's shop, it came to him that he never quite knew how

she would take—well, things. Of course he had never objected to her lunching with men; didn't she always say that so
much of her sort of business had to be done across the lunch
table? But he could not be altogether sure of the attitude she
might take toward his own little—er—er—

He retraced his steps, went into the florist's and bought a
dozen red carnations; as the woman was putting them into
the box he told her to add another dozen. For didn't his
Cookie—no, his Beatrice; it was absurd to call her Cookie—
didn't his Beatrice deserve everything he could give her of
flowers, ease, protection?

"Miss Lee telephoned she would be detained, Mr. Bronson,
and you weren't to wait for her," the maid informed him almost at the moment of his entering the house.

"Are you speaking of Mrs. Bronson, Hilda?" Henry asked,
stiffening.

The girl looked startled. "Yes, sir. I get so used to hearing
everybody—"

"That will do," said Henry, and left the florist's box on the
hall table.

The food was exceedingly good. He could not fail to remember that his mother always had to go into the kitchen
before dinner, or else apologize for something; it had been one
of the exhilarating marvels of his married life that Cookie's
meals never seemed to cause her the least concern, even
though he brought home extra guests, which he had never
dared risk in his mother's home. Oh, he knew his Cookie.

Abruptly his appetite seemed to become satisfied. But did
he know his Cookie—his Beatrice, confound it? Why, for example, was she dining out tonight? Had she ordered this particular dinner of things he liked that morning, or had she done
it by telephone after—well, after luncheon, in fact? Was she
punishing him, handing him coals of fire? He had encountered
the subtleties of Cookie's displeasure before now.

The evening seemed unduly long. He had a new *Life of Lincoln* to read, but it did not hold him; he thought he was getting
a sore throat, too, and remembered that he had forgotten to
have his gargle refilled. When at last he heard a latchkey in the
door he sat up and unconsciously braced his shoulders a little.

She came into the room with the florist's box under her arm, pulled off her hat and tossed it away.

"Hello, lamb," said she. "Lordy, I'm tired."

"It is after ten," said Henry stiffly.

"I thought it was midnight!" She dropped upon the down-cushioned sofa and bent forward to loosen the strap of her shoe. Then she slid her foot out of it and wiggled her toes through their silk stocking. "Whee-oo, that feels good!" said she.

"I see no necessity for your working until this hour of the night," said Henry. "That is—I suppose you were working, as you call it."

She was snapping the string of the box. "Well, what do you think I've been doing? Dancing?" She stared at him; then she grinned. "Oh, lambkin, I've worked out the most gorgeous scheme for the store! It's a job, you know, to tie a huge place like that together in one plan and do justice to everything. I've got just the spiffiest figures for the windows—glass, all flowing and gooey, like beautiful soft-boiled snakes. Billy Furness is crazy about them—we were unpacking them tonight."

"At luncheon, too, I suppose," said Henry.

She looked at him, her lips parted; then she laughed.

"This from you, Hank? Now don't turn my head, darling!"

Henry's frown deepened; but five years had taught him the advantage of registering the first score.

"It was—er—very embarrassing," he began; but apparently she was not listening at all.

She had dropped the lid of the florist's box on the floor. "Will you look what's here?" she cried. "Carnations—to me!" She leaned back, ran her fingers through her short hair until it stood on end like a boy's, and briefly laughed. "Now I ask you, do I, oh, do I look like a woman you'd send carnations to?"

"What's the matter with carnations?" Henry asked; and at the somewhat hoarse note in his voice she looked across at him. Her eyes softened; compunction, amusement, a lovely tenderness were there. She laid the box on the sofa.

"Ah-h-h!" The sound came from her throat, inexpressibly like the murmur from some deep copse that has caught an echo from the wind and releases it reluctantly. She perched on the arm of Henry's chair, pressed her cheek against his stiffly held head. "Oh-h-h, the lamb, the precious lamb . . . Did he bring me home those lovely flowers? What made him think I deserved them—oh, the precious—"

As always when she was in such a mood Henry's very knees felt weak; his eyes smarted.

"I thought you'd—like them," said he, and all his earlier emotions were now gone into the limbo of things that did not matter.

"Like them!" Her lips were on his. "But I'm just not—well, not good enough for carnations, darling!"

There it was! She could laugh in the most ecstatic moments. Henry stirred restlessly.

"I don't see why you accuse yourself of not being a—good woman," said he. "It is not the way to talk, even in joke. Goodness is above ridicule."

Cookie leaned back, her hands on his shoulders, slowly shaking her head. "Hank," said she, "I do think you are the most utterly wonderful man that ever lived. There's only one of you!"

"Oh, I know you're laughing at me," said he. "But just the same, I do want to give you things. Everything, in fact."

"Like carnations," she cooed. "Oh, you sweet! Oh, I do love you!"

Henry's arms made the most of her yielding mood. "Dear," he said, "I want all of you—I don't want to share you with anything any more. This—all this other thing has got to stop."

Cookie drew back. "What do you mean—any more?" she asked.

"This damned work of yours. I tell you, it's got to stop."

She got up; she had paled a little. "Do you quite realize what this—this damned work of mine means? Doesn't it occur to you that it may be as important to me and to a good many other people as yours is to you?"

"The most important thing in any woman's life is her home, where she belongs," said he. But he was not willing to let the earlier mood slip away so soon. He leaned toward her. "Dear, I do want to take care of you," he said.

She had listened with open mouth. "But why on earth should I want to be taken care of, as you put it? Not that you don't anyway, you lamb; but—"

Cookie dropped to a chair, her feet out in front of her. After a moment she laughed aloud.

"I don't think that is amusing," said Henry.

"Oh, neither do I! I just can't see myself as the sort of woman that men yearn to take care of!"

"Why?" he demanded.

"Oh, well—" She rocked with laughter; but at last she looked up at him, standing stiffly before her, affront in every line of him. She bit her lip, held her arms up to him, and her face. "Co-o-ome here, you lamb," she cooed.

"I—will—not!" said Henry. "And I don't understand what you're laughing at. I—"

"Hank," she asked, "do you honestly think you married me because you wanted to protect me?"

"Certainly I did. Every man wants to protect his wife. And I must ask you to stop endowing me with those ridiculous names—lamb, and Hank. And what is more, hereafter you are to use the name that is legally yours. I've had enough of this Miss Lee business. B. Cook Lee—sounds like a Chinese laundry."

When she got up, her eyes were no longer twinkling. "I'd have you remember it's a name I've made famous in my own line of work. And it is a name I intend—to continue—using."

"You shall not."

"I certainly shall."

"Do you mean to imply that you are not going to—"

"Give up my job? My job? Oh, my dear man! Go chase yourself."

Henry swallowed. He could not speak. He was baffled, and he knew it.

From the doorway, with the box of carnations under her arm, she said, "Don't let's be foolish! I guess we're both tired."

"I am not tired," said Henry with dignity. "I've got a sore throat, but I'm going out."

"If you're going out for your gargle, you needn't. I had your prescription refilled, and you will find that it's on the left-hand side of the third shelf in the bathroom—as usual!"

And there, thought Henry, there it was! That was Cookie!

A few mornings later she said to him as she rose from the breakfast table:

"Don't forget this is your mother's day for coming to dinner, lamb. She's bringing a guest with her, too, so you get home early, won't you? Because"—she added, slipping into her coat—"because I may be late."

"A guest?" asked Henry.

Cookie giggled. "Your mother says she is such a sweet little womanly woman," said she, "your lady friend from Ohio."

After all, she was home before him. He was delayed at the office; his mother and Mrs. Moffitt were entering his front door as he mounted the steps.

"My dear son!" From her long experience in speaking before women's clubs, his mother knew how to put a world of meaning into her tones. "My dear, dear son! Isn't it wonderful to have dear Addie with us?"

"It is indeed," Henry assented; and Mrs. Moffitt said, as he helped her out of the rather tight sleeves of her coat, "I think it was lovely of your wife to let me come—before she had called too."

The elder Mrs. Bronson had moved to the living-room door. But she had not entered; even before he and Addie joined her, Henry felt something strange in the atmosphere. Then, looking over his shoulder, he saw. Cookie and Billy Furness were seated cross-legged on the floor, a very large sheet of manila paper spread out between them and held down at the corners by books and candlesticks; with a carpenter's pencil Cookie was marking swirls upon it, and she was talking:

"Now don't be an idiot, darling, and pretend you don't see! Look—get your mauves and purples on this side, on the lovely green ladies, and your greens on the amber ladies over there. You might use the old Chinese stuff for a background. I wouldn't use any jewels—ivory, maybe, to tie it all together. Now you can do what you've got to! You can't hang on to mamma's skirts forever, you know—much as I know you love me."

Something roused her attention to the group in the doorway; she was on her feet in one lithe movement, and came forward, smiling.

"Oh—sorry! I didn't hear you come in, mother dear! I am so glad, so very glad to meet an old friend of Henry's too! So good of you to come."

She shook hands with Mrs. Moffitt, kissed Henry's mother; but Addie's eyes wore a startled look. That strange talk of amber ladies and green ones; that young man scrambling up from the floor, whom she had just heard called darling, who was surely the man of the restaurant . . .

There was silence until Hilda said from the door, "Dinner is served, m'm."

Yet in spite of Cookie's talk and her graciousness, at first that dinner was strained. For a time Addie kept her eyes on her plate, tactfully refraining from looking at Henry. For a time Henry did not speak at all, and Mrs. Bronson answered her daughter-in-law only in monosyllables. The food was excellent, but the delicacy of Cookie's table, like the invisible clockwork of her housekeeping, always suggested to Mrs. Bronson something vaguely reprehensible; the feeling matched her subconscious suspicion that to have your servants adore you must mean that you paid them too much.

But gradually the restraint wore off, melting away under Cookie's persistent charm like snow under a soft spring rain. Young Mrs. Bronson's interest in the forthcoming rummage sale that her mother-in-law was arranging for the Ladies Aid was really remarkable; almost shyly she made quite useful suggestions. Mrs. Moffitt could not fail to become interested when the talk swung to some of the latest things from Paris that had been brought over for the store. When, at half-past nine, Mrs. Bronson said they really must be getting home, Mrs. Moffitt felt that the evening had been very short.

"But you must not think of driving us home, my son!" Henry's mother protested. "You said your throat was sore."

"Where's my brown overcoat?" Henry asked, his face expressionless.

"The one you take hunting? On the right-hand side of the hall closet, isn't it?" Cookie returned lightly.

"Cookie and Billy Furness were seated cross-legged on the floor, a very large sheet of manila paper spread out between them." Illustration by Saul Tepper. From "Henry's Divorce," *Ladies' Home Journal* 46, no. 16 (June 1929), p. 17.

But when Henry, his car purring in front of the house, came in for the ladies, his mother exclaimed:

"I'm sure you are going to give me that coat for my rummage sale, dear."

Henry stiffened. "This coat? What's the matter with this

coat? I like it. I'm used to it," said he, and knew that the twinkle in Cookie's eyes was evidence that she saw through his little effort at assertiveness.

When he reentered the house a while later she was at the telephone; it was obvious that she was giving young Furness further directions.

"Can't you ever forget that confounded store?" Henry demanded. "Or was it just that you had to talk to that young ass?"

Cookie pursed her lips at him. "Oh, you're so sweet and cunning when you make believe you're jealous," she said. "And it flatters me so!"

"Jealous—rot!"

"Didn't we have a pleasant evening?" she asked, demurely smiling.

"Pleasant! Hell!"

"Really?" she asked, your eyebrows raised. "And I thought I was being so sweet and womanly."

How was it that she could always torment him? "Oh, Cookie, I don't know why you behave this way," he said miserably. "But I tell you, I've had enough of it."

Cookie crossed her legs, leaned forward with an elbow on her knee and her chin in her palm. "What way?" she asked. "Enough of what?"

"I tell you I've had enough of it," he repeated. "You're going to resign tomorrow."

"Just think of that!" said Cookie. But it must have been the look in Henry's eyes that brought her to her feet. She laid a hand on his shoulder. "Dear, dearest man," she said, looking up at him with the faintest, swiftest of quivers, "what is this all about anyway? Aren't we being a little ridiculous? Need we quarrel?"

His arm went about her. "No. But this ridiculous working— this Miss Lee—this being out at all hours—this—this—"

"This is not being a good old traditional kind of wife," she supplied softly.

He kissed her. "Traditional! I want my wife, my own wife, all of her," he told her, his voice choking. "Dear—I'm making money enough. Please—"

She shook her head slowly. "My dear, what you think you

want—maybe what you really do want—is a wife who will stay home and sew on your buttons, instead of paying to have them sewed on while she's doing something that interests her more. You want her to follow the good old pattern—do a little church work and play a little bridge; fiddle about the house and fluster the servants as our grandmothers did; set her clock by the time you go off in the morning and come home at night. You want a wife to share your own life; apparently you don't want to share all of whatever life there may be with her. You—"

Something was ringing in Henry's ears. "You mean you won't give up this—"

"I can't," said Cookie; and after a moment that was prolonged, Henry said, "I see."

In the morning he awoke to a miserable sense of everything being out of kilter. From the guest room he heard Cookie moving about, heard her go downstairs, a while later heard her leave the house. During the day, in spite of the pain in his throat, he worked with a savage energy that left his secretary with a sense of being abused. When his mother called up during the afternoon he sent word that he was in conference, and received a message asking him to stop at her house on his way home. When he left the office at five o'clock snow was falling; looking down at the flakes on his sleeve, he saw that he had worn the old brown overcoat. But it didn't matter.

"Why, Henry," his mother asked at once, "aren't you feeling well, dear?"

Henry was shaking Mrs. Moffitt's hand, shaking and shaking it.

A few days later he asked his mother, "Did you telephone Coo—I mean Beatrice?"

"Yes, dear, of course," she said, straightening his pillow. He hated having a pillow moved under him. "I didn't want to alarm her unduly, and so I only told her that you had decided to spend the night here. She said she quite understood."

"Oh," said Henry. "When was that?"

"I don't think you ought to talk, dear," said his mother. "I'm going down to get you some of the nice broth Addie has made you."

"I don't want any broth," Henry snapped. "Has—I suppose Cookie has telephoned since?"

"Now don't let anything worry you, my son," said his mother. "And don't put your arms outside of the covers. Wait—here's your dressing gown."

Obediently he thrust his arms into the familiar garment. Then he remembered. "Where did this come from?" he demanded.

"Dear Beatrice sent some of your things," said his mother, and left the room; but not before he saw tears well up into her eyes.

Some of his things. . . . And Cookie had said she quite understood!

The first day that he went downstairs his mother covered him up on the sofa so firmly that he felt as if he were upholstered. He even felt that he was slightly ridiculous; things that Cookie would have said kept coming into his mind. Yet undoubtedly the gentle feminine fussing that had surrounded him during the past week had been comforting; his mother, and Mrs. Moffitt, too, had been tireless in their efforts to keep him amused. They read aloud to him a good deal, his mother from the editorial and front pages of the paper, Mrs. Moffitt from the latest murder trial, discreetly skipping certain parts; neither of them thought it was good for him to use his eyes, or to bother his head about things like the stock market. They were very careful, too, about his nourishment; they discussed it a good deal. So Henry was fed to repletion; but when he was well enough at last to escape the semi-fluids of the trays and go to the table, he discovered that old Martha, who had tyrannized over his mother since he was a boy, never seemed capable of producing a meal at the same moment on two successive days. Yet if he came down late, his mother's eyes or her gentle silence reproached him.

"We have to consider Martha's feelings," she explained to Addie one day when Henry had observed that the roast beef was overdone, "because she's the only one I'm ever sure of keeping. It's really a most deplorable sign of the times, the way maids walk off and leave you nowadays."

Henry caught himself wondering about Cookie's maids; as far as he knew, they never produced their feelings.

Gradually—or possibly not so gradually—he became aware of other things about his mother's house that he had never observed before. There was not a reading light in any bedroom; when he asked for one his mother said she did hope he wouldn't think of straining his eyes by reading in bed. There was a fireplace in the living room, but it was swept clean of ashes. Why not, Mrs. Moffitt, asked, since the furnace gave perfectly adequate heat? Once, coming into the room at dusk, he stumbled over an obstacle and found it to be the mending basket; he might have looked out for it, since it was usually in evidence somewhere.

"I never do let my mending pile up on me," he had heard his mother say several times; but as far as he could observe, the contents of the basket remained about the same.

"Addie's little visit has been a real pleasure," his mother told Henry one day. "We have so much in common. I wish I could have her nearer, all the time."

And on an afternoon when his mother had been persuaded to go to the club, where she was to read a really important paper, and when Henry had found Mrs. Moffitt sewing under the red-shaded lamp, she said, "I'm so fond of your dear mother, Henry. How she does understand making a real, old-fashioned home."

"Yes, doesn't she?" Henry agreed, and opened the evening paper at the stock market page.

Mrs. Moffitt's eyes were on her sewing; probably she did not observe that Henry wanted to read. "She has been very much upset over all this," said she. "I think she has been very brave."

"There was nothing to worry about," Henry said shortly. "My throats never amount to anything."

"Why, Henry! You don't realize how ill you've been," Addie reproved him. "Nobody knows how much the flu takes out of one any better than I do. But that wasn't what I meant." Henry's eyes went down a column, but for some reason he was not concentrating. "I mean—this other thing," Addie explained softly.

"What other thing?" asked Henry.

"I've been through it all myself," said Mrs. Moffitt softly, and sighed. "So I know just how—well, how painful it is. Especially when neither party has any real—though of course, where they have, it is even—. Yet I do think divorce is often a blessing, Henry."

That evening Henry waited until he thought the two ladies must be asleep; then he crept cautiously down the stairs. He found his hat in the hall closet; there was no light there, and in feeling about for his overcoat he knocked over some strange thing that fell with a crash. When he emerged from the closet his mother was halfway down the stairs, wrapped in a substantial gray garment.

"Why, Henry!" she exclaimed, her eyes widely startled. "What on earth are you—"

"Where's my coat?" Henry demanded. "I'm looking for my coat."

She came all the way down to the hall. "But, my son, you cannot want your coat at this hour of the night! You can't be thinking of going out into the night air, when you haven't been out since—"

"Oh, come mother! Please tell me where my coat is," he said with obvious restraint.

His mother smiled, shook her head as one does to an insubordinate child. "Now, my dear, that coat was really not fit for you to wear again," said she. "So I sent it—"

But the front door had closed behind Henry.

The only light in the house shone dimly from the living room. That brought him up short on the doorstep. He remembered a spread-out drawing, young Furness there. Yet he went in.

The fire had fallen to that state of glowing embers that it reaches when a man has spent a peaceful evening before it. The only lamp that was lighted shone across the deep chair that he liked to read in; beside the chair was a small table with a *Life of Lincoln,* an evening paper opened to the stock market page. He saw the whole gracious quietness of the room as he had never seen it before; but at first he thought Cookie was not there. His heart sank, beat rather wildly. Then he looked at the sofa. That . . . that . . . He went closer. It was incredible, even impossible, but that surely was the coat he had been looking for at his mother's; and under it Cookie lay, asleep, a crumpled handkerchief under her cheek.

It may have been a sound from him or only his presence that waked her. Almost at the instant when her eyes opened she sat up, swung her feet to the floor, yawned.

"Hello, lamb," said she. Then she blinked, came fully awake, and said stiffly in quite a different tone. "Oh!"

"What," Henry demanded, pointing, "what is the meaning of that?"

Cookie looked down at the coat. "Why why—it's yours. Why shouldn't it be here? You can have it—I suppose you have come for—for all of your things."

"Cookie—Cookie—" He sat down on the sofa beside her. "Cookie, how did you get that coat?"

For a moment she said nothing; then slowly her face turned toward him and their eyes met. Her lips quivered.

"Well, I—I bought it! That's how it got here!" she told him with an elaborate assumption of defiance.

There was a smothered exclamation from Henry, and the next moment, cheek to cheek, heart to heart, she was sobbing in his arms.

"I just knew she'd send it to that rummage sale," she made him hear, between her broken breaths. "And you loved it so! I—I just slipped in and bought it. . . .

"Oh, my own darling, why do I love you so?" he asked, so much later that the embers had turned gray.

"Because I'm so sweet and womanly," she said, and giggled.

But he did not laugh with her. "You are," he said seriously, even devoutly.

She leaned away from him, put her hands on his shoulders, "Hank, I believe you're beginning to see!"

"I see there's nobody like you!"

"Oh, plenty! Of course there has to be all sorts, and I happen to be my sort. Of course I like my job. You like yours! But there isn't a woman alive who doesn't put something else first."

"Oh, my own sweet—what?" he asked with a choke.

She laughed again, looked away. "Oh, well—what do you think?" she murmured.

"I think you're yourself, and I love you."

"I'm only part of myself. You're the rest."

He was very serious. "And that is the marvel, Cookie. I don't know why you love me. I don't know why I love you so much."

"I think you love me because you do—oh, you do—understand me so well, my lamb!" He grinned, and she said again primly, "And you'll never be able to bore me, darling, because you do keep me so busy stirring you up!"

That time she yielded to his arms; presently he said, "Oh, it's been horrible, Cookie—like being divorced! And that flu was the devil."

She sat up, shook him a little. "You haven't been ill—not really? And you didn't—your mother didn't let me know!"

Actually there were tears in her eyes.

"Darling," he asked, a lump in his throat, a flood of sentimental warmth sweeping over him, "would you have nursed me?"

"Nursed you—I?" She stood up. "I should hope not! I'd have got you a nurse who knew something about it!"

And while Henry roared, she crossed to the sofa and picked up his coat.

"Such a disgraceful old thing," she murmured, and pressed her lips to it. "Look how they tore it at the rummage sale too! Oh, well—never mind! The seamstress is coming tomorrow."

BELINDA'S IMPORTANCE

Booth Tarkington

Booth Tarkington began this series on Belinda Dale in August 1929 for the
Ladies' Home Journal. In the first story, Belinda, nicknamed Pansy, is a
graduating high school senior, as is her best friend, Patsy Dorker, who is set
on engagement to a classmate. Pansy is alarmed by her friend's rush into
matrimony and unsuccessfully tries to dissuade her, while deciding she will
embark on a career the way a man would. Although her family is horrified
when she takes a factory job, Pansy is firmly committed to climbing the ladder
of success and to taking herself seriously. The first episode ends with her
reclaiming the name Belinda. In subsequent issues, Belinda becomes alienated
from Patsy, now a suburban, middle-class matron, and her boring husband;
but she meets various challenges at the factory so well that she is steadily
promoted to executive positions, in which she applies her decisive, competent
managerial skills and her innovative ideas. Eventually she becomes manager
of the firm. Throughout the six-month serial, a stark contrast is drawn between
Belinda's continued youthfulness, vigor, and attractiveness and Patsy's steady
deterioration, even though their social circle disparages Belinda with hurtful
talk about her unwomanliness and emotional instability. Her suitor, George
Hinchman, is an amateur ornithologist who has loved Belinda since high
school, but he cannot persuade her to marry because he wants a full-time
wife. In this last episode, they are both in their mid-thirties, and George is
able to accept Belinda's career.

From *Ladies' Home Journal* 47, no. 20 (January 1930). Reprinted by permission.

THAT brown and hardy traveler, George Hinchman, returning from a final excursion in Patagonia, and settling himself for the first time with the aspect of permanence in his native, comfortable farmhouse on the edge of Long Hills, most self-centered of suburbs, could not reasonably have expected his home-coming to be entirely unobserved by the community; but he was a quiet man, liking the independence found in obscurity, and he had little pleasure in the discovery that all talkative Long Hills felt his return to be a matter of romantic, and even dramatic, general interest.

It was his cousin, Maria Capoole, a lively and voluble matron near his own age, who helped him to make the discovery one springtime afternoon as they sat upon his veranda; indeed, since she delivered herself of all the information she possessed upon all other subjects, as she always did with everybody if pressure for time did not prevent, the returned traveler had little chance to escape hearing of the suburb's newly stimulated interest in himself and his affairs.

"But, my dear George, it's entirely flattering," Mrs. Capoole assured him, in response to some mutterings expressive of annoyance. "You can hardly expect to drop back in here as if you were nobody, can you? When a man so distinguished as yourself—"

"Good heavens!" he interrupted. "How do you persuade yourself to use such a word in speaking of me?"

"But you are!" she said, quickly emphatic. "Don't you know, yourself, that you're immensely distinguished?"

"I? Then all one has to do, in order to be 'distinguished,' is nothing of any benefit to anybody. All I've ever done has been to go poking around the world looking at things, and I couldn't possibly be called an explorer because I've never been anywhere that somebody else hasn't been before me. I've got a couple of small packing cases filled with manuscript notes I've made on a few kinds of birds; I haven't even put the notes in order, much less published 'em, and if I did straighten the stuff out and print it, only a dozen or so people in the whole country would feel the slightest interest in it; so just where do I qualify for—"

"Dear me!" she cried, and she laughed. "Do you think we

care, here, whether or not your name is known to the inhabitants of some little village in Nebraska? That's never been what Long Hills has thought of as distinction, George. I think you've never understood that for years and years we've all thought of you as becoming more and more a distinguished person; and I see that you've never in the least realized how or why. You've never had a good view of your own picturesqueness."

"Picturesqueness!" he exclaimed, objecting strongly. "Murder! Maria, I wish you wouldn't—"

"Yes, picturesqueness!" she insisted. "In the first place, you're what young people used to call 'mysterious.' Years and years ago you began going off to Greenland or Burma or Mozambique or Wrangel Island and nobody-knows-where—maybe I don't get the names of the places right, but they've always sounded remote and adventurous—and usually you'd be away for many months and even several years; then you'd turn up here at home again, and people would get glimpses of you for a few weeks at the Country Club, or maybe at a dance or two, and then you'd be off again to some place more nobody-knows-where than ever. Several times the newspapers have printed cables from places nobody ever heard of, or could pronounce, saying that you were lost in 'jungle morasses,' or something, or had broken your leg in the crater of a new volcano—things like that—and in time such a career of itself gets to be rather impressive, you know. All the more so because when you've made your brief reappearances here nobody could ever get you to talk—that is, if you ever did talk, it must all have been to the one person. Now do try to look a little pleasanter!" Mrs. Capoole interjected, as he made a gesture of protest and impatience. "I can't make anything clear to you at all if you aren't going to allow me to refer to her."

"You don't think you could leave all that out?" he asked with some gruffness.

"'All that?'" she repeated satirically. "'All that' meaning Belinda Dale! No, because I'm explaining your distinguishedness, and it's your attitude toward her that's the most essential part of it, George. What I was just talking about—your long sojourns in jungles or zones of ice—that's just the background part of your being distinguished. Your real distinction is your impossible and absolutely unheard-of fidelity to the romance of your youth. There's nothing like it outside of old ballads and medieval tales, and naturally all of us here in Long Hills are delightfully excited about having had such a thing happen in our midst. You couldn't expect us not to be buzzing about it—especially at this juncture, George!"

"Dear me!" he exclaimed crossly. "You women are terrible! What do you mean by 'this juncture'?"

"You don't see? It's not very intricate. Of course everybody's always known that you fell in love with Belinda Dale when she came out and that she didn't have sense enough to reciprocate. After that, every time you came back from every one of your long wanderings, nothing could have been more obvious than that it was to her alone you did come back. You never had eyes for anybody else; you haunted her, and though I'll do her the credit to say she never appears to have mentioned it, nobody has any doubt that every time you came back you proposed to her again, and always found her still unappreciative. Well, that's gone on—how long? She was eighteen when you began it and I'm afraid she's about thirty-six now, George. Distinguished? Why, it's magnificent! Men like you don't exist nowadays; we only read of 'em in old books—the new books wouldn't know what to make of you at all. And yet, with all this, you don't understand that you're distinguished and you get cross with poor old Long Hills for buzzing over you?"

"I believe you used the expression 'this juncture'," he said dryly. "What—"

"'This juncture'? Yes, indeed! For one thing, you see, your opening the old house and wearing the general air of a settled-down person—it's felt that a decided change of some sort has come upon you, and that you're now to become a regular feature of life in Long Hills. This suggestion of a change in you naturally brings up a vital question, George: Does it mean a change in your attitude toward Belinda? No! I'm not asking you; I don't mean that. I'm only quoting the question that excites the community, and the community certainly has nothing under its observation comparable to you. That's part of what I meant by using the expression 'this juncture,' George."

"What's the rest of what you meant by it?"

"Something that'll be perfectly absorbing to watch. Your fidelity to the old love is already incredible, and more than half of us, I should say, are betting that it simply can't last any longer. You see, some of the romance about you lay in the fact that you couldn't bear to stay here near her and not have her, so you fled away from the presence and buried yourself as remotely as possible, until you couldn't stand it any longer and had to come back. Well, now you've come back to stay, so it appears you've decided that at last you can bear to be near her. More than that, you're at the age at which bachelors, however faithful to old loves, pretty frequently fall for cunning little creatures of nineteen or twenty. Long Hills has a perfectly charming crop of those, George, and don't you see that it's all naturally felt to be quite extraordinarily dramatic!"

"Dramatic!" he said shortly. "Oh, dear me!"

"But yes!" she cried. "Belinda herself has always been almost as dramatic as you are, flying in the face of everything and everybody that had brought her up, and starting out as a factory girl—to 'learn the business' I believe she said—that sort of general defiance to Long Hills was pretty nearly theatrical, I think! She certainly did 'learn the business' too, we'll have to admit; when her father's investments turned out badly, it didn't make any difference in the Dales' way of living— Belinda was already too prosperous for that—and now she's generally spoken of, in a business way, with deep respect; so I'm given to understand. Yes, she's dramatic, though nothing could sound more prosaic than 'General Manager of the Farrier Textile Companies, Incorporated.' Poor George! Was it to possess this romantic title that she sacrificed you and her own youth?"

George's response was not amiable. "Rubbish!" was what he said.

But Mrs. Capoole cheerfully overlooked his ungraciousness. "I must say Belinda doesn't wear much appearance of having sacrificed anything. Nobody can deny she's a pretty strikingly fine-looking woman, though the wear and tear of business life couldn't very well have helped making her rather hard and dry mentally, of course. She's like an athlete for keeping 'in condition'; rides and walks, and every Saturday afternoon plays thirty-six holes at the Country Club—thinks she owes it to her business responsibilities; so many people's prosperity depending upon her, and all that, I understand. Anyhow, it's remarkable the way she's held her looks; but I'm certainly carrying coals to Newcastle in talking to you about Belinda Dale's good looks, George! Since your return you've probably spent as much of your time in her society as she's felt her business cares would permit."

The surmise of Mrs. Capoole's did not end with an interrogation point; but she paused, and the pause itself was undoubtedly inquiring enough to cause her cousin's dark cheeks to redden slightly. "No," he said, "my time's been pretty well taken up with getting things in order here."

"You mean you haven't seen her at all?"

"Well—no. No, I believe not yet."

"Indeed!" Mrs. Capoole stared at him with a strong curiosity, but tactfully decided not to give immediate expression to it. "Well, when you do see her," she said, "you'll find that Belinda certainly has the edge on some of her contemporaries who've merely been leading a normal and healthy married life, supposedly. Do you remember her great friend of the old days, Patsy Dorker—Mrs. Bayard Pelley? Belinda looks as if she could run a mile without being breathed; but Patsy is enormous—one of those terrible things, a discontented fat woman; but of course she's got a right to be discontented—with her husband! Lost all his own money and then spent all hers! None of the Pelleys have anything any more at all; nobody knows how they keep going; but there's a girl of the Clement Pelleys come out this year who's perfectly exquisite looking." Mrs. Capoole paused, then added thoughtfully, "You might like to meet her, George. Everyone says—"

"No," he said, and laughed, with some dryness. "I'm not a dancing man, Maria."

"Perhaps not; but you may be soon!" Mrs. Capoole returned gayly, rising to go. "Wait until you've seen a few of our lovely young things; you never can tell! This time, even if you do propose to Belinda again, you've already proved you won't mind the result so much as you used to. I'm afraid you'll find

her more difficult than ever, now she's become so important—important women are usually rather terrible, don't you
think? And it might even be that you won't ask her—
especially if you first happen to glance over some of our darling little beauties, like young Julia Pelley." Then, as she descended the steps to go to the automobile waiting for her on
the driveway beside the house, she said brightly over her
shoulder, "At any rate, George, it's going to be absolutely en-
thralling to watch!"

He did not appear to be much pleased with this prophecy,
and, after he had put her into her car and it had borne her
away, his gloom seemed to increase. He returned to his chair
upon the veranda and sat there, staring out into the apple orchard beyond the lawn. The trees had just come into young
spring bloom; but it was not of the lovely young creatures
extolled by Mrs. Capoole that they made him think. Long,
long years ago he had looked over a hedge and seen Belinda
Dale standing near an apple tree in April blossom, and, being
pretty young himself, had called to her that he couldn't tell
which was which.

"Important!" he murmured sadly. "I suppose so!"

Mrs. Capoole had not overstated the fact when she said that
Belinda Dale had become an important woman; but neither
Miss Dale's importance nor her business responsibilities pre-
vented her from wondering why her old friend had been in
Long Hills for three weeks without coming to see her. It was
upon the Saturday afternoon concluding this period that her
wonder was made rather poignant by the sight of Mr. George
Hinchman engaged in a foursome preceding her at some distance, as she played over the Country Club course with her
young cousin, Crowley Dale, a sophomore on vacation.

Moreover, an incidental dialogue she held with her opponent did not lessen her mystification; young Crowley had
been unusually silent until they came within sight of the foursome, and then he began to be earnestly voluble.

"The way I think things ought to be," he said to Belinda,
"well, when people are trying to enjoy themselves and get a
little pleasure out of this life, because everybody's got troubles
and worries enough the best way you can fix it, and the least

thing you can do when you do get a chance simply to enjoy yourself a little, it's not to go mixing things all up like that."

"Like what?" Belinda inquired; then, perceiving that his frowning glace was fixed upon the distance, "You mean those people yonder?"

"What I mean," Crowley explained, frowning more deeply, "I mean, you take an old man like that, and when he tries to go around and everything with people prob'ly a way under half his age, why, what's the result? Well, it's simply this: It makes everything kind of formal and embarrassing, and nobody gets any enjoyment at all. For instance, look at Ted Miller there, and Gracie Lang and Julia Pelley; why, they've got to be on their best behavior and all stiff and polite and constructed the whole afternoon because they've got the old man with 'em. Well, men of that age ought to stay with other men their own age, because of course, when they don't it makes 'em appear foolish, whether they realize it or not. People ought to think over things like that before they get mixed up in 'em. One way you might look at it, though, of course, it isn't so much his fault."

"Not Mr. Hinchman's fault, you mean, that he's playing with those three young people?"

"No. It's Julia's. I heard her ask him last night at a little party over at Mrs. Capoole's."

"Did she?" Belinda looked thoughtful. "Well, then, since she asked him, she must have wanted him, and so I don't see why you think that she at least isn't having a good time, Crowley."

"Oh, prob'ly she is," Crowley admitted. "Of course she's showing off at him, and I suppose that gives her a good time. She and all the rest of 'em were showing off at him last night at Mrs. Capoole's. It was kind of sickening." Here the note of complaint in his voice became acute. "What I don't understand is why a man's simply never liking to stay home for more than about a week at a time makes girls think he must be so fascinating and everything. To me it was terribly disgusting; you'd have thought that all in the world Julia Pelley ever cared about was geography!"

"Julia's generally thought to be the prettiest girl in Long Hills just now, isn't she, Crowley?"

"Just now?" he repeated, surprised. "Why everybody says she's the prettiest girl that ever did live in Long Hills, now or any other time! Didn't you know that?" Then, taking her assent for granted, he added. "Well, I suppose she's doing her best to have a good time with old Hinchman, after dragging him in the way she did! I kind of thought he was supposed to be your property, Cousin Belinda."

"My property?" Belinda laughed and paused, confronting the small, white wall toward which they had been walking. "I had an idea your generation didn't believe in any person's being any other person's property."

He did not speak until she had made her stroke; then, as they walked on toward where his own ball lay, he muttered, "Seems to me Julia's looking for some, anyway."

"Some what?"

"Property," he said grimly, and sent his ball far off the fairway.

When they returned to the clubhouse young Crowley disappeared indoors; but Belinda's name was called by one of a group of ladies approaching middle age who were refreshing themselves with iced tea in the shade of an enormous striped umbrella upon the terrace. She joined them, accepted a green chair and a goblet of their beverage; and then, becoming aware of something covert but eager in their glances at her, wished that she had continued upon her way without pausing. Beneath another brilliant great umbrella, at a corner of the terrace, sat the foursome of which her undergraduate relative had so eloquently complained; Mr. Hinchman's back was toward Belinda's group, but the sprightly loveliness of young Julia, who faced him, talking gayly and continuously, was revealed in full.

"Extraordinary thing, that child Julia," Mrs. Pelley said lazily, in her husky, pampered voice, continuing to eat bits of cake from a plate in her lap as she spoke. "You certainly are careless of your possessions, Belinda, to allow that sort of thing getting started. You'd better give him a talking to when he comes around this evening! They tell me little Julia's got a wonderful 'line' for boys of all ages, young and old. They say she handles them all beautifully from the cradle to the grave."

"Dear old George isn't exactly ready for the grave," another of the group said. "Talk about 'well preserved'! I suppose it's the outdoor life he's led, and, as far as looks go, it strikes me that anyone who didn't know his actual years might think him more appropriate where he is now than if he were sitting over here with us."

A stranger could not well have thought this a humorous bit of observation; nevertheless, all of the little circle, except Belinda, laughed with evidently genuine enjoyment, and Mrs. Bayard Pelley's small eyes, under fat eyelids, moved their gaze deliberately from Belinda to the youthful Julia and back again. "Belinda's spiritually head and shoulders above the rest of us," she said. "She'd never be small enough to begin to want to keep something she'd never cared about having just because someone else showed an interest in getting hold of it."

At that all of the group, except Belinda, laughed again, and this time heartily; Mrs. Pelley's sally brought to them an acute merriment, the almost openly revealed undercurrent of which caused a heightening of the color in Miss Dale's cheeks. She was impatient with herself that she could not suppress the token that these old friends of hers, companions of her girlhood, had found something vulnerable within her.

Belinda set her goblet upon the painted iron table, rose and moved away, although there were cries of protest quite genuine, her friends not desiring the conclusion of a juxtaposition so piquant. At the sound of the protesting voices, George Hinchman turned his head, saw Belinda, instantly jumped up and walked toward her; but at the same moment the most important financial personage residing in Long Hills, the aged, large and impressive Mr. Codman Sloane, emerged from the clubhouse and called to her in his imperious, dry, old voice, "Miss Dale!"

Belinda nodded to him, but turned to meet the advancing George, an action evidently not to the pleasure of the great man who had called to her. Frowning magnificently, Mr. Codman Sloane stepped forward and intervened between the two old friends just as their hands touched in greeting. "Ah—young Hinchman, isn't it?" he said, with an excess of his usual coldness of manner. "I'm afraid you'll have to wait; I've come here personally to take up a matter with Miss Dale that can't be held over until Monday. You'll have to wait, sir; you'll have to wait!"

"I was only saying how-d'ye-do," George explained meekly. "I—"

"You'll have to wait sir; you'll have to wait!" The overwhelming Sloane was already conducting Belinda away, if not by actual physical force, then at least by the power of his pompous will; and George turned back to the vivacious umbrella where sat young Julia. "I hadn't half finished asking you about Turkestan," she said reproachfully. "I spose a poor little American girl like me would have a perfectly terrible time if she ever tried to travel all alone among those wild Oriental races. Of course, though, we're pretty adaptable—or perhaps you don't think so, Mr. Hinchman?"

She went on chattering in her small, sweet young voice, while George Hinchman, seated facing her, had a view over her shoulder of what ere long appeared to be a momentous business conference. The ponderous Mr. Sloane had taken Belinda to a table under an umbrella remote from all others, and there, producing a small notebook, read aloud from it at some length, while she listened gravely yet in an attitude apparently noncommittal. Then Mr. Sloane seemed to be urging upon her some course of action to which she was disinclined; he became first insistent, then vehement; with his heavy arms he made impatient gestures, a remarkable thing for him to do, and finally his angry voice became loud enough for his words to be audible across the terrace: "You think you can go on saying no to me?"

Julia interrupted herself to glance over her shoulder. "Good gracious!" she said. "To think anyone in the world would have nerve enough to say no to Mr. Sloane! It scares me to death just to look at him, even when he's trying to be pleasant, and Miss Dale isn't only looking at him; she's actually smiling! I should think she'd just die! Well, of course I naturally admire her terribly, and she certainly is awf'lly dashing looking, for her age; but yet when you get right down to thinking about it you do kind of wonder what's the use of being a woman at all if you feel obliged to always go around acting exactly like a man. I should think it'd get terribly irksome; but I spose she prob'ly enjoys it, though. Do you think she does, Mr. Hinchman?"

"Yes," George answered with more melancholy than he intended to express. "I'm afraid she does."

Then, as Julia stared at him with surprised eyes in which there appeared to be a glint of disapproval, he observed over her shoulder that the business interview was concluding; but he did not move to rejoin his old friend and complete the interrupted greeting. Instead, he sat watching Miss Dale and Mr. Sloane as they crossed the terrace, and, to the increased disapproval of young Julia, his expression was visibly wistful. Belinda did not even glance in his direction; she walked into the clubhouse with the large old gentleman whom she had so seriously annoyed, and she parted with him upon no amicable terms under the porte-cochère at the other side of the building.

"You look out for your next stockholders' meeting!" he warned her fiercely. "You think you've got the whole thing in your hands because Farrier can't be detached from you and Mears and your bloc. You wait!" Then, as Belinda's only retort was a brief laugh of serenity, his temper got the better of him again. "Women in business! What's the matter with that Hinchman fellow? What's wrong with him he couldn't have married you long ago and got you out of it so you wouldn't be getting in everybody's way like this!" Evidently the question was rhetorical merely, since Mr. Sloane paused for no reply but, instead, said "Thunder and lightning!" in a voice of disgust, and entering his waiting automobile, was instantly driven away.

His question, however, remained in the mind of Belinda Dale, and she thought of it as she drove homeward a few moments later. How many times had George asked her to marry him and what was wrong with him that had always caused her to refuse? There was nothing wrong with George, of course; but was there something wrong in the way he had asked her? What was it he had said that last time, three years ago? "Aren't you ready even yet to give up this infernal plush business and come with me?" Yes, the wrong thing was there, Belinda said to herself, driving homeward; George had never understood in the slightest what she felt about the manufacture of plush and other Farrier textiles. Then, feeling lonely, she laughed to herself a little morosely. He'd never come back to Long Hills before without hurrying to see her on the day of his arrival, and she admitted, without resistance, that this three weeks' neglect hurt more than she could have expected. She had long known that she had a strong affection for him; she cared for him, certainly, though not enough to marry him— not even to save him from a beautiful child of eighteen who would still be eighteen at thirty-six.

Belinda Dale might not have seen the figure near the gateway of the great Farrier plants if she had not stopped her car there for a moment to wait for a better clearance of the crowded street; but, as she came to a halt, her eye, roving a little, became aware of a shaping and texture of garments not usual in that locality. Then, with an incredulity sufficient to bring instant color to her cheeks, she recognized this old friend who had let a month pass without coming near her.

"Why, what—" she said. "George Hinchman! How in the world did you ever happen to wander into this part of town? What on earth are you doing?"

"Why, I—I had an idea maybe you'd lunch with me and go to the races this afternoon; but—but—"

"But what?"

His glance again moved over the departing throngs. "But I suppose you wouldn't," he said.

"Why wouldn't I?" she laughed. "Get in, George!"

Upon that, his expression lightening, he stepped into the car, sat beside her and they drove away; but for a little while neither of them said anything further. Then Belinda inquired, as if casually, "Have you been home for some time?"

"For some time?" he repeated vaguely. "Well—I—I saw you at the Country Club a week ago today, you know. I tried to get a chance to speak to you, but old Sloane wouldn't let me. Perhaps you don't remember though."

"I meant before that."

"You mean, had I been home some time before last Saturday?" he asked, apparently a little surprised.

"Yes; I heard you'd opened your old house and intended to stay."

"Yes," he said. "Yes—I believe so. Probably that's correct."

There was another silence, then, "Where had you thought of lunching?" she inquired.

"Lunching?" he said blankly. "Oh, yes! Where would you like—"

"We'll go to the Oak Leaf," she said. "It's near the race track, and we can walk over there after lunch."

"The Oak Leaf? But you have to be a member to lunch there, don't you, and I'm not—"

"I am," Belinda informed him. "You'll have to lunch with me, George."

"But I—"

"No," she said definitely. "It's convenient and I'm sure of a safe parking space there. By the way, did you happen to notice the new arrangement of our factory buildings back yonder?"

"Notice? Good heavens!"

"Did you like it?"

"Like it?" He shook his head, not in negation but to express an amazed admiration qualified by personal gloom. "It's rather overpowering, Belinda. They tell me you run that whole show."

"I?" She laughed. "That proves what prestige will do, once it's started to grow. Out at Long Hills they used to say I was either crazy or disappointed in love because I was a working woman; nowadays they like to exaggerate my 'business success' and they say I'm 'hard and dry.' You've heard that, too, haven't you?"

"Well, I—"

"Of course you have!" she interrupted. "No doubt it's true too. But I was telling you not to exaggerate my prestige; Mr. Farrier is chairman of the board and still comes down to the factory for an hour or so several days in the week; I lean on him for advice in everything that's of great importance."

"I see. Were you leaning on him last Saturday, for instance, when you were getting old Mr. Sloane so upset at the Country Club?"

"Oh, you noticed that?" she said, and laughed. "Poor Mr. Sloane! No; that was about a matter Mr. Farrier had left to me and another of the directors, Mears, to decide. You see, when we incorporated, Mr. Farrier gave all the old employees a chance to take up stock, and he and Mr. Mears and I together now hold the greater part of it. Poor old Mr. Sloane can't help trying to get his hands upon anything he thinks is pretty good, and he thought if he could get us to do a little merging it might be very useful to him. He almost persuaded Mr. Farrier; but I told Mr. Farrier the story of the Arab and the camel, and he saw the point."

"Is that the way business is done? You tell a story and stop a merger?"

"Ah, but Mr. Sloane is so precisely like the camel that first got his head in the Arab's tent and then persuaded the Arab to let him squeeze a little more of himself in, and then a little more, until presently there wasn't any room for the Arab. It was pretty easy to show Mr. Farrier that old Mr. Sloane's whole career has been built upon a shrewd imitation of that camel."

"Was it?" George said, and muttered to himself so indistinctly that she did not catch the words. "Yet she says she doesn't run the whole works!"

"What did you say, George?"

"Nothing," he murmured, and the renewed silence between them was not broken until they had entered the green gateway of the Oak Leaf, left their car and seated themselves at a table in the flowering bay window of the grillroom.

Not far from them seven elderly grave gentlemen were excellently lunching at a round table, and the great back and bald head of the host of this little party, resembling a moderate hillock of gray tweed surmounted by the egg of an ostrich, were easily recognizable. Cracklings and growlings from the egg were audible; evidently Mr. Sloane's mood was not amiable, a circumstance upon which one of his guests a little later came to congratulate Miss Belinda Dale. As the luncheon party broke up, George Hinchman recognized the approaching figure as that of the preeminent member of the banking firm of Brookings Brothers; the lips of Mr. Brookings were twitching beneath his white mustache, his eyes twinkled behind his glasses, and altogether his emotional condition seemed to be one of hilarity just released from suppression.

"Miss Dale, you've certainly got the old boy going!" he said in a husky voice. "He was quite cheerful until he happened to see you come in here; then he began to lecture on women in business that's just ended. I represent the others, I believe, in coming to felicitate you upon doing more to annoy the old rascal than any of the rest of us have been able to do for a long time."

He departed, chuckling, and Miss Dale and her companion, having finished luncheon and a desultory conversation almost embarrassingly impersonal, presently rose and set forth upon foot for the neighboring race track. The crowds were thick, pushing and jostling were heavy. They were separated by a roughly pushing group of well-dressed young men, and George's height enabled him to see that one of these, a pallid and emaciated youth, lifted his hat to Belinda and that she smiled and nodded to him in return. Hinchman heard an exclamation of annoyance from Belinda, and, a moment later, as the crowd found space enough to spread fanwise, he was able to rejoin her.

"Did you call out?" he asked. "What was the matter?"

"My bag!" she said. "One of those young crooks got it."

"What! I saw you speak to one of 'em as if you knew him."

"I did. Oh, it wasn't he that took my bag!"

"What was in it?"

"Not enough money to be very important; but there were some memoranda I shouldn't like to lose."

"They've gone entirely out of sight," George said, looking about him. "And of course there isn't a policeman anywhere near just when—"

He was interrupted; the emaciated, pale boy who had spoken to Belinda appeared suddenly and quietly out of the spreading crowd. "I'm terribly sorry, Miss Dale," he said. "I wouldn't have had such a thing happen for a good deal; but that fool didn't know who you were. Here—" Touching his hat, he departed hurriedly.

George Hinchman inappropriately uttered a sound that bore some resemblance to a gasp of dismay.

"It's nothing," she answered him as they walked on together. "That poor boy has a brother we took on at the factory when he came out of the penitentiary two years ago; one of the first people I employed was a man just out of prison—an extraordinary man who is one of the powers in the business now. That began our policy of not turning down men because they've had a prison record, and we still maintain it, even though one does become hard and dry in business."

"I suppose you're too important to be sensitive," he suggested after a moment of rumination.

"No; I'm usually too busy to find time for it."

"Yes, of course. As soon as I got home I heard how terribly busy you were; that was one reason why I—"

"No, it wasn't," she returned quickly. "Never in the world was that the reason why anybody waited a whole month to look up an old friend."

"You mean you haven't understood—"

He was interrupted; they were passing near a group of lively young people clustered along the rail of the race course and exquisite young Julia Pelley extended her arm and tapped Mr. Hinchman upon the shoulder as he came by. "George!" she said. "I thought something funny about you last night. Drop around a little later and I might tell you!"

Belinda halted a few paces on, and observing the redness of her escort's face permitted herself to laugh. "But naturally I have," she said.

"You have what?"

"Understood," Belinda explained. "Shan't we go back and join those young people now, George? My cousin, young Crowley Dale's one of them, and there's something I want to talk to him about."

"All right; if you want to," George said, and to her astonishment she observed that his expression had suddenly become embittered. "Maria Capoole got me to her house one night and had the place full of 'em. Ever since that terrible little Pelley girl has seemed to take me for a contemporary! If you have something important to say to your young cousin, go ahead, but for heaven's sake let me find a place a little farther away where I can wait for you!"

Belinda looked at him gravely, then began to walk onward with him again. "No; it's nothing really important, and of course," she added, "what we came here for is to watch the racing."

"Is it?" he asked. "I don't seem to remember your ever showing any particular interest in racing, and, for my part, I'm like the shah of Persia who said he always had known that some horses are faster than others."

"Good gracious!" she exclaimed. "Then what in the world are we here for?"

With that, they looked at each other, laughed helplessly, and, without any more words upon the matter, began to retrace their steps. They returned to the small automobile in the yard of the Oak Leaf, immediately set forth and within a few minutes were driving at a decorous speed upon a quiet roadway that ran between green fields and woodland groves.

"But you're entirely mistaken about that," George Hinchman said, suddenly breaking a long silence with this apparently irrelevant speech. "I didn't do anything of the kind."

Belinda waited until they had rolled rumblingly over a little wooden bridge, the planking of which was loose; then she asked, "Of what kind?"

"Not coming to see an old friend for four weeks," he explained. "I mean I did come."

"Did you indeed? Strange I didn't know of it! You might have left a card mightn't you? When was it?"

"The day I came home—about three hours after I got off the train."

"George!" she exclaimed scornfully. "It's nonsense for you to make up things like that; they'd have told me at the house if you'd been there and I was out. Why do you—"

"It wasn't at your house," he interrupted. "I didn't go there. Today isn't the first time I've come to the factory; that's where I went at closing time the day I got back. I hoped maybe you'd notice me and pick me up as you came out; but you were having a great powwow with three or four men—one of 'em was Farrier—and you weren't driving this little machine; you had your big closed car with the chauffeur, and you took those men in with you and drove off apparently to some kind of business conclave. At any rate, you know, you were far too absorbed in talking to them to notice me. You didn't see me at all. Don't you believe it, Belinda?"

"Why—why, yes," she said and, frowning, spared him a glance sidelong from her driving. "I remember that day; I drove them out to old Mr. Sloane's house for our first talk with him. Why in the world didn't you—"

"Signal you to stop?" George laughed gloomily. "I felt too out of it; I daresay it was unreasonable, but somehow I felt a little snubbed, even though, of course, I knew you didn't see me. Maybe you'd understand better if you'd ever felt yourself to be a terribly unimportant person hanging round an important one. All those people pouring out of the gates, and that prodigious line of buildings—the size and power of that whole exhibit seeming to be pretty well concentrated in your hands— well, probably I'm not being very coherent, but I found it a little stupefying, Belinda. You see, it brought up recollections of my previous homecomings and things I'd said to you that became rather mortifying to remember, so I just sneaked back to Long Hills and began to get the old house fit to live in and kept busy with that. You see, that first sight of you scared me, and everything I've heard about you since has kept on scaring me more."

She shook her head. "I don't understand, George, I certainly never scared you before, did I?"

"No," he said. "That's what mortified me. I'd never realized before what you were and what I was. I hadn't ever realized what your business life meant or why you cared about it and were so absorbed in it. I hadn't understood you were trying to be a great part of a great thing, and what made me blush most was remembering that I'd always asked you to 'let me take you out of it'! I'd always had the Long Hills view of you, and the Long Hills view of me, too, I suppose. Even your own family, when they brag loudest of how important you are, still add a little apology for your being a business woman, I suppose you know?"

"Yes," Belinda said in a low voice, though she contrived to smile. "Even my father does that."

"And Long Hills thinks I'm not wholly unimportant,"

George went on. "So I suppose really I've thought myself not wholly unimportant; but your factory makes me know that I am, Belinda."

"Does it? How?"

"Well, I've got my whole life's 'work' in a couple of little packing cases at home and expect to put in the next several years straightening out and publishing what's in those boxes— some notes on birds that may slightly interest a few ornithologists. There's the climax of my immensely useful career, Belinda!"

"But I think that's splendid, George!" she said warmly. "I think it's a perfectly lovely thing for you to do!"

"Do you?" he asked, and laughed with some hollowness. "Do you appreciate the fact that you've just spoken to me very much as a kind and encouraging gentleman would speak to a young lady of her embroidering—'splendid' and 'perfectly lovely'?" Then, at her gesture of protest, he added quickly, "Oh, I don't mind! I'm only too pleased to get even that sort of approval from you. It helps me to feel I'm expiating some of my old foolishnesses about you."

"I see," she said slowly. "You mean it's mortifying to you, George, to remember that for a long time you thought you were interested in a woman who's turned out to be so hard and dry and masculine—a woman Long Hills says is 'exactly like a man'?"

"Good heavens, no!" he cried. "I meant my underestimation of you when I spoke of my old foolishnesses!"

"Oh!" she said, and she looked first startled, then dubious. "I think you exaggerate them and exaggerate me."

"How do I?"

"You exaggerate me when you think of the Farrier industries' seeming to be concentrated, as you said, in my hands; I'm only one of the thinking parts of that establishment—its size and power are impressive, as you say; but I'm not impressive apart from them."

"I'm afraid you can't help seeming so to me," he insisted, and then asked. "But what do you mean by saying that I exaggerate my old foolishnesses about you? Haven't you always thought me an idiot for wanting to get you out of your work just to come and be a housewife for me?" Uncomfortably he shook his head. "Offering you the privilege of pouring my morning coffee for me! Not having sense enough to be proud of what you are doing and—"

She interrupted him a little breathlessly. "What did you say, George? Did you use the word 'proud'? Meaning that you could feel that way about me—"

"Belinda! Do you suppose that even yet I don't know enough to be ashamed of ever having tried to get you away from your work? Do you think I'm too stupid and too embedded in Long Hills superstitions to be almost awe-strickenly proud of you?"

At that, Belinda's under lip suddenly began to be tremulous. During all her long struggle, from the time when in the face of family opposition and the chilling wonderment of all Long Hills she had gone forth to be a factory worker and "learn the business from the bottom up," not one of her own people had ever spoken of being proud of her, and the word coming from this old friend of hers had so great an effect upon her that the long country road stretching before her began all at once to wind and waver in a watery distortion; she had to stop the car and try to find her handkerchief.

"What on earth have I done?" George asked in sharp distress. "Of course I knew you'd say no again; I was only leading up to wondering if you couldn't stand it for me to sit at home over my embroideries, being proud of you until you should get back after your day's work."

Belinda had found her handkerchief and was weeping into it heartily. "George, did you—did you really come to the factory gates that first evening?"

A NOTE
ON THE WRITERS

JOSEPHINE DASKAM BACON

Born in Stamford, Connecticut, in 1876, Josephine Daskam graduated from Smith College in 1898 and married a lawyer, Selden Bacon, in 1903. They had three children. Between 1914 and 1924, she was a member of the Girl Scouts National Executive Board and in 1920 compiled the *Girl Scout National Handbook*. Like most magazine writers, Bacon was a prolific author; she published thirty-seven books between 1900 and 1941. She wrote juvenile as well as adult fiction and centered her stories on women, many of whom try to enter the male world of commerce and adventure. Bacon produced comedies and satires, primarily, but also published mysteries and romances. She made her home in New York City and died in 1961.

VIVIEN R. BRETHERTON

No information is available on this writer beyond her lifelong association with Portland, Oregon.

EDITH BARNARD DELANO

Edith Barnard was born in Washington, D.C., in 1875 and educated at Bryn Mawr. She married James Delano in 1908. A well-known contributor to all the leading magazines of her day, Edith Barnard Delano wrote such fiction until her death in 1946 at the age of seventy-one. She also published several novels during the 1910s and

1920s. She lived in East Orange, New Jersey, for a time, then Old Deerfield, Massachusetts.

JESSIE FAUSET

Jessie Fauset was one of the prime movers of the Harlem Renaissance, having been literary editor of *The Crisis* from 1919 to 1926 and the author of four novels: *There Is Confusion* (1924), *Plum Bun* (1929), *The Chinaberry Tree* (1931), and *Comedy: American Style* (1933). She is credited with discovering Langston Hughes, whose poem "The Negro Speaks of Rivers" was first published by her, and with getting the careers of Countée Cullen, Claude McKay, and Jean Toomer off the ground. Fauset was born in New Jersey in 1882 but was raised in Philadelphia by a minister of the African Methodist Episcopal church and his wife, Redmon and Annie Fauset. She was their seventh child. Jessie Fauset was a distinguished student, both in the all-white girls' high school she attended in Philadelphia and at Cornell University, from which she graduated Phi Beta Kappa in 1905. She was one of the very few black women to receive a college degree at the time and the first of her race and gender to be admitted to that honorary society. While Fauset coped admirably with being the only black female in her educational institutions, she suffered from racism, both materially and socially. She was denied entrance to Bryn Mawr, for example, on the basis of race (no Pennsylvania college admitted African-Americans at that time) and prohibited from teaching in the Philadelphia public schools upon her graduation from Cornell. There were, in fact, few secondary institutions for blacks in the nation, and Fauset had difficulty finding a position until she was hired by the best such high school, Paul Laurence Dunbar High School in Washington, D.C., where she taught Latin and French from 1906 to 1919. After she left for *The Crisis* and Harlem, having completed a master's degree in French at the University of Pennsylvania in 1919, Fauset devoted herself to publishing and writing literature that would advance the position of African-Americans. To this end, she deliberately wrote about middle-class black families and successful independent women in order to get away from racist stereotypes of poor, comic blacks speaking dialect. She was accused by some black critics of creating a false, white-identified image, but in recent years, scholars have recognized the progressive aspects of Fauset's fiction, including the antiracist, antisexist message behind her heroines. Fauset's own life was courageous and unconventional. She did not marry until she was forty-seven (in 1929), for instance, and continued a professional career beyond her marriage, teaching French at a New York City high school from 1927 to 1944. She also traveled extensively in Europe, went to Africa in 1924, and lectured actively until the last years of her life. After living in New Jersey with her husband for some years, Jessie Fauset died in Philadelphia in 1961.

ELIZABETH FRAZER

Elizabeth Frazer remained single all her life and was a contributor primarily to the *Saturday Evening Post* and *Good Housekeeping* until her retirement in the late 1940s, when she became a freelance writer. During World War I, Frazer served as an ambulance service nurse and then a war correspondent in France. She was born in California and educated at the University of California, after which she moved to New York City, where she died in 1967 at the age of eighty-nine.

ZONA GALE

Zona Gale is arguably today's best-known female author of the women's magazine writers represented here. She is the author of thirty-one books written between 1906 and 1939, one of which, *Miss Lulu Bett* (1920), was dramatized by Gale into a Pulitzer Prize–winning play. Other well-known works include *Friendship Village* (1908), *Neighborhood Stories* (1914), and *Faint Perfume* (1923). Born in the village of Portage, Wisconsin, in 1874, Zona Gale specialized in regional tales that lauded small town life and the strong women who dominated it. Graduating from the University of Wisconsin–Madison in 1895, Gale earned a master's degree from that institution in 1899 and an honorary doctorate in 1929. She eventually was a member of Wisconsin's Board of Regents from 1923 to 1929 and was instrumental in gaining support for creative writers there. A social activist and feminist, Gale was especially helpful to women, seeing to it that Jewish immigrant writer Anzia Yezierska received a fellowship to continue her work at the University of Wisconsin in the 1930s and promoting Jessie Fauset's novel *The Chinaberry Tree* (1931), for which she wrote the introduction. She also wrote the introduction to and made possible the publication of *The Living of Charlotte Perkins Gilman* in 1935. Gale was good friends with Jane Addams and active in both the suffrage movement and Women's Peace Party. She did not marry until the age of fifty-four, when she wed a manufacturer and banker from Portage. They adopted two daughters. Zona Gale died in Chicago, Illinois, in 1938, having lived most of her life in Wisconsin.

SOPHIE KERR

Beginning her professional life as a journalist, Sophie Kerr edited the woman's page for newspapers in Pittsburgh and then worked her way up to managing editor of *Woman's Home Companion*. She was born in Denton, Maryland, in 1880 and received a number of college degrees, including a master's degree from the University of Vermont in 1901 and a doctorate in literature from Washington College in 1942. In 1904, she married John Underwood but continued to write under her given name. Immensely popular in her day, Kerr published twenty-six books from 1916 through 1953 and regularly wrote for all the national magazines throughout the 1920s and 1930s into the 1940s. She specialized in romances about businesswomen, whose characteristics and circumstances Kerr used to reflect the changing mores of the era. Although Kerr wrote sympathetically of a neighborhood on the eastern shore of Maryland in many of her stories, she wrote many others in which the heroine leaves a conventional town for the excitement of New York, a city in which Kerr herself resided for most of her adult life. She had no children and died in 1965.

JENNETTE LEE

A New Englander, Jennette Lee was born in Bristol, Connecticut, in 1860 and lived much of her life in Northampton, Massachusetts. She married clergyman and writer Gerald Lee in 1896 and had one daughter. Lee's story "The Cat and the King" reflects her generation's familiarity with romantic friendships between women as well as her extensive experience with women's colleges. She received a bachelor's degree from Smith College (1886), taught English at Vassar from 1890 to 1893, chaired the English Department at Western Reserve University's College for Women (1893–96), and was a professor of English at Smith between 1901 and 1913. From 1926 to 1933 she and her husband directed the Training School for Balance and Coordination in New York. After her retirement in 1933, she devoted herself to writing and gardening. Lee published numerous stories in women's magazines and was the author of twenty books that appeared from 1900 to 1926. She died in 1951 at the age of ninety in Northampton.

EDITH MacVANE

Evidently a single woman, Edith MacVane was born in Boston in 1880 and educated at Radcliffe. Her father was a professor of ancient and modern history at Harvard. She contributed stories to several magazines and published six novels from 1906 through 1912, and was last reported living in Rome, Italy.

GRACE SARTWELL MASON

Grace Sartwell was born in Port Allegheny, Pennsylvania, in 1877 and married James Redfern Mason in 1902. Not much is known about her beyond the publication of her eight books between 1909 and 1933. She contributed to all the leading magazines and made her home in New York City.

RUTH COMFORT MITCHELL

The daughter of a hotel manager, Ruth Comfort Mitchell was born in San Francisco in 1882, educated at a private institute there, and married in 1914. She kept her given name. Like the heroine of "Call of the House," Mitchell was active in California politics as a Republican and married a state senator. She was also fond of riding horses. Her extensive involvement in professional women's organizations is too great to detail here, but it included the League of American Penwomen, the Women's Athletic Club, the California League of Business and Professional Women, and Pro-America, a Republican women's group. She was a prolific writer, publishing sixteen books between 1921 and 1944 as well as contributing to national magazines. In addition she wrote poetry and plays. While a political conservative, Mitchell was a pacifist during World War I and a feminist whose alliance with women is evident from her biography. She did not have any children and died in Los Gatos, California, in 1954 at the age of seventy-one.

EUDORA RAMSAY RICHARDSON

Born in Versailles, Kentucky, Eudora Ramsay received a bachelor's degree from the University of Richmond and a master's from Columbia University. She married Fitzburgh Briggs Richardson in 1917 and had one daughter, named Eudora Ramsay. Although it is not evident in the story "Men Are Like That," Richardson wrote many books on Virginia, where she lived most of her life. What is reflected in this story, however, is her extensive involvement in women's organizations and her support for feminist causes. She was, for example, field director for the National American Woman Suffrage Association from 1914 to 1917, and national field representative for the National Federation of Business and Professional Women's Clubs from 1932 to

1935. She was also the organizing president of the Virginia chapter of the American Association of University Women. Richardson was a leader in many other contexts: she directed the women's division of the War Loan Organization (1918–20), chaired the English Department at Greenville Women's College in South Carolina (1912–14), and directed the Federal Writers' Project (1937–39). In addition to co-authoring several military textbooks, Richardson contributed many essays, articles, and short stories to national magazines. She made her home in Richmond, Virginia.

MARY SYNON

One of a number of journalists in this group, Mary Synon worked as a reporter on the *Chicago Journal,* dramatically breaking through a prohibition on the employ of women reporters with her bold coverage of the great strike at the Union stockyards. She later went on to be a correspondent in Ireland and in London for the *New York World.* Synon was also a noted fiction writer, both for Catholic and mass market periodicals. Author of at least five novels, she tended to create stories of ambitious yet humanitarian career women located in urban settings. She was born in Chicago, but no record of her birth date or death date is available.

BOOTH TARKINGTON

The most famous of the writers included in this collection, Booth Tarkington became a millionaire as a result of his lighthearted novels about childhood, romance, and midwestern life. He won the Pulitzer Prize twice, for *The Magnificent Ambersons* in 1919 and *Alice Adams* in 1921. Many of his books became plays and movies, scripted by Tarkington and starring famous celebrities of the thirties and forties: Katharine Hepburn, Jackie Cooper, Jane Withers, Judy Garland, and Bob Hope, among others. Tarkington is, perhaps, best known for *Penrod,* concerning the adventures of boyhood. He was born in Indianapolis in 1869 and educated at Phillips Exeter Academy, Purdue University, and Princeton, which awarded him an honorary doctorate in 1918 as did DePauw (1923) and Columbia (1924). He was married to his first wife in 1902 and divorced in 1911, then married again in 1912. His only child, a daughter born in 1906, died at a young age. Tarkington was an immensely talented and energetic writer, producing forty novels and twenty plays between 1899 and 1946, despite poor eyesight leading to complete blindness in 1930, followed by the restoration of sight to one eye. No longer able to write or read very well, he dictated stories to a secretary until the end of his life. Tarkington traveled widely but made his home in Kennebunkport, Maine, and Indianapolis, where he died in 1946 at age seventy-six.

JULIET WILBOR TOMPKINS

Although she kept her given name, Juliet Wilbor Tompkins was married at some point. She was born in Oakland, California, in 1871 and graduated from Vassar College in 1891. From 1897 to 1901, she was associate editor for *Munsey's Magazine*. Tompkins made her home in New York City, publishing many short stories in national magazines and fourteen novels between 1908 and 1929. She died in 1956 and was buried in Pacific Grove, California.